For the Love of Labor

For the Love of Labor

The Life of Pauline Newman

CATHRYN J. PRINCE

UNIVERSITY OF
ILLINOIS PRESS
Urbana, Chicago, and Springfield

Manufactured in the United States of America
1 2 3 4 5 C P 5 4 3 2 1
♾ This book is printed on acid-free paper.

Cataloging data available from the Library of Congress
LCCN 2025032314
ISBN 978-0-252-04955-2 (cloth : alk.)
ISBN 978-0-252-08920-6 (paper : alk.)
ISBN 978-0-252-04870-8 (ebook)

The manufacturer's authorized representative in
the EU for product safety is Mare Nostrum Group
B.V., Mauritskade 21D, 1091 GC Amsterdam, The
Netherlands. Email: gpsr@mare-nostrum.co.uk

Pierre. Nathan. Zoë.

&

Marvin. Norma.

"A working girl is a human being with a heart, with desires, with aspirations, with ideas and ideals."

—Pauline Newman

Contents

Preface

Emerging from the tumultuous beginnings of the twentieth century, Pauline Newman stood as a beacon of resilience and determination. Along with a cadre of extraordinary women, she challenged the status quo while also forging a path toward personal independence and civic engagement.

As a young immigrant living in New York City, Newman immersed herself in the burgeoning labor movement after experiencing the harsh working conditions in the garment industry firsthand. Over time, she navigated the turbulent waters of union politics, her voice resonating with the hopes and demands of working women. Newman's unwavering belief in the power of collective action propelled her to the forefront of the Women's Trade Union League, where she tirelessly advocated for women's rights and economic empowerment. Her dedication to social issues went beyond the factory walls, encompassing a wide spectrum of causes, from education and health care to suffrage.

Newman also bucked societal expectations when it came to her personal life. While she lived with Frieda Miller and together they raised a daughter, she never spoke about her homosexuality. And yet, as fierce and outspoken as she was on working and voting conditions, she remained a closeted homosexual her entire life. This tension between her public and private persona offers a lens through which can we can consider the constraints on women like Newman, who clearly struggled with her sexual identity and desires in this time period.

Aside from being drawn to Newman's story because of the role she played during a pivotal time in American history, her story also resonated with me on a personal level. My paternal grandparents immigrated to the United States in the early 1900s from what is now Ukraine and Poland.

Like Newman, they fled violent pogroms and economic insecurity. My grandfather, Nathan Prince, traveled a similar route as Pauline, overland to England and then in steerage across the Atlantic Ocean before arriving at Ellis Island. He was a teenager when he apprenticed as a furrier in the garment district, eventually starting his own business, Fantasia Furs. My grandmother, Helen Prince, came into the United States through Canada and worked in various clothing shops while raising three children. My maternal grandparents were born here to immigrants who came from Lithuania and Belorussia. Milton Goldstein was a liquor salesman and his wife, Sara, a schoolteacher.

As I embarked on this first full-length biographic treatment of Newman's life, I decided the best way to tell her story was through her letters, diaries, her own unpublished manuscript, and interviews, as well as the writings of her contemporaries. Additionally, I mined the Arthur and Elizabeth Schlesinger Library at the Radcliffe Institute for Advanced Study, Kheel Center for Labor-Management Documentation and Archives at Cornell University, and the Tamiment Library and Robert F. Wagner Labor Archives at New York University for primary source documents, letters, and photographs.

As a journalist I recognize that history is a continual process and that to understand both the past and the present we must build on the works of the many scholars and writers who came before. In trying to understand Newman's life and the time in which she lived, I am indebted to many scholars, including, but not limited to, Annelise Orleck, Ann Schofield, Lillian Faderman, Dorothy Sue Cobble, and Alice Kessler-Harris. Each of them has written well-received books and essays that convey essential aspects of the labor movement, gender studies, early American history, and feminism that helped inform this book.

I hope readers will come away from this book with a better understanding of how Newman—a labor activist, socialist, and feminist—played a vital role in some of the most important social movements of the twentieth century.

Acknowledgments

My deepest gratitude to Jill D. Swenson of Swenson Book Development. Here's to 16 years of working together, to your calming presence, and to your always spot on feedback. Most of all, thank you for planting the seed that became this book.

Thank you to Alison Syring Bassford at University of Illinois Press for recognizing the importance of Pauline's story and being such an advocate for this book. Thank you also to Jennie Fisher, Leigh Ann Cowan, Kevin Cunningham, Tad Ringo, and the entire team at University of Illinois Press for helping shepherd this book into the world. Thank you to Jill Hughes for your keen editorial eye.

I am grateful to numerous archivists and librarians; without their assistance this book would not be possible. To start, thank you to the staff at the Arthur and Elizabeth Schlesinger Library on the History of Women in America at the Radcliffe Institute for Advanced Study for helping me navigate a treasure trove of papers, including those of Pauline Newman, Frieda Selke Miller, and Elisabeth Miller Burger. I'd like to add a special mention to Diana Carey who so patiently helped me secure many of the images included in this book.

At the Kheel Center for Labor Management Documentation and Archives at Cornell University, I would like to thank Steve Calco and Melissa Holland, both of whom graciously stepped in to scan and send research materials during the height of the COVID-19 pandemic when in-person research was impossible. Thank you also to the staff of the Tamiment Library and Robert F. Wagner Archives at New York University.

A heartfelt thank you to the early readers whose constructive suggestions helped shape the narrative.

I am grateful to Hugh and Michael Owen, for sharing their insights, memories, and photographs about their granny Pauline, and grandmother Frieda Miller.

To Amy Levine-Kennedy, thank you for being my shoulder to lean on and for our walk and talks. To Ingrid Warneryd, thank you for your friendship and support.

I am grateful for having parents who championed me every step of the way. To my mother Norma Prince, I miss you every day; you will always be the color of my life Z"L. To my father, Marvin Prince, for your strength and guidance.

To Nathan and Zoë—you constantly inspire me with your wit and wisdom. And to Pierre: You hold my heart.

Abbreviations

AFL	American Federation of Labor
AFL-CIO	American Federation of Labor–Congress of Industrial Organizations
CIO	Congress of Industrial Organizations
ILGWU	International Ladies' Garment Workers' Union
ILO	International Labor Organization
WSP	Women's Suffrage Party
WTUL	Women's Trade Union League

For the Love of Labor

1

The Land of Gold and Promise

"Quick! Into the boxes!"

The words sent Pauline Newman and the other children scrambling for cover inside the large cardboard boxes, already half filled with finished crisp, white shirtwaists.[1] Newman, whose tongue still tripped over English words, clapped her hand over her mouth. Counting herself lucky to have a job at the Triangle Shirtwaist Factory, she was petrified of coughing or sneezing, or saying something that might give away their hiding place.

At eleven years old, Newman was resigned to the fact that she would never join those children who sat behind desks in neat rows. She would never dip her pen into an inkwell and practice her penmanship under the attentive eye of a teacher. She knew she would never play hopscotch on the sidewalk in front of her family's tenement or spin tops on the stoop. Instead she was here, toiling alongside hundreds of other immigrants, mostly women and children, on the top three floors of the Asch Building.

It was 1902, and like the other children in the crowded workshop, Newman had no tailoring experience, other than knowing how to sew a button and darn a sock. And like the other children, she worked long hours in dangerous conditions similar to other such factories in New York City where profits were elevated over health and safety. Locked exits, a broken fire escape, a lack of sprinklers, windows painted shut, monitored bathroom breaks, stifling heat in summer, and numbing cold in winter were the norm. So too were periodic inspections by the city's labor department.[2]

Hence the hissed orders to be quiet from the floor supervisor as Newman and her coworkers heaped shirtwaists on top of the closed boxes. By the time the rubber-soled inspector from city hall approached, there was nothing to see but men, shears in hand, bent over swaths of cotton and silk, or stiff-necked women silently peddling the trestles of sewing machines. The inspector saw fabric scraps fluttering to the dust-covered floor and window sills coated in thick grime. What he didn't see were children. Thus, the fiction that no child laborers worked at the shirtwaist factory could live for another day.[3]

While child labor had been outlawed in a smattering of states since 1848, the laws were rarely enforced. As such, there was a movement afoot to stop the practice, not because managers and business owners felt moved to end the appalling conditions in which many children worked. Rather, the motivation came from both religious and secular groups who, for different reasons, were growing increasingly concerned about the persistent lack of education among school-age children and the number of hours they worked.

It was a movement that started nearly a century earlier. In New England, where the current of Puritanism ran deep, the notion that children couldn't read was disquieting: Illiterate children couldn't read the Bible. By contrast, the situation dismayed those in more secular circles who believed a democracy depended on an educated citizenry.[4] These groups had worked to change this circumstance for more than a century, and they did achieve a modicum of success. In 1813 the Connecticut state legislature passed a law requiring any child who worked in a factory to learn reading, writing, and arithmetic. In 1836 the National Trades' Union, the first federation of labor unions in the United States, urged states to pass legislation that set a minimum age for factory workers. Although the organization disbanded a year later, during the Panic of 1837, it nevertheless set the stage for future reform. In 1842 Massachusetts passed a law barring children under twelve from working more than ten hours a day. Connecticut followed suit, decreeing those fourteen and under could work no more than ten hours a day. By the 1840s all of New England passed similar laws. However, Newman lived in New York City in 1901 and most of those laws had not survived into the new century.[5]

That's how Newman—who first entered the workforce at the age of nine, not even a year after arriving in the United States from Lithuania—spent the better part of her childhood. So far, she had withstood three years of tedious, monotonous, low-paying labor. Sometimes her knuckles and feet throbbed with the dull ache of a woman five times her age. But it hadn't always been like this.

Born sometime around 1890 to deeply religious Jewish parents, Pauline Newman was the youngest of four children. Her father, Meyer, taught

Talmud to the more well-to-do sons of Vilijampolė, a tiny village on the outskirts of Lithuania's second-largest city, Kovno (Kaunas). "At times he would talk to me about things as though I was no longer a child. Our little community considered my father to be a scholar and a thinker. Some of the more affluent neighbors chose him to teach Talmud to their boys," she later said.[6]

There were few options for Jewish men and women to earn a living at the time. Aside from teaching, as Newman's father did, Jewish men could work as teamsters, coachmen, and unskilled laborers. However, legal restrictions barred them from making a thriving business out of it. Newman's father's work was steady, though by no means well paid. To supplement the family's income, her mother, Theresa, started her own small produce business. She bought fruit from nearby farmers, and then once or twice a week she walked to the village market and picked her way through the maze of crates, baskets, and wooden tables, hoping to sell the ripened fruit. On the days she couldn't sell anything, she bartered—perhaps a basket of plums for a bolt of cloth, a box of pears for a sack of barley, or a box of cherries for some butter.[7] She also kept the house with the help of her daughters. Together they baked, cooked, and washed their clothes in the river. Pauline's older sisters were dressmakers, but the work was irregular and so were their wages.

Inside the wooden house, the Newman family shared two rooms. One was a bedroom; the other room served as kitchen, dining room, sewing room, and an extra sleeping alcove. But "we had enough to eat and a roof above our heads—if only a thatched roof. However, it kept out the rain and the wind, and the cold," Newman later wrote about her childhood in her unpublished memoir.[8] The double windows also kept icy drafts at bay, especially during the four months of bitter cold that seized Kovno each winter. Come fall, Newman and her sisters helped their mother stuff bundles of white cotton into the space between the outside and inside windows. They spent hours decorating the cotton with colored paper, handmade clay figurines, pressed butterflies, and flowers. Each neighbor always tried to outdo the other in their "artistic effort."[9]

Living on the edge of poverty meant the family had little in the way of health care. They rarely, if ever, saw a dentist. There was no regular doctor to call upon. If someone in the family fell ill, they resorted to the counsel of the village apothecary. Despite all of this, Newman never lay awake at night with a stomach rumbling from hunger. Masterful at stretching ingredients, her mother oversaw the pickling and canning of vegetables and fruit each fall and planted potatoes on a stamp-size swatch of land behind the house.

As the youngest daughter, Newman never slipped her arms through a new woolen coat or laced up a new pair of thick-soled winter boots. If she was unhappy with her family's lot, she hid it well. "We and our neighbors were at peace with ourselves. We had little and expected less. Hence, no great disappointments or disillusionment. I do not remember anyone yearning for the unobtainable. We were, in fact, free from the desire to possess things. In short we were content with what we had," she said about her impoverished childhood.[10]

Like the other Jewish families living in Kovno, the Newmans lived across the Neris River from their predominantly Roman Catholic neighbors. During World War II the Nazis turned the already densely packed quarter into the Kaunas ghetto, but for now the two communities coexisted. They engaged in the occasional business transaction or exchanged polite greetings, perhaps while sending a letter from the post office, which, also serving as the postmaster's home, was the sole brick building in the village. That was as far as their interactions went. They rarely, if ever, shared a glass of tea or played a game of checkers or chess in the sole teahouse situated off the village square. Just beyond the post office rose one of several Catholic churches. The small synagogue where her father prayed and taught lay just beyond. There were just enough Jews in the village to have a synagogue, Newman later recalled.[11]

Each time Newman and her father walked past the squat brick synagogue, she asked him the same question: Why couldn't she sit with him when they went to services on the Jewish New Year or Shabbat services? "The answer my father gave was too complicated for my young mind to understand. But in later years I often wondered whether this early observation conditioned me to resent and to fight against all discriminations based on sex. I think it did," she later wrote.[12]

While she yearned to attend classes, it was the area beyond the village center that called to her. Surrounding the clusters of houses stood a dark, mysterious, and, in Newman's opinion, rather inviting forest. Stately Norway spruce trees mingled with silver birches. Scotch pine trees stretched skyward. In autumn the fallen pine needles turned russet and she thought, *This is what it must be like to walk on a carpet.*

Newman stood hypnotized as the serrated circular saw sliced a thick log into planks of equal size. The sawdust accumulated on the floor like so much snow. Her father, who occasionally took his children on small excursions around the village for a diversion, had arranged a visit to see the village's new sawmill. She decided it was interesting but not nearly as fun as what was arguably the most exciting time of the year. He would "take me to see the breaking of the ice. The harbinger of spring. This was quite an event in our village."[13] The more adventurous boys, including her older brother, would jump onto huge blocks of ice and "sail away" to the end of the lake.

When the last snows finally melted and she finished helping her mother beat the dust from the bedcovers and scrub the outside of the windows, she and friends ran off to the woods. There they darted between the sun-dappled trees, stopping now and again to pick wildflowers—tiny blue hepatica and little white blossoms that resembled stars. When the too-short spring yielded to the even shorter summer, the children scampered between the trees, searching for plump, wild raspberries that burst on their tongues.

Throughout the humid days of July and August, when the sun was at its hottest, Newman and her siblings cooled off in the crystal-clear lake. At twilight they climbed into wooden rowboats, the oars slipping in and out of the inky blue water. Low hills were silhouetted against the darkening sky. "Our voices sweet and low singing our favorite songs. During these hours peace took possession of our hearts and minds. We were happy," she wrote.[14]

In autumn she and her father often woke just after the sky turned pale with the first light. Pulling on extra sweaters Theresa had knit, they went to the forest to forage for mushrooms. They delighted every time they spied chanterelles, blewits, or morels poking through the chocolate soil. Back in the small kitchen, her mother turned the small harvest into a hearty mushroom barley soup. The earthy aroma mingling with freshly baked bread and plum jam was a true pleasure.

The first snowflakes swirled through the air just as the last brown, crisp leaves fell to the ground. Winter had arrived and now there were other ways to escape the monotony of chores. Newman was steady on her skates but not exactly graceful. On the other hand, her older brother "was known as the champion skater," etching lacy patterns on the thick ice that covered the river.[15] When they weren't skating, they were zipping down the sloping path behind the church on sleds. It was exhilarating to speed alongside the trees, now naked of leaves. The winter air bit their cheeks. Their woolen mittens, made of yarn the color of a winter sky, were often frayed, their coats frequently threadbare. Being underdressed was never an excuse to miss the fun. "Besides which, our homes, when we returned from play, were warm. The big Dutch oven in the living room—which we used for cooking, baking and heating—served us well," Newman wrote.[16]

When not playing down by the lake, or helping her mother at home, one of Newman's favorite places to roam was the garden path behind the church leading to the lake. It was, she thought, the prettiest place in the village. A fringe of light green grass edged it in spring; red berries dotted the shrubs in fall. She and other children were allowed to walk on it as long as they kept their promise not to stray from the path: "I still remember one pear tree with golden yellow pears—luscious in their appearance and so appealing to the palate! Of course we kept our promise and did not touch anything."[17] Sometimes Newman remembered hearing faint but melodious strains of music coming from the church. When she did, she hid behind the shrubs and lingered until the final notes floated into the air.

She and her friends also enjoyed playing in the meadows on the outskirts of the village, not far from fields of corn, wheat, and rye. "This particular field, then, offered us space to play, air to breathe—things which our homes did not possess," she said.[18] Although the buttercups that bloomed each May were enchanting, the train was the real draw. They stood shoulder-to-shoulder as close as possible to the tracks and waved to the passengers. Newman looked longingly at the people inside, wondering if she too would someday get a chance to sit on that train—or any train, for that matter. If she did, where would she go? It was a fleeting question, given the unlikeliness that she or anyone in her family would ever board a train. The cost of a ticket was too high. Besides, neither she nor her family had any business to attend to or relatives to see outside the village. Like the other Jewish families in their community, the Newmans stuck close to the village. And for good reason.

Before nearly 90 percent of Lithuania's Jews were murdered in the Holocaust, the Baltic nation was home to a large and thriving Jewish community. Lithuania's first Jews arrived in 1338, at the invitation of Vytautas, a ruler of the Grand Duchy of Lithuania. The nobleman granted them a charter that, among other things, allowed them to form a class of freemen subject in all criminal cases directly to the jurisdiction of the grand duke and his official representatives, and in petty suits to the jurisdiction of local officials on an equal footing with the lesser nobles and other free citizens. This relative easing of restrictions was short-lived.

In 1495, a little more than a century later, Alexander Jagiellon, the grand duke of Lithuania and later the king of Poland, expelled the country's Jews, only to reverse course and allow them back in 1503. Sixty-three years later, the Lithuanian statute of 1566 imposed several restrictions on its Jewish residents, including sumptuary laws that mandated Jewish men wear yellow caps and Jewish women yellow kerchiefs. These laws were meant to identify those deemed to be other and inferior. Defiance or failure to comply meant fines and imprisonment.

Jews were forbidden from owning property or engaging in business other than money lending, although small numbers of Jews were able to work as teamsters, draymen, coachmen, unskilled laborers, and farmers. However, legal restrictions prevented them from developing thriving businesses.[19] Despite these controls, the Jewish population of Lithuania increased from about 120,000 in 1569 to approximately 250,000 in 1792.

In 1793, after the Second Partition of the Polish-Lithuanian Commonwealth, Lithuanian Jews, known as Litvaks, found themselves subjects—not citizens—of the Russian Empire. Of course they could be, and were, conscripted into the Russian army. They were consigned to a territory called the Pale of Settlement, which included parts of northeastern Poland and areas along the Baltic Sea, where they could work as merchants and artisans. If they went beyond the designated territory, they risked arrest and imprisonment.

Nine years before Newman was born, violence once again erupted across the Russian Empire. On March 13, 1881, a member of the far-left revolutionary group called the "People's Will" hurled a bomb at Tsar Alexander II while he toured the streets of St. Petersburg in a bullet-proof carriage. The Russian government libeled the Jewish people, triggering pogroms—violent riots that targeted Jewish people. Dozens of Jewish men, women, and children were slaughtered and their homes plundered. This outbreak of pogroms triggered several waves of emigration. Between 1881 and 1886, more than 77,000 Jews from Lithuania, Ukraine, and Belorussia fled west. The number nearly tripled between 1887 and 1892 when 250,000 Jews left.[20] Of course, the exodus wasn't limited to those three countries; persecuted Jews from Austria-Hungary and Romania also boarded steamer ships bound for the United States, the United Kingdom, and Canada.

However, before the assassination, Lithuania's Jews enjoyed a relatively calm existence. In fact, from the eighteenth century and into the end of the nineteenth century, they thrived—so much so that the country became a renowned center of Jewish learning and religious study, with Vilna, present-day Vilnius, "the Jerusalem of Lithuania," as its heart. But Jewish people still could not own land and faced travel restrictions. Nevertheless, for the first time Jewish children attended public schools and Jewish men sat on governing boards of local public institutions such as hospitals, banks, and city councils. Yet, unlike their fellow nationals, the Jewish community remained responsible for most aspects of their daily lives, including the administration of charitable funds like the cost of education for orphans and poor children. But even as Vilna enjoyed a renaissance of sorts in these years—from telegraph and telephone networks that crisscrossed through the city to a municipal sewage system—the economic situation in the countryside worsened. Jews as well as Christians sought job opportunities in Vilna, which was an Eastern European center for education, culture, and politics.

The assassination of Alexander II ushered in a new era of societal crackdowns, mostly targeted at the Jews. During the next decade, tsarist edict after tsarist edict was handed down—each one delivering yet another blow to the tiny liberties the region's Jews now enjoyed.[21] First came the May Laws of 1882, which forbade Jews from living in rural areas, including villages where they might seize the opportunity to carve out a living in grain and timber, sugar mills and mines. Meanwhile, new laws restricted the number of Jews allowed to live in Moscow, St. Petersburg, Kiev, and other cities. By 1891 nearly thirty thousand Jews had been driven from Moscow.

Throughout this period, state-sponsored anti-Jewish pogroms continued unabated—encouraged first by Alexander III and then by Nicholas II. In 1896 an armed mob of Orthodox Christians attacked Jewish homes across Lithuania, including Newman's thatched-roof house in Kovno. Priests often led the mobs who cried "Kill the Jews." The local police made no attempt to check the reign of terror.[22] Not only did the local police stand idly by, but they also arrested any Jews who defended themselves.

This was the Lithuania in which Newman and her family lived. It was a country where she could etch lacy patterns in the ice in winter and hunt for mushrooms with her father but also one where she and her family might be killed for being Jewish.

More than anything else, Newman wanted to attend school. She longed to thumb through the hardbound books, the edges softened and rounded from years of handling. The village boasted one secular school, but to be eligible to attend one's family needed to own land. "We owned no land, hence no school for me," she wrote.[23] She was, however, allowed to attend Sunday school. Each week she walked there alone and looked forward to singing Russian folk songs and reciting poetry, "at which I was pretty good."[24] Those Sundays kindled her lifelong passion for poetry, as both writer and reader.

One of Newman's fondest memories was borrowing books from the school library, the only library in the village. "One Sunday, when the singing was over I was looking at the book case full of books, being little I could not reach the titles of the books on the upper shelf, at that moment the teacher passed by and saw me standing there on my toes," she wrote.[25]

"'What book do you want?' he asked.

"'*Anna Karenina.*'

"He just looked at me—as if seeing me for the first time—and then said—'no, no, not yet,' and handed me *The Uprising of Poland*!" Newman wrote.[26]

It wasn't enough. She craved more. So it was that each time she and her father walked past the local heder, a traditional school for Jewish children where Hebrew and religious subjects are taught, she tugged on his woolen coat sleeve. Please, she begged him, could she join his classes? She promised not to interrupt. She would just listen. It was a preposterous idea, he told her time and again. After all, only boys were allowed to take their place at the long wooden tables. Over time, his daughter's pleas softened his resolve. "He surprised everyone—including my own family, by doing that. Teach the Talmud to a girl? How ridiculous! My father laughed at the taunts and continued to keep me in the class," she reflected.[27]

Ensuring that his students studied history, geography, and arithmetic alongside the Hebrew texts, Meyer Newman's heder, one of more than a thousand in the country, became an outpost of Vilna's Russian Jewish nationalist and socialist movement. So Meyer's decision to allow his daughter Pauline a seat in the classroom was not solely because of her persistence; it also reflected the ideals of the Jewish Enlightenment, or Haskalah. With leaders like Haftali Herz Imber, who advocated for Jewish civil rights and cultural assimilation, and Moses Mendelssohn, regarded by many as the "father of Haskalah," the movement encouraged Jews to embrace mainstream European society and culture through secularization and modernization. Thus, for some of Meyer's students, the heder became one stop on the way to Berlin to pursue a degree in humanities or perhaps to Italy to pursue medicine at the University of Padua.[28]

Save for the family Bible handed down from generation to generation, Newman's parents had no books, nor could they afford to buy them. They made do with the Yiddish translations of Russian newspapers and pamphlets that Meyer brought home. "I remember one pamphlet in particular—it told how 'rain comes down and why.' I don't know who was responsible for sending these books and pamphlets. However, they did reach us. The person or persons who undertook to educate us must have had the spirit of a missionary," Newman recalled.[29]

As an important center for Jewish journalism, Vilna was home to a plethora of journals, such as *Pirhe tsafon* and *Ha-Karmel*, which published articles and columns about Jewish ideas and scholarship. There were also several Jewish publishing houses in Lithuania, the most prestigious being the nearly century-old Romm family printing house. It was so prestigious that in 1836, when Tsar Nicholas I closed all Jewish printing houses, he made an exception for the Romm, although the family was forced to pay five thousand rubles for that right. Alexander II rescinded the limitations on Hebrew printing in 1862 for an annual tax of twenty rubles for every manual printing press.

Vilna was now also the hub of Russia's Zionist movement as well as the emerging Jewish Labor Movement. One of the principle organizations was the Bund, or the General Jewish Workers' Union in Lithuania, Poland, and Russia. Heavily influenced by socialist and Marxist ideas, the Bund, whose members were predominantly wage laborers and apprentices, pushed for workplace reform, including an end to anti-Semitic discrimination and exploitation. It encouraged its members to join Yiddish-speaking school systems, drama societies, and adult evening classes.[30] This era also gave rise to the Jewish Socialist organization Poale Zion, which sought to braid together Jewish labor and Zionist nationalism.[31] These ideas would eventually provide the scaffolding for Newman's political views. Robust debate energized her parents. Later in life she recalled how they and their friends spent many an animated evening discussing how in 1894 the Jewish French artillery officer Major Alfred Dreyfus was convicted on trumped-up charges of treason and exiled to Devil's Island. "Of course we believed him innocent of the treason charges against him," she wrote.[32] She remembered how excited the adults' voices became when they argued over Theodor Herzl's push for a Jewish homeland. Occasionally, one of the men underscored a point in a voice that boomed like a bass drum. Mostly, though, she listened to the ideas as they drifted in the air like feathers for her to collect and examine later in the quiet.

Throughout Newman's childhood her father often fell ill. Yet, even as the sickness gnawed away at him, he continued to teach and find time for fun, so the family woke each morning fully expecting to see him heating a kettle on the stove for tea. But one morning in 1901, before the ice broke, when Newman was just about eight years old, Meyer died. The Chevra Kadisha, the burial society, came to the house and carried him away. They washed his body, gently wrapped it in a plain white cotton *kittel*—the one he had worn when he stood under the marriage canopy with Theresa so many years ago—and stood watch all night. In the morning, in keeping with Jewish burial custom, they placed his body in a plain, unfinished pine coffin and loaded it onto a horse-drawn wagon. The family and members of the Jewish community followed on foot, wending their way to the Jewish cemetery.

It took all the strength of the gravediggers to shovel a deep enough hole in the still-frozen ground. Standing with her mother and siblings, Newman watched as the first shovelfuls of dirt landed on her father's casket. Slowly her beloved father disappeared into the earth. Newman could not bear to think of a life where she would never again hear the sound of his voice or feel the reassuring weight of his hand on her shoulder. "It was a dreary day when we went to the little cemetery to bid good-by to my father. Being early spring his grave was bare—there no sign of grass as yet. A sturdy board which had his name carved on it stood watch over his remains," she wrote. "Here was he whom we loved . . . It hurt to leave him there, alone in the cold earth. Henceforth, there will not be any one to look after his new home."[33]

Several months after Meyer died, Theresa decided it was time for her and her daughters to leave Lithuania. Her three older children had moved to New York City several years earlier, and when they learned of their father's death, they urged their mother and remaining siblings to come. Pauline's older brother provided the necessary proof that the family would not become public charges, that he would help support them until they got their footing. Her brother had already left for South Africa, influenced by some neighbors who had already emigrated there hoping for a safer and more secure economic future.

On the morning they were to leave, Newman heard the familiar clip-clop of their neighbor's horse outside the window. The neighbor offered to take the Newmans to the train station in his wagon. Last kisses and hugs were exchanged with their neighbors. They knew they would never see each other again. Once people emigrated, they rarely, if ever, returned.

Moving to America was a logical move for a Jewish widow of meager means. There was no business for Theresa to take over, and as a woman she most certainly could not run the school. She had depended on Meyer financially for the duration of their marriage, and there would be scant support from the community. She also knew she would never earn more than a pittance acting as a middle woman between farmer and market. Moreover, if Theresa elected to remain in Kovno, her children's marriage prospects, especially those of her daughters, would be slim. If her children were to have any chance at a future, they needed to move elsewhere and if not reinvent themselves, at least reinvent their situation. Thus, the Newman family became just one more Lithuanian family that left for the United States because of economic dislocation, antisemitism, or some combination thereof. While some Lithuanian Jews sailed to South Africa and others for the British Mandate of Palestine, Theresa chose America. She scraped together enough money to cover the cost of the tickets—they were thirty dollars each—and the passport fees. Owning neither suitcases nor trunks, they packed their possessions into cloth bundles. They also filled their pockets with freshly baked rolls; Theresa wasn't going to let her children leave without a bite of home.

Between 1870 and 1900, more than 12 million Jews left Eastern Europe for the United States. Another 9 million left between 1901 and 1910.[34] Every act of emigration, every tallit tucked into a packed bag, every bindle slung over a shoulder, every door shut on a thatched-roof home symbolized a hope that things could get better.

As the village roofs receded in the distance, Newman understood she would never again walk past her father's classroom, pluck ripe berries in the woods, or hang her woolen socks to dry over the Dutch oven in her family's house.

At the station the Newmans boarded the train to the port city of Libau, known today as Liepaja. After a long day of waiting, the foursome boarded the boat. And so began Pauline Newman's first leg of a long journey to the land of "gold and promise."[35]

2

"Will It Ever Be Different?"

Newman clutched her mother's worsted wool skirt. Together with her sisters, they walked across the top deck, past several crew members and passengers, to an opening that revealed a steep, dark stairway. Down they went. Among them were fellow Lithuanian Jews hoping to get to South Africa or the United States. Some were fleeing economic uncertainty and political violence; others were evading conscription into the Russian army.

Leaving Lithuania was an extraordinarily expensive and difficult undertaking. First the family took the train from Kovno to Vilnius. In Vilnius they boarded a ship bound for Liverpool, England, where Newman saw a banana for the first time and mistook a tomato for an apple. There a shipping agent directed them to the steamer they would take, which would stop in St. John's, in the Canadian province of Newfoundland and Labrador, before hugging the Eastern seaboard until it reached Ellis Island.

Newman dreaded the crossing. She overheard the adults talking about how rough the seas could be, how people got sick, and, most frightening, how some people died on the way. She heard they threw the dead overboard.[1] She thought of their bunk in steerage as a life raft of sorts. Sitting on a burlap-covered, straw-filled mattress, she studied the faces of the other adults and children. With no more than about two square feet of space per person, there was no privacy. It was never quiet. Rats and mice scratched and scurried along the wooden floors; roaches skittered into dark corners. Soon her skin was dotted with tiny red bites from fleas and lice. Typhoid, cholera, and dysentery spread among the passengers.

Most of the passengers stayed belowdecks for the duration of the six-week-long voyage. The intrepid few who felt strong enough ventured to the upper deck, where they greedily inhaled the cold and salty air. However, finding the wind too strong and the air too cold, most of them hurried back down the wooden stairs, where the stench of paint, oil, damp, and sour bodies hit like a wall. Unable to avoid the pools of vomit on the floor, they clambered back onto their bunks. Because the bathrooms were on the deck above, most passengers relieved themselves in metal buckets, which flipped and tipped during storms. During storms the crew shut the hatches to stop flooding. "I have never forgotten those days—they were days of gloom and distress," Newman wrote.[2]

Hunger pangs beset Newman. Her mother had packed their own provisions, but somehow they never quite satisfied the growing young girl. The acrid water also tasted funny. She tried not to complain, but judging from the way her mother looked at her, she could have tried harder. One afternoon an English sailor brought Newman an orange: "Another day, he picked me up and took me out on deck for a bit of fresh air, but it was so stormy and so cold that he took me down again, and that really shows you that I couldn't have been more than a kid, or I wouldn't have gone back [to the deck]."[3]

Three weeks later Newman happened to be on deck when she spied a towering woman wearing a crown and holding a torch aloft. Less than an hour later, the ship moored at Ellis Island.

Forty-one years after the legendary gangster Albert W. Hicks, forty, became the last man hanged in New York City for the federal crime of piracy, Ellis Island no longer represented a portal to death but rather a gateway to a new life. Nearly eight out of ten immigrants would be processed through what became known as the Island of Tears.

Hungry and scared, bedraggled and bewildered, Newman tried to hold her own tears back as her mother gripped her small hand. Each of them carried a bundle, though they arrived with fewer possessions than when they had left. The list of things Newman and her family lost during the crossing was long: copper pots and bedding, linens and utensils. There was also the family Bible in which Meyer had inscribed the birth date of all four Newman children on the flyleaf. Newman never knew exactly what day or year she was born. "There was no registration in that village. And so I can be a hundred and five or sixty-five, I don't know," she later quipped.[4] A few years later she picked October 9 as her birthdate, choosing it because it coincided with the start of the Russian Revolution.[5]

Shortly after they disembarked, the family passed through the doors of the Great Hall, or Registry Hall, a place of a thousand sounds. Here they were jostled and poked. White-faced parents, fearing they would be summarily turned away, held their crying babies close. Others whispered warnings about being shortchanged at the currency exchange window. Stories swirled about a Lutheran minister who was arrested for trafficking young women.[6]

Theresa's eyes darted about, looking for someone, anyone, who might help them. At the time, representatives from the National Council of Jewish Women, which was founded in 1893, were stationed at Ellis Island. These women, fluent in English and Yiddish, walked up and down the lines looking for newly arrived immigrants who needed help interpreting, directions for what to do after they passed the inspection, or where they might find short-term lodging. They also made citizenship guides available to newly arrived immigrants. Single women traveling alone could sometimes find temporary guardianship. Some single women were able to stay at the Clara de Hirsch Home in New York, the Home of Jewish Working Girls, or the Josephine Club. The Ruth and Miriam clubs in Chicago and the Rebecca Gratz House in Philadelphia offered room and board to hundreds of young women who might not be able to stay with a private family.[7]

Before the Newmans knew it, they were standing before a uniformed inspector seated on a high stool behind a wooden desk. The questions came fast: Are you married? Do you have a job? Do you have a contagious disease? Criminal record? What did you do before? What is your destination? With whom are you going to be living and what is the exact address? Theresa had memorized her responses during the crossing. In English flecked with Yiddish, she answered: Widowed. No. No. No. Sold fruit. 311 Madison Street, Manhattan. A wrong answer, or too halting an answer, could condemn them to being sent back to the shtetl from whence they had fled.

On any given day, government agents might detain half of the Jewish immigrants, ultimately sending them back across the rolling ocean. Those among the nearly 5,000 immigrants who arrived daily who did pass muster spent only a few hours on the island before continuing on their journey. By the time the Newman family arrived, more than 250,000 people had already made the crossing. About 64 percent of all Jewish immigrants who arrived between 1899 and 1910 remained in New York City, most of them settling in the Lower East Side. Others traveled on to Philadelphia, Boston, and Chicago.[8]

After the questions came "the line," shorthand for the six-second medical inspection. Inspectors peered into mouths looking for rotten teeth, and then, using a button hook, they flipped eyelids looking for signs of trachoma, a highly contagious bacteria that can lead to blindness. Finally, the Newman family was cleared to continue to the mainland.

They boarded a ferry, and less than a half hour later they stepped onto the cobblestone streets of Battery Park. "I never saw so many people on the streets, shouting, going in all directions. Having come from a little bit of a village with a few houses, it was to say the least disturbing," Newman recalled.[9] Filled with bedding and belongings, the wagon they rode in jostled and bounced its way over the streets from Battery Park to the Lower East Side, where nearly five hundred thousand Jewish, Italian, and Irish immigrants lived, squeezed into two square miles.

The first Jews arrived in New York City in 1654 from Recife, Brazil. Descendants of the hundreds of thousands of Jews expelled from Spain and Portugal during the Spanish Inquisition, they were a group of twenty-three Sephardic Jews of the Dutch West India Company, which was headquartered in Amsterdam. Some of them escaped to Turkey and points farther east; others eventually made their way to Holland. Among those who settled in Holland, many sailed for Recife, then a Dutch colony. Life for Jewish people was relatively quiet until 1654, when war erupted between the Portuguese and the Dutch. After the Dutch lost the war, the Inquisition extended to Brazil and the small group of Jewish people fled. Carrying four Jewish men, two Jewish women, and seventeen children, their ship arrived in New Amsterdam after an arduous journey. Along the way Spanish pirates robbed the passengers, stole their ship, and dumped their belongings in the West Indies. A Montreal-bound French vessel then agreed to take the group to New Amsterdam—much to the dismay of Peter Stuyvesant, the colony's antisemitic governor. He dispatched his letter to the Dutch West India Company headquarters and awaited the reply. In his letter he implored the company that "the deceitful race . . . be not allowed to further infect and trouble this new colony."[10]

Weeks later Stuyvesant received his response. As much as the company wanted to fulfill his wishes "that these new territories should no more be infected by the Jewish nation," they told him that disallowing their entrance would be unfair to the many Jewish people who supported colonization, so "these people may travel and trade in New Netherland and live and remain there, provided the poor among them shall not become a burden to the company . . . but be supported by their own nation."[11] The twenty-three Dutch Jews were thus released from confinement and began to build a life on the twenty-four-mile stretch of land between the Hudson and East rivers—a synagogue here, a business there. The first cemetery in New Netherland was incorporated in 1683 in what is now Chatham Square in Chinatown. While the Jews enjoyed the privileges common to the other inhabitants of this town, they did not escape discrimination. Nevertheless, as their numbers grew, so too did their civic engagement.

The Jewish community would go on to help finance the construction of Trinity Church. They also fought in the Revolutionary War, and during the Civil War they sold $200 million in bonds to help support the Union Army.[12]

By the time the Newmans stepped off the boat almost two hundred years later, there were several Jewish organizations where they could get help. There was the Hebrew Immigrant Aid and Sheltering Society, which Lower East Side Jews founded between 1881 and 1883. There was also the Henry Street Settlement, founded by Lillian Wald in 1893, which helped newly arrived immigrants assimilate. The settlement offered English and cooking classes and provided health services.[13]

Wedged between her mother and sister as they explored their new surroundings, Newman couldn't absorb the sights fast enough. Buildings rose several stories in the air, and people walked around in all manner of dress. Other than their stop in Liverpool, Newman had never spent time in a city. Whatever images she had conjured on the nearly two-month-long trip across the Atlantic, nothing prepared her for what she saw now.

The wagon slowed upon reaching Hester Street. Newman's brother and his wife waited on the sidewalk in front of the five-story tenement. After spending all that time squished together during the trip across the ocean, after a childhood living in two rooms with parents and siblings, it was time to split up. Theresa moved into her brother's, apartment. Pauline and her sisters, Fanny and Sarah, were parceled out to their brother's tenement, where they would all live crowded together. Once inside, Theresa's sister-in-law opened the door to a dark and stuffy space and pointed her to a bed in the living room. "It was not much better than a cellar," Newman wrote.[14]

At five stories high, Newman's brother's apartment was a typical "dumbbell" shaped tenement. The design was supposed to create an air shaft for fresh air to circulate. It didn't work. Only one room boasted a street-facing window, and it was a basement window at that.[15] Next on the tour, such as it was, was the bathroom. There was one toilet per floor, which they shared with three other families. As for bathing, Newman would learn to make do with a sponge bath at the kitchen sink. Every time she turned the rusty faucet, it squeaked in protest. For this, Newman's brother paid twelve dollars a month. In time, Newman counted herself lucky, for she soon met people who were even worse off, including some "friends and neighbors who lived in tenements where the toilet was in the yard, with no heat, except if you were able to own a stove. And that stove served for cooking and heating as well."[16]

Certainly the Newmans knew life in America was going to be different; still, they envisioned better living conditions than what they found. Yes, their thatched-roof home had felt cramped, but it was clean and tidy. The tenement was dark and in disrepair. Here even fresh air was a luxury. Here housework quickly proved a Sisyphean task. The soot and grime followed them in from the outside. The idea that everything could have a place to be neatly tucked away was a joke in a space where a table pulled triple duty as bed, work table, and ironing board.

Newman's first days in Manhattan were a blur. She quickly learned to feed the kitchen stove with coal and wood and how to cook soup the way her sister-in-law did. Missing her mother, she was afraid to fall asleep in her bed. Speaking only Russian and Yiddish, she was scared to venture outside alone. Impatient for his younger sister to learn English, her brother tried immersion. In short, he spoke only English to her. He gave up after a couple of weeks. Slowly Newman picked up a word here, a phrase there. When she finally mustered up the courage to go outside, she tucked a bread roll into her pocket.

The pace of city life overwhelmed Newman: "There was always such crowds of people! People walking, standing, pushed each other; arguing, shouting, drinking soda water at one cent a glass . . . There were men speaking from soap boxes . . . There was the Salvation Army with music and song and of course, the ever-present push carts."[17]

The pushcarts occupied nearly every inch of the sidewalk and side streets. There was nothing that couldn't be hawked from a wagon: bandannas and tin cups for two cents, a quart of peaches for a cent, and hats for a quarter; plucked chickens and geese, well-worn coats and trousers with holes at the knees. Newman marveled at the offerings.

From the first crack of light in the morning until well after midnight, the streets pulsed with life. Freshly laundered sheets, dresses, shirts, and trousers danced from rooftop clotheslines. Women rushing to work in factory lofts dodged boys playing stickball. Crossing the street amid horses and pushcarts tested one's nerves. Young children with smudged faces and scuffed shoes scurried down the sidewalks carrying unwieldy bundles of unfinished garments or boxes of sewing supplies. Manufacturers relied on these children, or "schleppers" to deliver the parcels to lofts, row houses, and tenement house workshops where, amid the whir of sewing machines and kitchen tables that doubled as workbenches, adults put the finishing touches on shirts, pants, and dresses.

Every few feet stood a pickle kiosk, where customers could pluck half of a sour pickle from a wooden barrel for less than a nickel. But on the rare occasions when Newman's brother pressed a few pennies into her hand for candy, she preferred buying a copy of the *Jewish Daily Forward*, published in Yiddish at the time. She read about the continual rent hikes and what it was like to live under the constant threat of eviction. She saw how the police harassed the newly homeless. She didn't understand why her brother scolded her for reading the paper. "One evening, while we were at supper, my brother said that he had noticed me reading *The Forward* and that it being a 'socialist' paper, he disapproved of my doing so," she later wrote.[18]

Founded in 1897 by the socialist and intellectual Abraham Cahan, the paper helped shape the Lower East Side into the capital of American Jewry, influencing Yiddish literature, Jewish American literature, Yiddish theater, the burgeoning Yiddish film industry, and, in time, the anticommunist direction that American socialism took. On Election Day people went to the building where the *Forward* was published and waited as the returns came in. The paper ran popular columns like the advice column "Bintel Brief," meaning "a bundle of letters." With its devoted readership, the paper served as a secular Bible for Newman.

Less than two months after Newman arrived on her brother's doorstep, he told her to find a job to help augment the family's earnings. The next morning, after scrubbing her face at the sink with a sliver of soap, she closed the door to the tenement and walked down the dark hallway, down the staircase with its peeling paint on the walls. She walked up and down the streets looking for "help wanted" signs. Along the way she passed several open-air labor markets. At the Chazir-mark, or "pig market," on Hester Street were bunches of Russian Jewish immigrants vying for jobs as merchants, butchers, and chicken sellers. There weren't many things that they, as unskilled foreigners with little English, could do, but they were willing. At the "tailors market" on Ridge and Delancey streets men, some with sewing machines strapped to their backs, hunted for jobs at any one of the hundreds of hot, dusty tenement shops that lined East Broadway and Clinton Street.

She found nothing the first day. Nor the second. Nor the third. On the fourth day she went outside again. It was late autumn and she couldn't believe it was possible to be this cold. The buildings were like wind tunnels, trapping cold air. Her smocked dress was too thin and her coat too threadbare. Her toes felt like frozen stubs. She walked up and down Canal Street. Nothing. Next she tried West Broadway and then Lispenard and Walker streets. Still nothing. Finally, on the fifth day she saw a small board nailed to a building. "Young girls wanted; experience not necessary" read the sign in Yiddish. She pushed open the door and climbed the partially broken stairs up four flights to a hairbrush factory.[19]

There was no job interview. There was simply a list of rules. Nine-year-old Newman was expected to remove wood splinters from horsehair eleven and a half hours a day, six days a week. On Mondays through Fridays she worked from 7:30 a.m. until 6:00 p.m. On Saturdays she worked from 7:30 a.m. to 4:00 p.m. For this she earned $1.50 a week.[20] After she weighed the hair, the foreman took it to another group of workers, who tied it into knots with twine. Another group of workers then guided the bunches through machines, which drilled holes in the stocks. Then another group dipped the bristles in heated pitch. It was as grueling as it was dull.

Negotiating for improved conditions was impossible for these newly arrived immigrants, who, because of their class, gender, and lack of English, were forced to bow before management. Conditions were even worse for Black Americans, particularly Black women, who, because of racism and classism, were even more vulnerable to exploitation, abuse, and wage theft.[21]

Still groggy from sleep, Newman and the other neighborhood children chatted and sang as they walked to work. Their ranks dwindled as one by one they arrived at their particular jobs. One child turned in to a basement-level cigar shop. Another girl arrived at a hat finishing factory. Newman turned the handle on the door to the hairbrush factory. When the children met again twelve hours later, it would be dark and they would be too tired to sing.

Finding work was relatively easy, but keeping a job proved harder. Factories didn't guarantee employment. In fact, many closed soon after they opened. It was an industry in constant flux. Most jobs were seasonal, so they hired and fired workers constantly. If a worker wasn't fired during slack season, that time of year when demand declined, factory owners frequently reduced their salaries. Predictably, the hairbrush factory where Newman worked shuttered just weeks after she was hired. It was a month before she spied another "help wanted" sign: "Girls wanted to make cigarettes by hand."

Invented by Don Luis Susini of Cuba, the first cigarette-rolling machines appeared in 1867. Because the earliest models were finicky, the wrapping paper often catching and tearing, they weren't widely adopted. Instead, employers preferred to hire girls and women to hand roll them, largely because they could pay them less than men. Newman welcomed the twenty-five cents she earned a day—ten cents extra for rolling more than her quota—but she did not welcome the way the thin paper sliced her hands.

Much to her and her family's disappointment, Newman was fired two weeks later. Overstocked, the factory no longer needed her and the other recent hires. Fortunately, as quickly as she was fired, she was once again hired. This time she found a job earning thirty-five cents a day sewing buttons onto shirtwaists in a shop located on the top floor of a five-story walk-up on Jackson Street. Threading her needle, the ten-year-old stared out the factory windows, which faced a park. "Often I longed to join the youngsters in the park and to breathe the cool fresh air. After all, I was not much older than they were!" she said.[22] Less than a mile away the East River shimmered.

On her way home from work she bought a copy of *The Forward* (formerly known as *The Jewish Daily Forward*), eager to read it before dinner. That January 8, 1902, two trains collided in the Park Avenue tunnel, killing seventeen people and injuring thirty-eight. Uptown she could see the triangular shape of the Flatiron Building slowly rising on the corner of Fifth Avenue and Broadway. When completed, the limestone and terracotta building would stand twenty-two stories—an imposing sight for a rural girl.

The arrival of summer meant the end of the Jackson Street job. Now nearly twelve, Newman was once again hunting for work. She hoped to find something that lasted longer than a few weeks. Luck was on her side. With the help of her cousin, she landed a job at the Triangle Shirtwaist Factory, the largest manufacturer of shirtwaists in New York City. Max Blanck and Isaac Harris, both Russian immigrants, opened the business off Washington Square Park in 1901.

Before Washington Square Park became one of New York City's most fashionable addresses, almost two-thirds of it served as a potter's field. In 1797 the city purchased an old farm for forty-five hundred dollars and used the land to bury the impoverished there in mass graves until about 1820.[23] Although most of the remains were later reinterred, some can still be found beneath the paths and green plantings. Nevertheless, by 1827 the space was reimagined as a public square, and soon townhouses with windows and iron balustrades rose up as a sort of boundary between the monied classes and the factories and tenements that extended from Broadway to the east and south.

Perhaps Washington Square was not an ideal location for a factory; the unofficial garment district was actually located more to the north and west. However, businessman Joseph J. Asch favored the site. He envisioned renting out space to retail shops on the first floor and renting floors two through ten to a factory. In this case it was the Triangle Shirtwaist Factory, and though it was of no concern to him how Max Blanck and Isaac Harris, the "Shirtwaist Kings" managed their shop, he involved himself in the building's design.

Worn tucked into a separate ankle-length skirt, with its front opening tailored like a men's dress shirt, the shirtwaist, or blouse, first made its debut around 1890. It fast became a symbol of female independence, sending a sly sartorial message that women belonged in previously male-dominated realms.[24] Wealthy women, college women, and office workers all wore the high collared, wide-sleeved cotton blouses. American illustrator Charles Dana Gibson popularized the garment. It was he who dreamed up the "Gibson Girl," an idealized and stylized white European American woman who, under a cloud of blonde or light brown hair, gazed serenely into the distance while wearing a snow-white shirtwaist. Advertised in *Ladies Home Journal* and *McClure's Magazine*, the blouse promised independence. But while its sharp creases and neat pintucks suggested freedom, its stitches told another story: one of sweatshops and child labor.

Before the fabric arrived in the Asch Building, it was a cotton bud on a plantation in the South. Nearly a thousand miles away, children labored alongside their parents and grandparents under the searing sun picking cotton for subsistence pay. The plucked and raw cotton was then loaded onto trains and shipped to mills in New England where textile workers, many of them children between nine and ten years old, spun the puffs into thread and dyed them different hues.[25] Hunched over looms, the children wove the thread into cloth. Injuries were commonplace. Some children lost fingers since the looms lacked safety devices like guardrails and automatic shutoff switches.

Until that time, ready-made clothing was mostly for sailors, miners, and soldiers. It was either homespun or custom-made clothing. It was only in the later part of the nineteenth century that standard sizes were introduced through firms like Sears, Roebuck and Co. The increased demand meant an increase in the need for labor. At the same time, a growing number of girls and women were entering the workforce. Whereas they accounted for about 18 percent of the US workforce in 1890, they comprised about 25 percent in 1920. A number of factors, including industrialization, urbanization, and the need for additional income all played a role in this steady growth.[26]

Adopting an unmechanized assembly line approach called the "task system," the Triangle Shirtwaist Factory was the future. It opened just as women's clothing production began its steady migration from apartments and small shops to factory lofts. In 1895 there were about six shirtwaist firms in New York City. By 1909 there were nearly six hundred shops, employing about thirty thousand workers and producing about $50 million a year.[27] It was one of the fastest-growing sectors of the garment industry, according to the 1900 US Census. Several factors made such growth possible, including the increase in skilled labor, machines that could cut and sew, and available loft space where the finished product could be stored until it was sold.

One group of workers cut sleeves, lapels, and other pieces of the garment into small, medium, large, and extra-large sizes.[28] A good cutter could slice through sixteen layers of cloth at once into identical shapes that fit together like a jigsaw puzzle. The hand-basted pieces were then sent to the sewing machine operators. Using treadle sewing machines, which Isaac Merritt Singer introduced in the 1850s, a good sewing machine operator could sew up to four hundred stitches a minute versus thirty-five by hand. Working at 240 machines arranged in 16 parallel rows, the factory's sewing machine operators occupied almost the entire ninth floor. Wicker baskets rested at the feet of each woman. A grooved wooden shelf was suspended just under the table to catch the oil drippings from the machine before they could dribble onto the highly combustible fabric.

Another group of workers, called finishers, added the linings, decoration, and buttons. The garment was then handed off to the "kindergarten," where for nearly fourteen hours a day, young children handled scissors too large, and in some cases too heavy, for their small hands. That's where Newman worked. "We were too young to do anything else but clean the threads off the shirt waists when they came to us from the operators and were piled into the large cases that were taller than some of us were," Newman said.[29] Once the children snipped off the stray threads, the garment was sent on to the pressers. Applying hot irons that weighed up to twenty pounds, the pressers removed wrinkles. This was the shirtwaist's last stop before being inspected, boxed, and sent uptown to department stores like Lord & Taylor and Bergdorf Goodman.[30]

Newman trained herself to avoid repeatedly glancing at the clock—not an easy accomplishment for a twelve-year-old. Finally the hands of the clock struck noon. Newman rushed down the narrow staircase as fast as possible. Once outside, she reached into the pocket of her cotton dress for the 10 cents it cost her to purchase a coffee and sandwich, or 3 cents for soda pop. This was the only time she could grumble and chat with her workmates. At day's end Newman was either numb with cold or soaked with sweat. She would smell the peculiar odor of sweat, oil, and lint long after she left work for the day. The odor was still there the next morning when she waited impatiently at the corner of Hester Street for the 6:40 a.m. horsecar. If it arrived late, she would be late for work. And if she wasn't at her work station at precisely at 7:30 a.m., her pay would be docked. "That these deductions meant less food for the workers and children bothered the employers not at all," she said.[31] The trolley cost 5 cents a ride, or 30 cents a week—precious coins, considering she earned only $1.50 a week. Newman spent every morning a bundle of nerves.

Once she walked through the factory door, she remained at her station, except for lunchtime, until 6:30 p.m. However, the reality was that she usually worked until 9:00 p.m. unless it was Shabbat. Then the supervisors would allow the workers to leave around 4:00 p.m. At the time that Newman worked at the Triangle, about 40 percent of New York City garment workers were Jewish immigrants, compared with about 27 percent who came from southern Italy. Newman would have spent most of her time working alongside Jewish workers.[32]

Overtime pay was nonexistent and the company's management never supplied dinner on those nights Newman did work late. Instead, the workers got a "nickel's worth of pie."[33] At the end of each week, Newman turned her unopened envelope over to her mother, who doled out a portion to her brother. Newman's sisters, Fanny and Sarah, earned $6.00 a week. Together the family brought in about $7.50 a week. At this point Theresa was taking in a little laundry to earn extra money. She carried the water up the stairs in buckets, trying not to slosh water over the sides. Then she soaked the dirty clothes in the kitchen sink overnight. After scrubbing them on a washboard in the morning, she wrung them out and then carried them up to the rooftop, where she clipped them to a clothesline. It was hours of work for pennies. Yet, bit by bit the coins filled the little jar she kept in the kitchen.[34] Twelve-year-old Newman's wages, like those of countless other young women, were vital to an immigrant family's survival. Parents expected daughters to hand over pay envelopes to the household financial manager, which was the mother in the case of Italian and Jewish households. In return, most received a small allowance. Fathers and sons, however, could justly open their own envelopes before returning home and extract sums for their own leisure.

Before the Industrial Revolution there were few women wage earners, except perhaps in domestic service. Occasionally a widow took over a husband's business or found work as a dressmaker. Working outside the home did not begin in earnest until the close of the eighteenth century, when the New England factory town grew. In 1880 a little more than 14 percent of females over ten worked outside the home; by 1890 that number increased to nearly 17 percent.[35] Families relied on their breadwinning daughters. The US Immigration Commission found that about 40 percent of foreign-born Jewish girls fourteen and fifteen years old, worked outside the home.[36]

Newman knew she held one of the highest-paying jobs in the garment industry, even if her salary fell far below that of a male worker. For example, a skilled cutter earned an average of $7 a week. The most qualified among them might bring in over $20 a week. Not only did the men earn more, but internal subcontracting effectively trapped women on the lowest rungs of the ladder. Although some earned between $7 to $12 a week, women typically earned between $3 and $4 a week. As Newman later said, "It was a world of greed; the human being didn't mean anything."[37]

Factory owners determined everything. They set the wages, they worked people around the clock, they hired and fired at will, and they fined workers for whatever they deemed a misstep, like taking a minute too long in the restroom or fixing a hairpin before 6:00 p.m. dismissal. Of course, neither Newman nor her fellow workers dared complain about the conditions; to do so was to invite summary firing. And you knew you were lucky to have a job. The idea of changing a job was a luxury the workers could ill afford. After all, as Newman remembered it, there was a sign by the elevator that said: "If you don't come in on a Sunday, you need not come in on a Monday!"[38]

Every evening Newman was required to queue with the other workers to have her bag searched. Then she was disgorged into the fresh air. Walking home via Houston Street, she thought about how "these crowded streets, these ugly tenements, the poverty, the squalor depressed me. As time went on they became familiar scenes," Newman said. "Every day the same foreman, the same forelady[,] the same shirt waists. The same machines, the same surroundings. The day is long and the task tiresome. In despair I ask 'Dear God, will it ever be different?'"[39]

After a year on the job, the odors and long hours no longer fazed Newman. Neither did working in near silence. She shrugged her shoulders when floor managers barked their orders. But she never got used to the scrutiny—scrutiny that was made easier for managers because of their rubber-soled shoes. Now nearly ubiquitous among employers, they added one more element of stress to an already stressful job. "You never knew when they would sneak up on you, spying, to be sure you did not talk to each other during work hours."[40]

The conditions in which Newman labored were neither better nor worse than any other shop in New York City. The tenement in which she lived was certainly no better or worse than those where her colleagues lived. The factories were swept once a year at most, usually before a Jewish holiday. There was never enough heat in the winter, and in the summer it was quite suffocating. "The early sweatshops were usually so dark that gas jets burned day and night. There was no insulation in the winter, only a pot-bellied stove in the middle of the factory," she said. "You got out of the workshop, dark and cold in winter, hot in summer, dirty unswept floors, no ventilation, and you would go home."[41]

As Jacob Riis, a Dutch immigrant who also worked as a police reporter for the *New-York Tribune* and *The Sun*, described in his book *How the Other Half Lives*:

> Every open window of the big tenements, that stand like a continuous brick wall on both sides of the way, gives you a glimpse of one of these shops as the train speeds by. Men and women bending over their machines, or ironing clothes at the window, half-naked . . . The road is like a big gangway through an endless work-room where vast multitudes are forever laboring. Morning, noon, or night, it makes no difference; the scene is always the same . . . whirring sewing machines behind closed door betraying what goes on within.[42]

Inside the shop Newman made fast friends with some of her workmates. Later some, like J.A.H. Dahme, would send her letters that seemed like fan mail: "Yes, I understand you to that depth of thoroughness as only one who has long suffered can! . . . From the deepest place of my bosom let me utter the words, 'we shall be friends in joy and sorrow!' what is there sweeter in life than the sympathy between woman and woman—what purer than the sincerity of hearts—what greater than the harmony of minds? . . . yours in friendship and socialist comradeship."[43]

Sitting at a wooden desk in her father's classroom was a mere fragment of a memory. If she tried hard enough, she could remember how the pages smelled when she opened her book, how she crossed her ankles while reading a particularly difficult passage. However, as much as she wanted to, she rarely allowed herself the luxury of thinking about returning to school. It wasn't that the possibility didn't exist; there were evening schools attended by immigrants from the world over, including Turkey and Russia. As tired as these people were after working all day in a sweatshop or factory, they went so that they could learn English.[44] Nevertheless, attending evening school after hours spent in a confined, crowded factory where the whir of machinery ground all day was not an option for Newman, or for most working poor. Most children in the garment trade dropped out of school before completing eighth grade. About 41 percent of milliners left before eighth grade, as did 55 percent of dressmakers and 49 percent of artificial flower and feather making workers.[45]

As such, Newman satisfied herself with an informal education. She continued to read the newspapers and to buy the occasional book from a pushcart. Her first purchase was Charles Dickens's *Great Expectations*. Whether she identified with Pip, Estella, or Biddy, she never said. For her, the novel was simply a key to unlocking English. Indeed, reading became a favorite pastime of hers. Newman remained a puzzle to many of her coworkers, who couldn't understand why after twelve hours on her feet she preferred to read the paper rather than splurge on a movie or a soda. "You could go out probably and join the other girls on the sidewalk and jabber and just sit on the stoop: you could go to sleep. But you also could use your mind if you had any, use your brains in order to hear," she said.[46]

Before long the papers and books were not enough to satiate her curiosity. Enter the Socialist Literary Society. Of course, socialism, which pushed for societal change through democratic means, was one of several competing political philosophies that ripened in this corner of Manhattan where people lived crammed into tiny apartments, worked in dangerous and exhausting conditions, and were confronted daily by squalor on the streets. There were also communists, who favored the overthrow of capitalism and anarchists, like the Lithuanian-born Emma Goldman, who wanted to dispatch with government all together. Newman, for her part, remained drawn to socialism and to the literary society, which, although egalitarian in theory, barred women from becoming full members. They were, however, allowed to attend the free lectures and literature classes. If she didn't dawdle when the final factory whistle blew at 6:30 p.m., she could get there in time to hear Dr. Henry Neuman, a professor of English literature at City College of New York. A dedicated teacher, Newman was impressed with the care her professor took to make sure students understood the work and to determine if they needed more help in learning English.[47] In time, the society became more than an education folded into a distraction. It became what Newman's father's classroom signified for her back in Lithuania—a gateway to the world. She was becoming a voracious reader and read everything from Shakespeare to Thomas Hardy to Charlotte Perkins Gilman, who once lectured at the society.

One evening Newman was reading George Eliot's *The Mill on the Floss*. Its themes of education, debt, and a woman's place in society resonated with Newman, who was now nearly fifteen. After the lecture, just as the librarian in Kovno did some years earlier, Professor Neuman invited Pauline to borrow as many books as she wanted with the expectation that she be prepared to read with him on Tuesday and Thursday nights. Her English quickly improved and her social circle expanded.

Among the many people Newman met at the society was Clara Lemlich, who arrived in New York City from Ukraine in 1903, and Rose Schneiderman, who immigrated to the United States from Poland with her Orthodox Jewish parents when she was eight. Two years after the Schneiderman family crowded into a tenement on Ludlow Street, the father, a tailor, died. The family was plunged into poverty. Schneiderman and her siblings were parceled out to orphanages and then to relatives' homes, always dependent on charity and whatever their mother, a custom seamstress, could earn by way of boarders and piecework. At thirteen Schneiderman found a job making cap linings. She and her friends often met during lunch or after work and, in English flecked with Yiddish accents, discussed what they were reading.[48] On the rare occasion that the young women found an extra few coins in their change purses or pockets, they might meet on the corner of Essex and East Broadway and get a bite to eat at Madison Square Garden. "After meetings, which usually lasted till long after midnight—they were held on Saturday night, so if you didn't have to work the next day you had an evening free, we'd go to Central Park and watch the moon arise, sometimes to watch the sun rise. We had a lot of fun despite everything," Newman wrote.[49]

Newman also attended Marxist theory classes at the Socialist Party's Rand School. Whereas she once rejected the idea of night school, she now felt inspired to get out of the shop to learn; education became the dominant force in her life. She and the other girls who attended liked to take turns reading poetry and Dickens and George Eliot in English to improve their understanding of the language. "I remember when we first heard Thomas Hood's 'Song of the Shirt' I figured that it was written for us. You know, it told the long hours of stitch, stitch, stitch. I remember one of the girls said, 'He didn't know us. Did he?' And I said, 'No, he didn't.' But it had an impact on us," she said. Clearly, lines like "It is not linen you're wearing out, But human creatures' lives!" and "Sewing at once, with a double thread, A Shroud as well as a Shirt" resonated.[50]

Five years after Newman first climbed the dark steps of the hairbrush factory, her mother had finally saved enough money for them to move uptown. It was 1906 and the small family now occupied a railroad flat at 307 Madison Avenue that boasted two bedrooms, a living room, dining room, and kitchen. The bathroom in the hall was the height of luxury. But while they had saved enough money to move, the city teetered toward an economic collapse.

3

East Side Joan of Arc

Pauline Newman poked the fire and stirred a can of beans. Clara Lemlich was chatting with Rose Schneiderman, looking out from their campsite high above the Hudson River. The trees were turning red and yellow. It was warm enough that boats were still sailing up the river. It was summer 1907 and the city was teetering on the edge of a full-blown financial crisis.

Together with Charles W. Morse, F. Augustus Heinze, one of Montana's "Copper Kings," and his brothers Otto and Arthur, tried to corner the market on United Copper Company. Their venture sent the New York Stock Exchange plummeting by 50 percent; so began the first major financial crisis of the twentieth century. One week into the crisis, banking magnate and Gilded Age financier J. P. Morgan announced he would not bail out the Knickerbocker Trust Company. The decision not only caused the collapse of the city's third-largest trust, but it also sent regional banks into a tailspin as customers frantically withdrew their deposits. All confidence in the financial system had evaporated. Ultimately, public calls for reform would lead to the creation of the National Monetary Commission, which in turn led to the establishment of the Federal Reserve System in 1913. Yet, outside of New York, life carried on; even Theodore Roosevelt wasn't terribly flustered. In fact, the barrel-chested, bespectacled president still went on his bear hunting trip in Louisiana with John Avery McIlhenny, the owner of Tabasco hot sauce.

But in the city, rising rents coupled with climbing unemployment meant forced summer furloughs for sixteen-year-old Newman and her friends. Deciding to take advantage of this enforced leisure, the group pitched tents on the Palisades. Below the steep cliffs, the waters of the Hudson River raced. From June through September the girls read Jewish poets like Morris Rosenfeld by day and David Edelstadt by night. "We lived on baked beans . . . morning, noon and night there was nothing but baked beans . . . [I] can still see the black iron pot in the improvised outdoor grill full of beans," Newman said.[1] They passed books back and forth, hiked, and sang Russian and Yiddish songs.

Thrilled to be away from the smothering city life, but less thrilled to lose her paycheck for these weeks, Newman bonded with Schneiderman, Lemlich, and the others who joined them. For Newman, who had shed the rituals of religion soon after arriving in America, there was something spiritual about gathering in the open air. Far from the watchful eyes and prying ears of the factory supervisors, the girls relished the chance to speak freely. They complained about the unfairness of worker speed-ups and wage cuts. They grumbled about being forced to pay for their own thread and needles. They ranted about being timed when they went to the bathroom and about earning pennies in comparison to what the men earned. "The employers didn't recognize anyone working for them as a human being," Newman said.[2]

Then almost as quickly as it began, the three-week-long banker's crisis, later referred to as the Panic of 1907, ended. Morgan pledged his own money and purchased New York City bonds to stanch the city's financial hemorrhaging.

Newman and her friends folded their tents, stuffed their tin coffee cups into their bags, and returned to their homes and jobs on the Lower East Side. They also returned realizing they could, and should, turn their friendship into action.

Back at the apartment, Newman trudged up the stairs. Her knuckles ached; her ankles ached. If she closed her eyes, she could still hear the whirring of sewing machines. Working in the Triangle Shirtwaist Factory was a grind. It was also oddly rewarding, in that for the first time since she had arrived in the United States, she no longer felt so alone. Here too were other young immigrants in similar circumstances.[3] Upon opening the door, she found her mother, Theresa, standing at the sink, hands red and raw from detergent, complaining about money, picking up where she'd left that morning. Somehow there must be more money, Theresa told her daughter. There never was. No matter how long Newman toiled at the Triangle Shirtwaist Factory, her pay envelope never grew any thicker.

It was the same each week. If Newman didn't go to the Socialist Literary Society on East Broadway, she went directly home, checked the mailbox, and then went upstairs to their tenement. Most evenings Newman, who had since moved out of her brother's apartment, pushed open the door to find her mother scrubbing dishes, rinsing out laundry in the kitchen sink, or preparing dinner for her and her sisters. On paydays Newman turned her envelope over to her mother, who promptly inspected it several times to make sure none of the bills were stuck together. Then she meticulously counted them, designating some for rent, some for groceries, and some for heat. There was scarcely any left for an emergency.

So when the Newmans' landlord threatened to raise rent—again—Newman had had it. Her mother had had it too. Theresa refused to pay one cent more unless the landlord installed windows in the bedrooms. She refused to pay one cent more unless the landlord installed a bathroom in each apartment so that they no longer needed to walk four flights down to the outhouse that occupied the bit of land he insisted on calling a yard. "And the landlord wouldn't do it, so we didn't give any increase," Newman said.[4]

Across the Lower East Side evictions were rampant. Each day another family was turned out of their home, another pile of belongings and furniture dumped onto the curb. Some families tried to preempt the indignity and upheaval of eviction by moving into less expensive housing. Yet, moving was costly and it was unclear if anything more affordable would be available. Already there was a squeeze on housing. The authorities evicted thousands of families from their homes to clear a way for an entrance onto the newly built Manhattan Bridge just as they had done three years earlier, when seventeen thousand residents were evicted so that the city could begin construction on the Williamsburg Bridge.

Property owners knew they maintained the advantage and could hike rents upward of 20 percent with no consequence.[5] For too long landlords ignored tenants' requests to do basic repairs and make sure the living spaces met basic health and safety codes. Just two years earlier, on March 14, 1905, a fire swept through an overcrowded tenement at 105 Allen Street. Twenty people died; numerous people were injured. Landlords had always determined rent according to family size—charging fifty cents additional per child above the base rent. Leases were nonexistent. Landlords were capricious. Despite this situation, tenants shied away from rising up for many reasons. Some accepted their living situations—several people crowded into one or two rooms with a shared bathroom down the hall—as normal. Others believed that as bad as conditions were in New York, they were worse in Europe. Still others felt they simply had no recourse.

As for Newman, she knew she could not stand one more conversation about rent or the need for their own bathroom. She could not bear one more paycheck that never quite stretched far enough. She realized her family's only recourse was to act, just as the women in her neighborhood had done five years earlier when the price of kosher meat jumped from twelve cents a pound to eighteen cents a pound.[6] On May 15, 1902, Jewish women from Brooklyn to Harlem and from Williamsburg to Brownsville had spilled into the streets. They flung raw meat onto the sidewalks to protest the Meat Trust, a group of meat wholesalers. They boycotted the kosher butcher shops. They were just getting warmed up. To ensure this wasn't a onetime occurrence, several of the initial protesters formed committees. They patrolled the streets to make sure the boycott held. They barred people from entering shops. They marched. They visited the kitchens of their fellow neighbors and peered into pots to double-check that no one was secretly buying meat and serving it up in soups or stews. They raised bail money for those who were arrested. They passed out fliers decorated with skulls and crossbones warning, "Eat no meat while the Trust is taking meat from the bones of your women and children."[7]

The New York City police didn't abide the protest. On one occasion five hundred police officers responded to a demonstration and reportedly attacked the protesters. "More than a score of prisoners had been taken to different stations, several men and women had been slightly injured by missile[s] hurled from the mad crowds, and the foreign-born population for a square mile around Broome and Essex Streets," the *New York Times* reported, packing xenophobia and incendiary language into one paragraph.[8] When the strike ended, at least seventy women and fifteen men had been arrested for disorderly conduct, a justification police and city officials used time and again to quell social unrest. But the women learned something: Striking works. The price of meat fell back to within two cents of its prestrike cost.

Though a child during the meat strike, Newman knew enough of the affair to form her own plan. She started organizing her peers. Every day after snipping stray threads for twelve hours, she went home and gulped down dinner rather than go to the Social Literary Society. Then she spent several hours knocking on doors in the neighborhood. By the time the leaves started dropping from the trees and it was too cold to sleep on fire escapes, she had successfully convinced nearly four hundred young women to come together under her leadership. Under Newman's direction, the young women started working to convince the housewives to join in combating the rent situation. They spoke with weary housewives, some skeptical of the earnest young woman standing before them. They spoke with men too tired to listen but who listened anyway. They spoke about how rent would continue rising even as their salaries continued falling. It was slow work but Newman was patient. She drew upon the same powers of oratorical persuasion she had once used to convince her father to let her attend school so many years ago. She also intuitively understood that reform was more possible if the women banded together.

She knew women were the key to implementing change. They were experienced consumers and managers of the household budget, skills that translated into organizing. It was the women who would convene and discuss strategy. Newman helped establish canvassing committees. Pairs of women went knocking on apartment door after apartment door, working to organize the tenants of each building into groups, all mobilizing for the cause. Her appeals struck a chord. The neighbors and others trusted her. After all, she wasn't an outsider coming in; she lived in the same deplorable housing conditions. Naturally there were skeptics and those who were worried about covering household costs. Newman tried to reassure them, telling them that if they were to receive an eviction notice, the Socialist Party would help cover the cost to go to court. Her deft handling of the situation impressed community leaders, many of whom she had met with, many of whom had read her articles about the strike for *The Forward*.

Her dark hair twisted into a bun, Newman climbed atop a soapbox, an American flag behind her. The crowd nodded their heads as she appealed to them in Yiddish and English to hold firm with their refusal to pay: "Come down or no pay," they chanted.[9] She fed on the energy from these street-corner meetings, delivering fiery speeches that talked about citizens' right to fair rent and their right to live in safe apartments. She tried to model herself after the Ukrainian-born Theresa Server Malkier. A suffragist and educator, Malkier was the first woman to rise from working in a factory to holding a leadership role in the Socialist Party. Malkier, who had organized married housekeepers into the Woman's Progressive Society of Yonkers, mentored Newman, showing her the power of speaking directly to the people. As a result, Newman started getting invited to speak at meetings and her interest in this and other social issues started growing.

Seizing the moment, Newman urged the protesters to resist a rent freeze. She urged them to settle for nothing less than an 18–20 percent reduction in rent. If the landlords refused, then the tenants would refuse to pay any rent at all.[10] If landlords handed out eviction notices, the tenants would demand case-by-case hearings in court. The chants reached a crescendo: "Come down or no pay." Newman reminded the crowd that if landlords got their way, then perhaps as many as one hundred thousand men, women, and children would be forced onto the streets with nowhere to go. The chants grew louder still.

By the time the rent strike started on December 26, 1907, ten thousand households agreed to withhold rent. The story captivated the press; they especially liked Newman's confrontational style. "The rent war begun yesterday on the Lower East Side is led by a frail-looking little woman who is hailed throughout Grand Street section as the East Side Joan of Arc," reported the *New York Times*. "The young woman who is recognized as the real leader of the movement is Pauline Newman[,] who is employed at a shirtwaist factory in Grand Street. Spends most hours in the factory but will then visit tenements to see what's up."[11] Newman enjoyed the attention: "The press gave us front page publicity and my own photo was carried under the caption 'Leader of the strike.'"[12]

Newman may have enjoyed the ear of the neighborhood, but she drew the ire of the landlords. This wasn't the first time tenants complained about rent, so the landlords laid siege. Some shut off the water supply to their properties. Others ordered the immediate eviction of their tenants. Katz & Co., one of the city's largest owners and rent collectors, announced plans to close more than one hundred tenement houses rather than lower rates. Several other landlords were able to get three-day eviction orders for upward of six thousand families. And yet the tenants remained steadfast under Newman's leadership. They would not pay more than they were paying now.

The strike spread "greater than any that has occurred in this city before."[13] Most nights, the women, many of whom were unemployed, convened at the Socialist Party headquarters at 313 Grand Street. They hashed out a multipronged strategy. One, they would make a case of the cost effectiveness—or lack thereof—regarding a rent hike. According to their calculations, evictions would cost landlords about eight dollars per family. Therefore, they argued, it made more sense to simply lower the rent by at least a dollar. Along those lines, families could decide to move anyway since housing was cheaper in Harlem or Bushwick. In short, if landlords didn't want to lose tenants, they should lower rent. Two, the protesters told landlords that if they hiked rent, they would begin reporting every single sanitary law infraction, no matter how trivial, to the Metropolitan Board of Health. In the past, the majority of tenants kept their mouths shut, fearing reprisals from their landlord.[14]

They met at night and demonstrated during the day. The demonstrations occasionally turned violent. On December 28, the protesters assembled in Rutgers Park. Police reserves from the nearby Madison Street police station "were sent double quick to break it up. They did so most effectively, charging the crowd with their night sticks," according to the *New York Times*.[15] The police denied protesters the right to parade through the streets.

Police officers weren't the only ones to view the protesters with disdain. As the strike continued, some in the press started framing the protesters as dangerous and unruly. Headlines and articles in various publications described the protest as an "uprising" or a "rebellion." This kind of rhetoric gave cover to landlords, who weren't shy about hurling racist insults. It wasn't unheard of to hear them tell tenants, "If you don't like your rents get out. If you are not satisfied with our system of rents go back where you came from."[16] Undeterred, the tenants continued to make their demands heard. They picketed outside the homes of landlords and distributed thousands of leaflets printed in Yiddish.

Days before a seven-hundred-pound iron and wooden ball adorned with one hundred 25-watt lightbulbs became the first to drop in Times Square, Newman met with strikers and explained that more than rent was on the line. She told them it was time to take a stand against the system itself. Having attended meetings at the Socialist Literary Society for several years now, the teenager became an official member of the Socialist Party. She earnestly believed "that justice and freedom and everything else we desired would be there under socialism and that your job was to bring it about and you did what you could."[17] Her principles guided her in the way she spoke to people about the landlords. To Newman, the misery and indignities so many of them suffered in their squalid flats was because of landlords and capitalism.[18]

As labor historians like Dorothy Sue Cobble have pointed out, Newman's growing political awareness aligned with the Progressive Movement. Anchored in the latter third of the nineteenth century, a time of rapid and rampant industrialization and urbanization, the movement aimed to tackle poverty and workplace exploitation, health care and corruption, through social activism and political reform.

Newman's activism caught the eye of local social reformers, including Lillian Wald and Mary Kingsbury Simkhovitch—the former of the Henry Street Settlement and the latter of the Greenwich House. In Newman they spotted someone who embodied the spirit of social reform. Her obvious commitment to improving her neighbors' and fellow workers' lives dovetailed with programs run by settlement houses like Henry Street and Rivington Street. Indeed, Newman's talent for firing up crowds not only caught the eye of women like Wald and Simkhovitch, but it also landed her invitations to speak at meetings, welcome opportunities for the young immigrant who still swapped her Vs for Ws to practice her diction and delivery.[19]

As Abe Cahan, the editor of *The Forward*, wrote a few years earlier, "The spirit which impels one to struggle for his rights, to combat robbery, has imbedded itself in the hearts of our workingmen . . . This is the case with the present rent strikes."[20] For many protesters, it was unconscionable that the city could spend forty thousand dollars on fireworks to celebrate the opening of the Queensboro Bridge but nothing to provide decent tenements for its working class.[21]

The strike dragged on. January turned to February and the city's police continued to disband and arrest protesters. Courts upheld eviction notices. Magistrates reprimanded strikers, telling them they were lawless citizens who would not be able to hide behind a strike to avoid paying rent.[22] In the end it was the sheer number of eviction notices that put an end to the strike. It was anticlimactic and disappointing in that Newman and her fellow protesters weren't able to enact lasting change. For example, they didn't make permanent committees that would continue the fight against capricious landlords, nor did they secure any kind of tenants' rights. However, the strike was not a complete failure. Of the ten thousand families that participated, two thousand received rent reductions.[23] During the height of the protests, the Yiddish press carried daily stories about them, and the poet Morris Rosenfeld based a one-act play, *Rent Strike*, on the protests. Yet, Newman's leadership laid the groundwork for rent control, which became instituted in the 1930s. It also showed her and those around her that she could lead. "The success of the strike depended both on shop floor networks of teenaged girls and in networks of neighborhood housewives and mothers. In a small way, I became the voice of the less articulate young men and women with whom I worked and with whom later I was to join in the fight," she said.[24]

It was a fight she wanted to continue in her forthcoming campaign for secretary of state in New York. The way Newman, now a neighborhood celebrity, comported herself during the strike impressed the Socialist Party, so they tapped her to run on the 1908 Socialist ticket, which would include women's suffrage in its platform even though predominantly outside of New York the party was less animated about female suffrage.[25] The dailies mocked the idea of a "skirted Secretary of State," and she was often heckled when giving speeches.[26] Additionally, since women didn't have the right to vote, it was more symbolic than anything else.

Even so, Newman used her campaign as a platform from which to stump for women's right to vote. Driven by a desire for equal rights and continued civic engagement, these socialist women considered suffrage to be the skeleton key that could unlock widespread social and economic reforms. As a bonus, she was invited to ride with Eugene V. Debs on his "Red Special" train as he hit the hustings for his presidential campaign. An American union leader and socialist politician, Debs was the founding president of the American Railway Union. Because of his role in leading the Pullman Strike of 1894, a major labor conflict that resulted in a nationwide railroad strike, he was arrested and imprisoned. Calling his train the "Red Special" was a nod to both his role in the strike and to Pullman cars' signature red color.

Newman's family did not share her enthusiasm about her forays into politics. In fact, her brother was angry. He barely tolerated her role in the rent strike and the press coverage that came along with it. However, the idea that she would run on a Socialist ticket was too much. The idea of running for anything was anathema to him, and, frankly, to her sisters and mother as well. Like many of their fellow immigrants, he didn't want to call attention to himself. He just wanted to fit in and earn a paycheck. It was time to set aside childish notions. Newman was nearly seventeen, old enough to marry and build a family. Her close friend Rose Schneiderman was hearing similar admonishments, her own mother cautioning her that if she didn't forgo life in the public eye, she would never find a husband.[27]

Newman scoffed. Her brother tried another tack. Knowing how much his younger sister missed the classroom, he offered to pay her college tuition. Newman thought about it for as long as it took to finish her soup. No, thank you, she told him. She hated her job, but she now knew she could make a change. After all, she countered, they were paying less rent because of her. And she was getting noticed in the movement; she was being asked to take on larger leadership roles. She was also starting to have some success in getting her work published.

So rather than pack a cardboard suitcase to go to college, she vowed to spend even more time at the Socialist Literary Society, where she and her friends Schneiderman, Lemlich, and Fannia Cohn dissected the latest articles in the Jewish press and listened to intellects, politicians, and authors like Jack London, the 1901 failed Socialist candidate for mayor of Oakland, California. London, the author of *Call of the Wild* and *White Fang*, was an ardent Socialist. He had launched the Intercollegiate Socialist Society in 1905 to spread and advocate for socialism among Ivy League students, most notably at Harvard and Yale.

Not so long ago, Newman had spent a pleasant evening at the Socialist Literary Society when London was the guest speaker. His most recent work, "The Scab," had caused a stir for its powerful and violent prose: "After God had finished the rattlesnake, the toad, and the vampire, He had some awful substance left with which He made a scab. A scab is a two-legged animal with a corkscrew soul, a water brain, a combination backbone made of jelly and glue. Where others have hearts, he carries a tumor of rotten principle." Centering on a striking teamster who takes a strikebreaker into an alley and breaks his arm with an iron bar, the short story resonated with Newman.

Newman gushed. She told London how much she enjoyed the short story and, more so, his novel *Martin Eden*. She was particularly taken with his portrayal of one's yearning for education and literary fame. "He said 'oh, did you like ME?' I said, 'Very much.' He said, 'well, I only slept three hours a night while I was writing that book. I had a job in the daytime, and I could only write during the nighttime," Newman said, recounting the exchange many years later.[28]

Newman and her friends also listened to the millionaire socialist Henry Gaylord Wilshire, who would lend his name to Los Angeles' Wilshire Boulevard, and to New Yorker Meyer London, who became one of the first socialists elected to Congress. Listening to these lectures was grist to her mill. "My world of ideas and ideals began to take shape. Reading became my chief occupation (outside my work)," Newman said.[29]

Unlike most of her coworkers, who favored dime store romances, Newman preferred more serious fare. Aside from newspapers, she enjoyed reading books like *Comrade Yetta* or *Women in Industry*. Whenever she felt a bit tetchy, she couldn't refrain from scolding women who didn't take the time to read "GOOD fiction, fiction that is to an extent a reflection of life." She admonished them to stop reading books that "take you into a fairy land and introduce you to a Prince who falls in love with you. You are wasting your time reading such books." Although her tendency to speak her mind was appreciated in meetings, it also grated on some people.[30]

Newman's ideas were evolving as fast as the neighborhood in which she lived. Pushcarts still sold all manner of provisions from herring and smoked fish to challah and pickles, but most were now packed inside the Essex Street indoor market. Dotted among and between the kosher butcher shops and candy stores were new delicatessens, ice cream parlors, and coffeehouses with gleaming sinks and tiled floors.

Newman generally steered clear of the restaurants, as enticing as their appetizing dishes were. If she and her friends were going to splurge, it was not going to be on a five-cent cream soda or charlotte russe. Instead the five cents would be used to cover the cost of going to the movies or seeing her first play in English: *Peer Gynt*, starring Richard Mansfield, billed as "An Ibsen Fantasy with Plays of Lighter Sort. Mansfield to Act Ibsen's *Peer Gynt*."[31] As the velvet curtain rose on the stage at the New Amsterdam Theatre, the curtain was also going up on another show: the trial of William "Big Bill" Haywood. The founding member of the Industrial Workers of the World was charged with ordering the assassination of Frank Steunenberg, the former governor of Idaho. Clarence Darrow, then the nation's most renowned defense attorney, successfully defended Haywood.[32] But Haywood's freedom would be short-lived. In 1918 a jury convicted him of violating the federal espionage and sedition act for calling for a strike during wartime.

In 1908, shortly before the trial, Newman found herself at the Grand Central Palace, a grand name for what was essentially a function hall. On that particular night, a ball there was very well attended by members of the Socialist Party and emerging labor unions. Everyone wanted to see Bill Haywood, Newman included. When she was introduced to Haywood: "He looked down upon me—he was so tall, close to six feet I'm sure. He looked down at me, and he said, 'Would you like to dance.' Well, I couldn't refuse."[33] And so it was that she waltzed across the dance floor in a borrowed gown.

The evening was a welcome diversion in the teenager's life. Still working at least twelve hours a day at the Triangle Shirtwaist Factory, Newman found little time for leisure. What downtime she did have she usually used to read and to sharpen her writing. She was now writing for *The Forward*, the very newspaper she once used to learn to read. The paper, which introduced socialist and trade unionist ideas to Yiddish-speaking immigrants, was on its way to boasting a circulation of nearly two hundred thousand readers.[34] It was also one of the first newspapers in the United States to hire women writers; including the Russian Jewish author Mary Antin, and the anarchist writer, poet, and political activist Emma Goldman.

In her pieces, Newman described her experience working in the garment industry, where the majority of the "so-called factories were located in old wooden walkups with rickety stairs, splintered and sagging floors. Where the few windows were never washed and broken panes were mended with cardboard."[35] She wanted readers to feel what it was like to work where the "warmth rarely reached the workers seated near the windows" and how in summer the constantly burning gas jets stank and added to the already "intolerably humid and oppressive atmosphere." She wanted their mouths to feel parched as they read about the lack of available drinking water, and if their skin crawled while reading about how the "vermin were as much a part of the surroundings as were the machines and the workers," she felt satisfied.[36]

If the Social Literary Society shaped Newman's politics, then the International Ladies' Garment Workers' Union and the Women's Trade Union League helped her put her principles into practice. Almost a century before Newman was born, trade assemblies and unions began emerging in cities across the United States. Most started out as small fraternal societies of immigrants who hailed from the same villages and cities in

Europe. Over time, they grew into mutual aid organizations that pooled pennies to help members with things like burial plots, medical care, and, on occasion, leisure activities. For example, in 1878 the International Labor Union was established to represent unskilled textile workers. However, it lasted only about five years.[37] Less than a decade later, in 1885, the first Yiddish-speaking union in America, the Russian-Jewish Workers' Union, was founded on the Lower East Side. The United Hebrew Trades followed in 1888. Both were closely related to the Socialist Party, which was founded in 1901; Newman was now a full member.

Nevertheless, getting individual trade groups to unify on a larger scale remained elusive—that is, until June 3, 1900, when eleven delegates from local unions came together.[38] They came from several cities, including New York City and Baltimore, and represented nearly two thousand workers, mostly Jewish immigrants, mostly socialists.[39] Thus was born the International Ladies' Garment Workers' Union (ILGWU). Agreeing to join forces with the American Federation of Labor (AFL), which was founded in 1886, the ILGWU elected Herman Grossman as its president and Bernard Braff as its secretary-treasurer. The AFL expressed support for women; in 1903 it passed several resolutions calling for the appointment of women organizers and for the executive council to prioritize unionizing working women. It also appeared to endorse suffrage. However, to Newman those were fine but shallow steps. While the AFL had hired a woman organizer in the early 1890s, it would not do so again for another twenty years. Their resistance stemmed partly because the majority of its leadership was American born and tended to look down on immigrants and women, viewing both groups as threats.[40]

Of the eleven original local unions, only four received charters: the Cloak Makers' Union of New York, Local No. 1; the Cloak Makers' Protective Union of Philadelphia, Local No. 2; the United Cloak Pressers of Philadelphia, Local No. 3; and the Cloak Makers' Union of Baltimore, Local No. 4. As the umbrella body, the ILGWU would help organize local unions nationwide, mediate problems between locals in the same city, and enforce boycotts when they arose.

As Fannia Cohn would later write in her unpublished history of the ILGWU, it made sense that the union sprang from the women's garment industry. Women were entering the workforce at an accelerated rate. Indeed, by the start of the 1900s women comprised about one-fifth of the labor force.[41] While most women worked out of economic necessity, some pursued employment for fulfillment outside the home. Regardless of why they worked, they discovered a paternalistic environment that infantilized them at best and oppressed them at worst. They were sick of not being able to do mundane things like having time to deposit paychecks or have enough money to see the doctor for that persistent cough. The women were sick of paying for their needles, thread, machine parts, and other supplies. They were sick of working more than sixty hours a week for as little as six dollars a week. They were sick of earning substantially less, as much as 20 percent less, than what men earned.[42] Yet, despite banding together because of the unfair trade practices in an industry dominated by female employees, the ILGWU paid scant attention to the women's concerns. They were "merely tolerated by union men, who still believed that girls were in industry only a short time until their marriage."[43] In a nutshell, young women workers were considered expendable.[44] As labor historians have documented, the paternalism and misogyny of the ILGWU's leadership meant that even though it would elect a female vice president in 1914, and although it played an indispensable part in female garment workers' lives, its executive board would remain the domain of men. Indeed, by 1935 only 10 percent of its executive board members would be women.

That attitude helped lead to the creation of the Women's Trade Union League (WTUL) in 1903, when a group of like-minded activist social reformers like Jane Addams and Emily Greene Balch, a Wellesley College professor of political economy, and settlement house residents gathered in Boston for the AFL's annual convention. During the convention, these activists held a side meeting at Faneuil Hall. A meeting place for patriots during the American Revolution and abolitionists during the Civil War, the red brick building was a fitting place to launch the new organization.[45]

Ironically, the organization owed its existence, in part, to a man: William English Walling. Hailing from a wealthy Kentucky home, Walling, who would eventually leave to help found the National Association for the Advancement of Colored People (NAACP), turned his back on his family's money.[46] After graduating from the University of Chicago, he attended Harvard Law School. From there he moved to New York City. Working as a factory inspector, he lived on a worker's wage. In 1902 the Socialist Republicans met with a British organization of the same name. He imported the idea to the United States and to Mary Kenney O'Sullivan and Nellie D. Parker of the Women's Label League; Walling and the two women served as delegates to the American Federation of Labor.

The WTUL's ranks were comprised of feminist middle- and upper-class, white Protestant "allies" on one side and wage-earning, largely Jewish immigrant workers on the other. The latter became the organization's most active workers. Over the years, this mix led to points of contention. Moreover, though it worked with Black-led organizations and had ties to the NAACP, the WTUL remained predominantly white through the first half of the twentieth century.[47] Nevertheless, it stood as the first organization to center on the lives of working-class women, pushing class equality and democratic governance.[48] Believing that partnerships that crossed socioeconomic lines would be indispensable to their success, the group started recruiting in earnest. They wanted college-educated women and women on the social register, but they also wanted working-class women. Among their first recruits were Margaret Daly and Leonora O'Reilly. O'Reilly, who became one of the WTUL's prominent leaders, was teaching sewing at the Manhattan Trade School when she met Walling. Witty, sharp, and quick to anger, O'Reilly had started working in a shirt factory when she was just eleven years old. The experience convinced her that women from all walks of life must work together: "Are we not all sisters of one another and should not a woman's heart thrill at being called upon for help?"[49] O'Reilly also recruited the socialites-turned-social-justice-reformers Margaret and Mary Dreier. Newman's close friend and confidante, twenty-three-year-old Rose Schneiderman, rounded out the roster.

In Mary Dreier, Newman found both a friend and a benefactress, who enjoyed the financial wealth to fund their work. She would open the way to a cross-class sisterhood where middle-class and upper-class suffragists and reformers partnered together with women who worked in the factories. It was an alliance that would be tested over time, but for now Dreier pushed Newman to realize that securing the right to vote was essential if they were to exact change.

During those first early years of recruitment, the WTUL struggled to find the best way to recruit dues-paying members. It often hosted parties and dances, picnics and "pink teas." The latter were gatherings where delegates served as voluntary stewards for WTUL leaders, carrying around trays laden with cake and tea for labor union leaders. According to the *New York Times*, "The experience they declared was a delightful one and as the labor men sat on the edges of the chairs and handled the teacups in a gingerly way they said that they never enjoyed themselves better."[50] The light touch didn't translate into lasting ties. Sipping tea from a saucer was a lovely way to while away a few hours in the afternoon, but it didn't pay the rent or shorten the workweek. Clearly, the leadership thought, a more aggressive approach was required, so by the end of 1905 the leaders began preaching the gospel of trade unionism outside the factory door.

Toward the end of 1908, the US Supreme Court upheld the constitutionality of *Muller v. Oregon*, one of the most important pieces of labor legislation of the Progressive Era. The ruling upheld Oregon's law that limited the workday for female wage earners to no more than ten hours a day. The court deemed the state's interest in protecting women's health overrode its interest in protecting the "freedom to contract." Simply put, the ruling allowed for the protection of employees from state interference in the contracting of wages, hours, and working conditions.

One of the opponents arguing before the court was Louis D. Brandeis. At the time, he argued that the state mandating fewer work hours for women than men could open the question of whether women possessed the same ability to negotiate their contracts with employers as men. Additionally, there were women who opposed the ruling on the grounds that such laws were rooted in stereotyped gender roles and ultimately restricted women's rights and financial independence. Lastly, opponents argued, protective laws of this nature protected only white women who worked in agriculture or food processing. Although Newman wasn't involved in the case, she and many others in the movement, including Schneiderman, Lemlich, and Cohn, would become loud proponents of protective labor legislation. To them it was the only way to begin to protect women against the conditions they all experienced as young children.

Meanwhile, Newman lost her bid to become secretary of state. Not only that, but upon quiet reflection she realized that her success in the rent strike was modest at best. Still, she had proved to leaders in the movement that she would not hesitate to assert herself when it came to championing a cause. In turn, they encouraged her and she remained wedded to the work. Some months later, with those themes and ideas tucked squarely into her pocket, Newman made her way to Cooper Union.

4

Corsets and Cloak Makers

The sewing machines went silent in factory after factory as hundreds of garment workers, most of them teenage girls, walked off their jobs on a cold, gray November morning in 1909. For nearly two hours they remained as still as the statues on Central Park's Poet's Walk. Finally the suspense became too much and one of the girls phoned the Women's Trade Union League. The woman on the other end of the line instructed them to come to Cooper Union, a red brick building located just a few blocks away. Whether there would be a general strike to protest working conditions in the garment industry would be decided in a matter of hours.

Less than twenty-four hours earlier, Pauline Newman had stepped into the auditorium of Cooper Union. Arriving well before the speeches started, the nineteen-year-old slid into a seat just feet from the same stage where, fifty-one years earlier, Abraham Lincoln had denounced slavery. She waved to Rose Schneiderman, her first and closest friend. She smiled at Clara Lemlich and nodded to Fannia Cohn, who also started out in the garment industry, albeit as an educated, middle-class woman who entered the trade with the intention to reform it.

A few weeks earlier, Newman and her fellow garment workers and union members had spent several days passing out fliers and brochures printed in Yiddish, Italian, and English advertising the meeting. Now, much to Newman's delighted surprise, the hall was packed. Lemlich would later remark, "I did not know how many workers in my shop had taken the oath at that meeting. I could not tell how many would go on strike in our factory the next day. When we came back the next morning to the factory, though, no one went to the dressing-room. We all sat at the machines with our hats and coats beside us, ready to leave."[1] This moment would not have happened without the four-year-old Ladies' Waistmakers' Union Local 25. Lemlich and six other women from her shop at Leiserson's Shirtwaist Company were all on the executive board of the all-women's local.

Theirs was not a new fight. Workers had been pushing for more reasonable hours for decades; from New England textile workers who sat before looms weaving an average of 11 hours a day to bakers in the Midwest who kneaded and pounded dough between 80 to 120 hours; from New York City cigar makers who rolled and cut cigars upward of 90 hours a week to the cloak makers and dressmakers whose eyes struggled to thread their needles in dim factory light.[2] It's important to note that since the majority of Northern mills prohibited hiring Black workers during this period, the Northern US textile industry remained predominantly white.[3] Indeed, in 1883, seven hundred of those cloak makers and dressmakers, 50 percent of whom were women, walked off their jobs in what some in the New York press dubbed the "Emigrants' Strike." At that time, the *New York World* described their action as "not a strike but a revolt for bread and butter."[4]

More recently, separate and spontaneous strikes took place in the garment district. In July, two hundred workers at Rosen Brothers went on strike. Five weeks later, employers conceded to the demands and signed an agreement with Local 25. Workers in other shops followed suit. Next the local zeroed in on Max Blanck and Isaac Harris, the Shirtwaist Kings, and Leiserson's. The latter two ended without reaching settlements. In each case management hired replacements for the striking workers and cracked down on the unions, firing several workers for supporting union efforts.[5] This prompted Lemlich and several of her coworkers to implore ILGWU leadership, as well as Samuel Gompers, who now headed the American Federation of Labor, to call a general strike in the garment industry.

Newman, who was still working at the Triangle Shirtwaist Factory and by this time was a member of the WTUL, rooted for a general strike. Nevertheless, like many of her colleagues, she worried that a general strike would end like so many smaller, isolated strikes: with broken contracts, the firing of participating workers, and, finally, the clipped wings of the fledgling union.[6] Those smaller strikes—Rosen Brothers, the Shirtwaist Kings, and Leiserson's—helped set the stage for this moment, which saw hundreds of workers assembled inside the historic auditorium. The atmosphere was electric. Newman looked to the stage. Labor movement luminaries gazed out at the crowd from underneath the lights. Abraham Rosenberg, president of the International Ladies' Garment Workers' Union sat next to John Dyche, the secretary-treasurer. Bernard Weinstein, head of the United Hebrew Trades, sat patiently. Mary Dreier, president of the

Women's Trade Union League, waited to read her prepared remarks as did labor lawyer Meyer London.

All eyes fixed on Gompers, who they believed would sympathize with their cause. After all, at thirteen he had been put to work as a cigar maker. Gompers, a London-born immigrant who now lived between a slaughterhouse and a brewery, had risen through the ranks to become first president of the Cigar Makers' Union and then president of the AFL. "A man would be less than human if he were not impressed with your reception. I want you men and women not to give all of your enthusiasm for a man, I would prefer that you put all your enthusiasm into your union and your cause," Gompers said. The crowd met his lukewarm words with tepid applause.[7] Gompers continued. Like Dyche, Gompers thought strikes were too expensive and were best avoided. Yet, he also seemed to be saying that if the women didn't strike now, they might as well "rivet the chains of slavery upon our wrists."[8] He seemed to be contradicting himself and the crowd began losing interest.

Then Jacob Panken, a Socialist leader and cofounder of the ILGWU, rose to his feet. The genial attorney barely uttered six words before Clara Lemlich interrupted him. "I want to say a few words," she said.[9] It was a breach of protocol to be sure. She was supposed to wait quietly until after the official speakers finished delivering their remarks. But Lemlich was tired of quietly waiting. The audience was also tired of listening to the men. Benjamin Feigenbaum, who would later be elected to the New York Assembly on the Socialist ticket, agreed. Lemlich turned and faced the crowd. "I am a working girl, one of those who are on strike against intolerable conditions. I am tired of listening to speakers who talk in general terms. What we are here for is to decide whether we shall or shall not strike. I offer a resolution that a general strike be declared. Now!" she declared.[10] Feigenbaum seconded the motion. The crowd jumped up. "Everyone shouting an emphatic affirmative, waving hats, canes, handkerchiefs, anything that came [in] handy. For five minutes, perhaps, the tumult continued," reported the *New York World*.[11] So began the "Uprising of the 20,000," the largest strike in the garment industry to date, and Newman had a front row seat.

This "wisp of a girl," as the press described Lemlich, knew what she was doing.[12] The twenty-three-year-old, five-foot-tall woman already counted seventeen arrests to her name. She had also been brutally beaten nearly as many times, most recently during the aforementioned strike at Leiserson's. During that strike, factory owners unleashed labor enforcers, like Dopey Benny and the Jewish Black Hand, a criminal extortion ring that preyed on budding unions, on the picket line. At the end of it, the enforcers left

Lemlich, whom they considered a "pint of trouble for the bosses," with six broken ribs.[13] She not only returned to the picket line, but she also refused to whisper a word about the assault to her parents or the police. The latter choice was less to do with her stamina than the fact that Tammany Hall ran the New York Police Department and that "Big Tim" Sullivan, the Tammany leader in the Bowery, was known to side with factory owners.

Although Newman had not felt handcuffs snap around her wrists, she understood the stakes. "During the weeks and months of the strike they would go hungry. Many of them would find themselves without a roof above their heads. All of them would be cold and lonely," she wrote.[14]

The next morning at precisely 10:00 a.m., an ILGWU representative in each shirtwaist factory gave the signal. He, or she, pushed a button and turned off the lights. The strike was on. Across the city, presses cooled and shears were laid down. At a waist factory at 536 Broadway, 450 girls walked out despite a number of forewomen screaming at them to stop.[15] "Ten thousand, twenty thousand, thirty thousand—this is more than any one of us dared to dream of or to hope for! This is not a strike—this is an uprising and an uprising of youngsters at that! It is cold, but the picket line is intact. Some are arrested. There are others to take their posts. Some are in jail. There are enough to fill every jail in town, and there would still be enough to keep the police busy on the picket line. The city is aroused," Newman said.[16]

At the time of the strike, about 60,000 of the 125,000 people who worked in manufacturing women's garments nationwide lived in New York City. They earned a pittance compared to the revenue the product generated. For example, in 1900 the Triangle Shirtwaist Factory paid workers a total of about $19,333,239 in wages for a product valued at $99,464,693.[17] The protesters reflected the demographics of the industry: Of those protesting poor working conditions and low wages, 90 percent were Jewish and 70 percent were women. Over the next few weeks, more than 40,000 female, mostly Yiddish-speaking, New York City factory workers came on board. Like Newman, most of them were just children when their parents sent them to work.

After the first adrenaline-fueled days of the strike subsided, the leaders turned their attention to maintaining their stamina and sharpening tactics. Newman, Lemlich, Schneiderman, and Cohn knew they needed to create a culture of unity. They needed to get garment workers to think of themselves as part of a whole rather than as disparate groups separated by "kinship, class, race, ethnicity and relation."[18] To boost morale, they sang working-class songs in Yiddish and Italian. They also belted out "The Internationale" and "The Marseillaise." They designed eye-catching posters. Though some of the messages were a bit wordy—for instance, "A strike is not a crime, a striker is not a criminal, peaceful picketing is the right of every worker"—they were on point. In no time the women would be dodging fists and elbows and trying to avoid arrest.[19]

But for now they focused on cultivating allies among the middle-class suffragists and reformers. They wanted their support, both financially and politically. That's why a few days into the strike Newman met with WTUL leaders like Helen Marot, Ida Rowe, Violet Pike, Alice Bean, and Mary Dreier, whom Newman described as "a person you rarely meet. First, her concern for others, considering that she grew up a very rich person and came from a very rich family."[20] Newman, who grew up on the edge of poverty, was initially surprised that these better-off women were ready to use their wallets to help those on strike.

The union needed to cultivate the support of middle- and upper-class allies like Margaret and Mary Dreier. Margaret met her husband, Raymond Robins, at a white-tie dinner. A Christian Socialist, Robins was a Congregational pastor and a lawyer who had struck it rich during the Alaskan gold rush. After their wedding, the couple enjoyed a sumptuous honeymoon in Florida. It was one of the last times they so indulged. In 1907 the newlyweds moved to Chicago and took up residence on the top floor of a tenement near Bickerdyke Park. Located in one of the city's most congested wards, the cold-water flat featured a coal stove and little else. In fact, it didn't always have water as factories in their district used the same water lines. After settling in, Margaret started volunteering at Jane Addams's Hull House on Halsted Street. It was an education for her, and she realized this was the kind of work that fulfilled her. Eventually she would become president of the national WTUL after having served as president of its Chicago chapter.

Born in Cedarville, Illinois, Addams was a social reformer who had once studied medicine. In 1889 she and her friend and fellow social reformer Ellen Gates Starr founded Hull House, one of the first settlement houses in North America. Modeled after London's Toynbee Hall, a charitable institution that Addams had visited, it provided child care, cultural training, education, and other services like US citizenship classes to Chicago's immigrant population. During the movement's peak, there would be as many as four hundred such houses nationwide.

Meanwhile, Margaret's younger sister Mary lived in New York City. She too was drawn to social reform. While working at the Asacog House, a settlement house in Brooklyn, she met Leonora O'Reilly and got involved in the WTUL. Now Mary was president of the organization's New York branch and was working to direct as many resources as possible from the

New York Women's Trade Union League to help support the garment industry strikers. Both sisters introduced Newman to key politicians and invited her to fund-raising events where she could meet celebrities and activists like the Connecticut-born author and feminist Charlotte Perkins Gilman. Of the two, Newman felt closer to Mary, recalling:

> And the first time I met CPG was at a ball for the benefit of WTUL. And I'll never forget Mary Dreier that evening. She wore a sort of rose-colored dress and her eyes were sky blue. So pretty! And, of course, in those days, they don't do it today, but in those days, before midnight, there was a march around the hall. The leaders of the union were in front, of course, and we followed. And then, Charlotte Perkins Gilman, I remember, wore a beautiful shawl—she was a very attractive person.[21]

Newman never remarked on whether she knew Gilman was also a racist who espoused eugenicist beliefs, including the idea of selective breeding, which maintained only "fit" individuals should be allowed to reproduce.

Of course, there were no delicately woven shawls on the picket line or inside the cramped rooms and hallways of Clinton Hall, the WTUL headquarters. It was so crowded that some strikers took to sleeping on the sidewalk. They wanted to stay close to the action rather than go home and possibly miss an important decision.

When not in meetings, Newman worked on enrolling as many women in the union as possible. She visited workshop after workshop; her reputation for tenacity was well earned. Next, she and the others worked to sign up manufacturers who would accept the terms. It was tedious work; then again, she could draw from her experience of the 1907 rent strike. Although some manufacturers claimed they wanted to end the strike, they said they preferred to make in-house improvements without recognizing a union. To that end they established Employers Mutual Protective Associations, which were intended as a bulwark against the rising tide of unionism. Newman saw this as a delaying tactic.

Ostensibly for workers, such associations were expressly loyal to management. For example, during the Jewish High Holy Days, some workers at the Triangle Shirtwaist Factory suggested donating ten dollars apiece to those in need. Management rejected the idea; rather than donate the money, they decided they would loan the money.[22] On other occasions when union representatives came to speak with workers, management spies made a record of those who attended. Anyone suspected of being pro-union was fired. Union leaders also faced resistance from workers who believed that employers should be allowed to run their businesses as they saw fit.

The days slipped into weeks. The strikers marched. The strikers chanted. They made their demands heard. Some demands were old: fewer hours and higher pay, no more child labor. Some were new: no more tenement house work, no more charging workers for the use of machines, no more inside subcontracting. Strikers also wanted a permanent board of arbitration to be ready to resolve disputes.[23] After a few days, it seemed their demands were finally being taken seriously.

The first attempt to settle the strike through arbitration came on December 10. On one side of the table sat Morris Hillquit, a union lawyer and Socialist leader; John Mitchell, former president of the United Mine Workers and vice president of American Federation of Labor; and Marcus M. Marks, president of the Association of Clothiers and uncle to John D. Marks, who went on to write "Rudolph, the Red-Nosed Reindeer." On the other side sat attorneys representing the Cloak, Suit, and Skirt Manufacturers' Protective Association as well as the Associated Waist and Dress Manufacturers. The negotiators faced a formidable situation.

The union made it abundantly clear that the workers would not settle for anything less than higher wages and a fifty-two-hour workweek. They also insisted on a "closed" shop, meaning workers were required to join the union in order to get hired. Ironically, many of the workers who stormed out of Cooper Union that autumn afternoon were earning decent wages, relatively speaking. For instance, the cutters earned between twelve and fifteen dollars a week. Yet, they chose to strike "on behalf of those poor girls under the sub-contractors" who earned about five dollars a week.[24] Among the women, Lemlich was taking home almost three times what most workers earned, but for her it was never about her own earnings. After all, she entered the industry because she wanted to reform it from within. She was there to make sure all workers earned a decent wage.[25]

The striking employees also wanted an end to night work, except when necessary. They also wanted the establishment of a committee to arbitrate wages. Several grueling hours later, the two sides reached an agreement on two issues: The shirtwaist factories would institute a shorter working day and an end to the hated contract system. Next, they tackled the only question that mattered to some on the picket line: Would the manufacturers consider a proposal involving a more explicit recognition of the union? An I.D. Hyman of the Associated Waist and Dress Manufacturers was quick to respond: "Not under any circumstances. We insist upon an open shop, the right to employ union and nonunion employees without discrimination, and from that stand we will not budge."[26] Likewise, the shirtwaist makers, who met in jam-packed meeting halls across the city, would not budge. They would not accept an open shop, so the strike would continue.[27]

Most nights, if Newman didn't stop off at the marble and art deco palace that was Child's restaurant for a slice of pie and a hot cup of coffee, she tramped up the dark and musty stairs to the apartment she shared with her mother. Mother and daughter briefly chatted. Unlike the rent strike, which directly affected her, Theresa wasn't invested or interested in the uprising. "I don't think she has any particular feeling, either for or against. I don't know how much she was concerned with things outside the house," Newman said.[28] However, her sisters, Fanny and Sarah, now married and living in their own apartments, were quite invested. One worked making skirts; the other worked at a small shirtwaist factory a few blocks from Triangle. Both sisters joined Newman on the picket line of what was now the largest strike initiated by women in American history.

Meanwhile the strike was manna for more than a dozen of the city's fifteen daily newspapers. Readers eagerly plunked down a penny to read all about it. The strikers were considered to be either troublemakers, disrupters, or immoral. Or they were saintly, thinly clad charity cases. They were "little" and they were "girls." Most outlets were keen to cover the women's dress rather than their demands, writing about the event as if it were a party, where "the girls went out with a whoop . . . Laughing and shouting, the girls dropped their work and ran for their hats and coats."[29] Many articles fed the public a diet of preconceived notions about how a deserving protester should dress; the subtext, of course, was whether women enjoyed the right to be political actors and whether their grievances were legitimate. Magazines like *Collier's* described workers as wearing ruined clothing and bedraggled bows. It was a stinging editorial swipe aimed at those who had the audacity to turn their backs on the four pillars upon which a proper white woman should aspire to stand: piety, purity, submissiveness, and domesticity.[30]

Dorothy Dix, the pen name used by Tennessee-born advice columnist Elizabeth Meriwether Gilmer, wrote frequently about the strike for William Randolph Hearst's *New York Evening Journal*. Although she typically covered crime, Dix, who often brandished words that undermined women and reinforced gender stereotypes, spilled a fair amount of ink on the strike. While she acknowledged that many shirtwaist workers were impoverished and labored under harsh conditions, Dix also made sure to weave little details into her articles that suggested the protesters weren't quite so serious because sometimes they bought "a pretty dress, or a book." In other words, the picketers were undeserving of living wages because they squandered what they earned on frivolous things. Coverage was also sexist in that most papers either neglected to mention, or played down, the fact that male strikers comprised 15 percent of striking workers and that nearly 100 percent of ILGWU leadership was male.

Even mainstream outlets sympathetic to the cause were careful to reassure their upper- and middle-class readers that the only thing the striking women were upset about were working conditions. Indeed, even the unions were not yet advocating equal pay for equal work. In fact, there was disagreement about what entailed a fair wage for women. Some held that an ideal wage was one that allowed for a woman's individual subsistence but not one penny more. In their mind, wages were not meant to allow for the purchase of "extras" like a book, a movie ticket, or a tube of lipstick. Others maintained that a woman's wage should never threaten a man's primary position at work or home.

Articles in the *New York Times* and the *New-York Tribune*, which targeted middle-class readers, were careful to stress business interests. In the *Times* one might read articles about the "little strikers" alongside advertisements for robes and messaline waists, $2.98 for black and $17.98 for chiffon at Bloomingdale's. With headlines like "Girl Strikers Dance as Employers Meet: The Waistmakers are holding impromptu parties in their headquarters," the insinuation was clear. The strikers were unserious and undeserving of support. When the picketers got arrested and the police violence began, the *New York Times* described the strike as a riot, where "the girls kicked, scratched, pummeled each other until the street was littered with torn and tattered millinery. Bleeding faces and blackened eyes were the general rule."[31]

Newman, for her part, continued to write for Socialist and workers publications. She would later describe the work in detail:

> All we knew was the bitter fact that after working seventy and eighty hours in a seven day week, we did not earn enough to keep body and soul together. This much we did know only too well. No economist, researcher or statistician could teach us anything on that score . . . Indeed—all of them also knew and understood that their own courage would warm them; that hope for a better life would lift their spirit. They were ready and willing to endure hardship of any kind until victory was in sight. And fight they did . . . the strike continued, no end in sight—yet. January was followed by February. The strike continued. Pickets were arrested. Some of them jailed, others sent to the workhouse on Blackwells island.[32]

Yet, some in the WTUL leadership also played into the way the strike was being framed. Well aware of the bias and the need to win public support, they advised strikers and union members to don their best skirts and smartest blouses. In organizing meetings, Newman taught the workers not to provoke police or name-call the replacement workers whom management sent to break the line. In short, they needed to show the public that immigrant women were responsible people who only wanted fair treatment. Above all, it was necessary they maintained their solidarity and not give any hint that they might back down. The more persistent the strikers grew, the greater the risk of violence. "I wouldn't call it violent compared to what we sometimes have today, you know," Newman said. "But there was plenty of clubbing on the part of the policemen on the pickets . . . A lot of girls were clubbed."[33]

Factory owners with more money and clout, like Blanck and Harris of the Triangle Shirtwaist Factory and Leiserson's, "hired thugs and prostitutes to abuse strikers" and non-union workers to take strikers' places. Police officers threatened "to break skulls" and came close to doing so many times.[34] For the scores of women who found refuge in America from countries where Cossacks rampaged through towns and villages, the sight of club-wielding policemen was traumatic. Knowing that, Mary Dreier and other women from her social milieu, like Ava Belmont and Anne Morgan, joined the picket lines in a show of solidarity as a way to offer protection.

Belmont was born in 1853 to slaveholders in Mobile, Alabama. The family moved to New York City after the family's finances grew shaky. When her mother died in 1871, Belmont's father found himself living like a character in a Jane Austen novel; he had four daughters to marry off and little money. So when William K. Vanderbilt, Cornelius Vanderbilt's grandson, asked for Ava's hand, she married him—despite having no love for him. Vanderbilt wasted no time in having an affair, leaving his self-respecting wife with little choice but to divorce him. In 1896 she married Oliver Hazard Perry Belmont, and by all accounts theirs was a happy but brief marriage. He died twelve years later. Once again Belmont found herself a single woman, which in 1908 was not a secure place to be. Both a divorcée and a widow, Belmont was tired of the way a woman's status depended on her husband's behavior or health. An epiphany struck her: If it was this way for the wealthy, it was even worse for the female factory workers who worked without any protection from their male bosses. According to Belmont, "If you are at the top of 'fortune's wheel' you must by every law of human nature aid those so well placed, for it is only by chance that you are there, and not because of any merit of your own."[35]

So Belmont, a woman of wealth and social power, saw the 1909 strike as an opportunity to push for more equality between the sexes, including the right to vote. It was a view that resonated with Newman, who understood that labor rights, suffrage, and civil rights were linked. Absent the right to vote, women were powerless to make, let alone influence, policy that directly affected their lives and livelihood. Furthermore, as long as women earned less than men, their work did not hold the same value in the eyes of their employers. Fundamentally, without the vote they would never achieve an "equal footing in the workplace."[36]

College-educated women like Inez Mulholland, a law student at Vassar College, and Violet Price, another college student, also joined the striking shirtwaist workers. They knew the public would condemn any police officer who dared beat up a wealthy, white, educated woman. However, they weren't prepared for the derision and cynicism their involvement engendered in the press, which viewed them as interlopers. A *New York Times* article reported the following:

> Police have discovered, and bosses, whenever there is a scrimmage, there is certain to be a girl "from the league" to see pickets have fair play . . . Now the volunteer picket, who has good training and college for this sort of thing is craftier than the boss . . . If arrested she goes to the station . . . She has a way of putting things which makes the man who "pulled her in" most uncomfortable.[37]

Readers like Irving E. Doob also weighed in on the involvement of the city's social elite. In a letter to the editor, he wrote, "The misguided women on strike are but puppets of a new show. They provide a pleasant escape from ennui. Once the player tires of the game the pieces will be discarded and left to their fate."[38]

Whatever their fate, the strike could not halt the holiday season. Outside Macy's department store on Herald Square, children and parents gazed at window displays. Inside the Colony Club, 150 "jeweled, befurred, belaced, begowned women" sipped tea and ate canapés off bone china while "10 wage slaves, some of them mere children," shared their stories.[39] Once a venue for lighthearted luncheons, the exclusive club on Madison Avenue mailed engraved invitations to artists and writers, politicians and economists, to lecture about a myriad of topics, including politics and industrial economics. That afternoon society's crème de la crème listened as young woman after young woman told their stories. "Also, it is true that I made $15 a week. I did not strike because I myself was not getting enough. I struck because all the others should get enough. It was not for me; it was for the others," said one striker.[40] Another young striker from Harlem told her she earned $6 a week as a finisher. "Yes, I get 4 cents a dozen for waists. A priest came to our shop and told us girls that if we struck we should go—excuse me—please ladies—to hell."[41] Before the last gilt-edged chair was pushed in, $1,300 had been donated to the cause. The Shuberts,

Broadway's theater royalty, pledged 50 percent of all New York theater receipts toward the strike. Mary Dreier, the event's organizer, beamed.

Six days later, on December 21, 1909, Belmont and Morgan, cocooned in furs, sat ensconced in a gleaming sedan. They were in the first of fifteen chauffeur-driven cars to motor down Fifth Avenue to the Lower East Side. Department store windows gave way to placards with messages like "The Workhouse is no answer to the demands for Justice," "Votes for Women," and "Strikers and Socialites Together." The women organizers, whether they were working class or upper class, realized that as long as employers paid women less than men, their work would not be valued the same as that of men. They needed the vote as a key to unlock a fair workplace.[42]

Schneiderman and Newman appreciated the way the "Mink Brigade," as it was dubbed, "lent prestige and, more important, an aura of respectability to our demonstrations. This was most important for it helped to weaken the attempts of the unsympathetic to force the women back to work through prison sentences and physical violence." However, the women were aware that the presence of the Mink Brigade came with complications. For instance, Jane Addams worried about differences of culture, mores, and goals between the wealthy class and the working class. To be sure, she did more than scrunch her brow; she joined the picket line, raised money, and donated food to strikers. Of course, some female philanthropists donated time and money and never made demands, while others donated only to see their name on union letterhead or to land a seat on the board. That's partly why Schneiderman never fully trusted the role these well-dressed benefactors were playing.[43]

Working well over eighty hours a week organizing and strategizing, Newman still managed to make time to pen a regular column for ILGWU and WTUL publications, in which she reflected on the strike and its aims. She considered it part of her mission to make the women who purchased factory-made shirts, hats, and dresses think about the women—and men—who made them. Maybe that was the only way you could buy something so "cheap"—to imagine that nobody was forced to work standing bent over for more than half a day, earning barely enough to pay rent, and forgo school, she wrote. It was imperative for consumers to recognize that every product of modern industry exacted both a monetary cost and a social cost. "Some articles that we seem to be getting very cheap will be found to be costing us very dear," Mary Dreier later wrote. "The costly social price appears when we consider vagabonds who were child laborers, and disinherited women who worked in sweatshops and department stores."[44]

The WTUL rented meeting halls, set up telephone networks, and, sorely lacking in funds, hired attorneys to defend strikers pro bono. There was "not even enough to pay for the halls where the meeting[s] took place,"

Newman said.[45] The wealthy women members donated money and sometimes houses and property for collateral for bail for picketers, soup kitchens, and relief funds:

> Some of the richest women in the country felt it. Mrs. O.H.P. Belmont, mother of the Duchess of Marlborough, felt it. Miss Anne Morgan, daughter of J. Pierpont Morgan, felt it. Mrs. Belmont sat up nearly all night in the night court to save some accused strikers from the necessity of spending Sunday in the Tombs, and, at three o'clock in the morning gave her Madison Avenue mansion as security for the appearance of the strikers in court the following day . . . The daughter of another rich woman induced her mother to deed the family mansion to her in order that she might sit in court, day after day, and give bail for arrested girls.[46]

On the other side of the picket line, management used ethnicity, religion, and class to try to drive a wedge between the strikers. They pitted Jewish women against Italian women, rich against poor. They knew fear of discrimination deterred individual workers from fighting for the enforcement of the sanitary and fire laws.[47] "The first thing employers do when their girls begin to speak up for better conditions is to play one class of recent immigrants against another," one striker said. They questioned the morals of the picketers. After all, only working women and immigrants would dare act in such a disruptive manner. Some employers even insinuated that the striking women were prostitutes. These tactics failed. The strikers carried banners emblazoned with Yiddish slogans: "We Are Not Slaves." And they sang Russian folk songs like "Ekh, Dubinushak," which told of how landowners beat peasants.

The government response was as swift as it was harsh. From inside his office at city hall, far from the noise of the strikers, New York City mayor George McClellan met with Police Commissioner William Baker, who had only recently replaced Theodore Bingham. The latter blamed immigrants for the city's crime wave. McClellan made it clear the patrolmen could deal with the picketers as they saw fit. Like the shirtwaist factory owners, both those in city hall and the police insinuated that picketers were sex workers as a way to discredit them. They too exploited the social convention that "good" women listened to men, employers, or police and that only "bad" women were assertive and independent.

The misogyny didn't stop on the sidewalk. It sat on the bench alongside black-robed magistrates in courtrooms across the city. Miss Bertha Eltren of 35 Market Street found that out after she was arrested and stood before Magistrate Peter Townsend Barlow in night court. He admonished her not solely for her presence on the picket line but also for using the word "scab," saying, "If these girls continue to rush around and cry 'scab' I shall convict them of disorderly conduct. There is no word in the English language so irritating as the word scab."[48]

While most women were fined upward of $5,000 and sent home, others, like Eltren, who could not afford the $2.50 bail, were tried, convicted, and sentenced to up to three weeks on Blackwell's Island for disorderly conduct.[49] Well aware of the possible consequences, the women nevertheless stayed on the picket lines. Disorderly conduct was defined as "offenses less than felony against the peace of good morals of the community," according to *Abbott's Cyclopedic Digest of All the Decisions of All the Courts of New York from the Earliest Time to the Year 1900*. In truth, disorderly conduct was whatever the judge, a man, decided it was. The judges brooked no tolerance for the strikers. As City Magistrate Willard H. Olmstead put it, "You are on strike against God and nature, whose firm law is that man shall earn his bread in the sweat of his brow. You are on strike against God."[50]

The police made 723 arrests during the first month of the strike. Of those, 19 women were shipped to the notorious Blackwell's Island, present-day Roosevelt Island. Some women, like Eltren, chose to go to prison to make a stand.[51] After a woman like Eltren was sentenced, she was removed from the Tombs (as the municipal jail was called) and taken to the docks at the foot of East Twenty-Sixth Street. Under cover of darkness, the convicted striker would be put on a Department of Public Charities and Correction steamboat and ferried across the East River to the New York City Lunatic Asylum and Penitentiary. Established in 1849, the complex was built from Fordham gneiss. Formed during the pre-Cambrian era more than 1.1 billion years ago, the gray rocks lent a gothic air to the place. It was the very same institution where intrepid journalist Nelly Bly spent ten days undercover to research her 1887 book, *Ten Days in a Mad-House*.

A woman's crime and sentence were subsequently entered into the admission book along with her occupation and place of birth. From there the matron escorted her to a bath, where she was made to scrub in the same dirty bathwater as everyone else. Then she was handed an ill-fitting striped dress that was either too large or too small. Once processed, she was assigned a job. She might labor in a cigar shop or hoop skirt factory; she might spend her time cooking or scrubbing. When not working, she was locked inside one of 150 cells in the women's wing.

While but a temporary stop for the strikers, the 147-acre, two-mile-long strip of land was the last stop before death, dissection, and burial in a potter's field for hundreds of criminals, mentally ill, and indigent. It was a far cry from the *The Bridge, Blackwell's Island*, George Bellow's 1909 sundrenched painting of the prison island.

After completing her sentence, a protester would then be ferried back across the East River at night and deposited on the pier at the foot of East Twenty-Sixth Street. Stepping off the ferry, she "was royally received . . . by a reception party of 50" that included Dreier, Schneiderman, O'Reilly, and Newman. She was "escorted by a cheering crowd of strikers and strike sympathizers."[52] Women like Eltren often posed for pictures, wearing the court-ordered sash that said "Workhouse Prisoner" as a badge of honor.

With the arrival of 1910, there was still no sign that a resolution to the strike would be reached. Again, management agreed that workers would get a raise and that working conditions would be improved, though how exactly they did not say. Still, union recognition remained a sticking point. To no one's surprise, the picketers rejected the deal. They insisted on union representation. Negotiations continued.

"Shirtwaist Girls Say They Won Strike!" ran a headline in the *New York Times*. On February 15, 1910, nearly three months after Clara Lemlich cried "Now!" it was over. Both sides claimed victory. The ILGWU reached a settlement with 339 firms, 19 of which were open shop. The cost of the strike was about $100,000, of which 60 percent was for strike benefits. Of the 353 Associated Waist and Dress Manufacturers firms, 339 signed contracts that granted workers a fifty-two-hour workweek, four paid holidays, no discrimination against union loyalists, the provision of tools and materials without fee, and an equal division of work during the slack season so that no one was laid off.[53] The strike came during what was a new period for the United States in terms of industrial advancement. New manufacturing advancements, like the assembly line and electric power, meant new conveniences like automobiles, telephones, refrigerators, and indoor plumbing were on the horizon for the middle class at the same time that a majority of workers lived in slums with no recourse against landlords or management.

Ultimately the "Uprising of the 20,000" lit the match for a decade of labor unrest in the garment trades. Between 1909 and 1920, waves of strikes and mass organizational campaigns rippled across the country. After the strike in New York City, fifteen thousand women waist makers in Philadelphia strode out of their factories. The next year, forty-one thousand men's clothing makers in Chicago laid down their tools of trade. And young women button makers in Iowa would soon fight for union recognition. Women led the way in all cases. As the lyrics in an undated ballad went: "In the black of the winter of nineteen nine, / When we froze and bled on the picket line, / We showed the world that women could fight / And we rose and won with women's might."[54]

The strike also led to a spike in union membership. About 85 percent of shirtwaist makers joined the ILGWU.[55] By the end of World War I, workers in all sectors of the garment trade would be some of the most organized members of the nation's workforce. As for Local 25, membership jumped from one hundred members to twenty thousand. Perhaps more importantly, Gompers, the reluctant striker, said the strike

> brought to the consciousness of the nation a recognition of certain features looming up in its social development. These are the extent to which women are taking up with industrial life, their consequent tendency to stand together in the struggle to protect their common interests as wage earners, the readiness of the people in all classes to approve of trade-union methods in behalf of working women, and the capacity of women as strikers to suffer, to do, and to dare in support of their rights.[56]

Gompers's reluctance to support the strike was due in part to his worry that a failure would bruise the AFL's reputation. Once it became clear the strike might actually succeed, his posture shifted.

Also taking note was Eleanor Roosevelt, who would join the WTUL in 1923. As someone already steeped in social justice work, having worked at the Rivington Street Settlement House starting at age eighteen, she wrote about how "women of leisure and women of wealth became interested in the problems facing working women."[57] Other unions took notice too. A representative of the New York City–based Corset and Brassiere Workers' Union said, "Let no member share the mistaken idea of many unorganized workers that Union or no, conditions would have been improved anyway, in accordance with the general improvement in trade. The employer concedes only as much as he is compelled to."[58]

The ILGWU also took notice, particularly of Newman's talents. The union made the bold step of hiring her as their first woman general organizer. In Newman they saw a level-headed, unflappable young woman who paid meticulous attention to the details. They noticed how she ran daily shop meetings and arranged strike rallies, how she commanded crowds when she spoke. She was on her way to becoming one of the Progressive Era's star speakers, making speeches until her throat hurt and she was barking in a whisper. Soon the ILGWU gave Newman her first official assignment, even before the strike concluded: raise funds and recruit union members in the Northeast. She wasted no time preparing notes and packing a suitcase. "We are off," she said, shutting the door to her apartment.[59]

5

The Union Label

When Pauline Newman stepped inside Penn Station one late winter morning, she saw possibility and purpose. Completed in 1910, it was "the largest building in the world ever built at one time."[1] With its vaulted ceilings, Roman colonnades, and four pairs of sculptures by Adolph Weinman, it seemed like an art gallery. The beaux arts–style building, designed by McKim, Mead and White, not only linked New York City to points south, but the station's intercity trains could take you almost anywhere you wanted to go.

Newman located her platform and, handing her ticket to the conductor, boarded the train. Putting her small valise between her feet, she leaned back in her seat and exhaled. Moments later the train departed in a puff of smoke and a whistle blast. Her much-hoped-for sleep didn't come. She didn't buy a return ticket, as she had no idea how long she would be away on this extended organizing and fund-raising tour. By now the garment industry encompassed several cities beyond New York City; upstate New York was just the beginning. As it turned out, Newman would spend the next four years touring factories at the behest of the ILGWU and the Socialist Party. She would meet and talk with people of all backgrounds and faiths—Irish and Polish, Protestant and Jewish.

It was uncommon to see a woman traveling alone in 1910. There were some women-only train carriages, and of course automobiles provided an alternative, but they weren't always safer and were always more expensive—besides which, Newman didn't drive. To fend off would-be gropers, some women secreted a hatpin or two in the folds of their skirt or in their handbags.[2] As Theodore Roosevelt said, "No man, however courageous he may be, likes to face a resolute woman with a hatpin in her hand."

After an uneventful train ride—no hatpins required—Newman arrived in Buffalo. The train station was crowded, and, unsure of where to go, Newman gave the address of the ILGWU headquarters to a porter, who told her which trolley to take.[3] The route took her past Wippert Hatter and Furrier and More's Hatterie. A few stops later, Newman stepped off into the cold, and with her shoulders hunched against the wind, she entered a squat building. Charles Ball, the local labor leader, ushered her inside, where hot coffee and a sandwich waited on a table. A potbelly woodstove radiated just enough heat to defrost her cheeks and hands.

Located at the head of the Niagara River and home to flour and steel mills, Buffalo was Newman's first stop. As she later recalled, "The union sent me out to raise money for the strikers. I apparently was able to articulate my feelings and opinions about the criminal conditions, and they didn't have anyone else who could do better, so they assigned me. And I was successful getting money. After my first speech before the Central Trade and Labor Council I got front-page publicity, including my picture. I was only about fifteen then."[4]

She arrived several months after local switchmen staged a strike, demanding a six-cent-an-hour pay raise and double time for Sundays and holidays.[5] As one of the nation's largest grain ports and as the second-largest railway hub after Chicago, Buffalo was a center of manufacturing. Even so, the city had yet to develop a strong union presence. Newman was there to change that. The ILGWU leadership had sent her because of her performance during the shirtwaist strike.

Alice Paul, the firebrand suffrage activist, had also recruited Newman to speak to working-class groups after seeing her in action during the 1907 rent strike. A prolific activist and writer, Paul was born in 1885 to Quaker parents. She first encountered the pugnacious tactics of the British suffrage movement while studying social work in England. In 1910, several years after she had returned stateside, she joined the National American Women Suffrage Association and in due course became the face of the organization.[6]

Although Newman answered the call without hesitation, she initially worried that her membership in the Socialist Party might disqualify her from the full-time job. Carrie Chapman Catt, a devout Quaker and suffrage leader whom Newman knew, assured her she needn't worry; many people in the union were Socialists.

Fresh off the picket line in Manhattan, Newman felt fairly confident in her ability to energize people. She felt less sure of her ability to raise money. Having never solicited funds before, she cautioned Ball that she would be lucky to raise even five dollars. After all, not only was she an unfamiliar face in the city, but the idea of organizing was still new to her. The two hashed out a plan and reviewed points Newman could include in her talk. A few hours later, she checked into the hotel, where the clerk handed her a note. A Miss Laverack had telephoned to iron out the details of the following day's talk at a local women's club. She wanted to confirm that Newman would discuss the arrests and the factory conditions that led to the "girls strike." She also wanted reassurance that any money raised would be donated directly to the local chapter of the ILGWU.

The next morning, Newman coiled her brown hair and buttoned her white blouse. She straightened her wide black tie, smoothed her black skirt, and slipped her wire-rimmed glasses into her handbag. Buttoning her coat, she felt a slight case of nerves. Standing atop a soapbox on Mott Street in the Lower East Side was decidedly not the same thing as standing before a gathering of socialites garbed in silks and wool, seated on smartly upholstered chairs.

Laverack introduced Newman in glowing terms and then, without further ado, told her, "Go, tell the ladies how the strikers live, the conditions under which they work . . . friend and foe alike."[7] Any trepidation Newman felt evaporated the moment she began telling the story of the strike. Mindful of her audience, she sometimes tried to hide her Yiddish accent underneath a vaguely sounding British accent and avoided Yiddish phrases and words.[8] Her appetite for reading informed the content of her speeches. She wasn't shy about referencing Jack London or Charles Dickens—nothing could be more Oliver Twist than young children working in sweatshops where haranguing supervisors scrutinized them for hours on end.[9] According to her grandson Hugh Owen, "She had an innate sense of pace and tone, and preternatural ability to connect with an audience emotionally when she spoke."[10]

The women listened, engrossed as she described the "unspeakable exploitation of men, women, and yes, of children, too." They were silent while she told them how children as young as nine worked in factories where the air was stale and sooty. They gasped when they heard how little money one young mother with a nursing baby at home earned. They listened as she told how workers lived in constant fear of losing their jobs if they complained about anything, no matter how serious. They were surprised to learn how employees were docked pay if they were even a minute late to work, whether it was because their trolley was late or because they had to see a younger sibling off to school. The room erupted in applause before she could finish explaining why the union so desperately needed their donations. One woman announced that she was giving a hundred dollars to the cause. One by one, the rest of the women opened their purses. By evening's end, Newman's purse was full of cash. "Not a bad beginning, not bad at all. For the first time women, rich and poor alike, now know of the conditions under which the clothes they wore were made," she later wrote.[11]

The day's success convinced Newman that the ILGWU was right in inviting upper-class philanthropists into the movement to work alongside working-class women. The WTUL was already effectively using this strategy—hence her trip to Buffalo. After her fruitful afternoon, Newman realized that the more middle- and upper-class women she could get to align with the organization's cause, the more clout it could have. To be sure, such a partnership could only work if the wage earners took the lead and decided how to allocate funds. She knew that overreliance on wealthy women risked allowing them a chance to exert undue influence. She wrote to Rose Schneiderman to say she had found that "the 'cultured' ladies may be very sincere" but that "because their views are narrow and their knowledge of social conditions limited, they cannot do well as some of us can."[12] Schneiderman shared her friend's reservations, saying, "I could not believe that men and women who were not wage-earners themselves understood the problems that workers face."[13]

It was imperative that the WTUL and the ILGWU implemented safeguards to ensure working women maintained 50 percent of the leadership roles. Newman believed having women like the Dreier sisters hold leadership positions with the WTUL was fine, but one needed to be careful not to cede too much ground. For example, with Margaret "Mary" Robins paying everybody's salary and other expenses, there was a risk she would gain too much control. "Now you know I think an awful lot of Mrs. Robins—but the only fault I find with her is that she has made all the girls of the League think her way, and as a consequence they do not use their own minds and they do not act the way they feel but the way Mrs. R wants them to," Newman wrote to O'Reilly.[14] Nevertheless, others chafed at the way Morgan and Belmont tied donations with ribbons of demands. Moreover, they were upset that the two wanted to bar Socialists from becoming union members. "If the help of benevolent ladies is to be bought at the price of free speech [then] it comes high!" Leonora O'Reilly said.[15]

Matters of speech and funding aside, it wasn't all work in the Nickel City. Two mornings after arriving, Newman took her first-ever car ride. Glass vases with fresh flowers were mounted to the car doors and thick plaid rugs covered the floorboards. The car was better appointed than her hotel room, and it would be a most comfortable way to travel the two hours to Utica.[16] During their drive, Newman thought about what topics she wanted to discuss with Herve K. Fiske of the Utica local organization.

Like Newman, he was a member of the Socialist Party. Although this would be their first meeting, the two had previously exchanged several letters and book recommendations as well as ideas on the future of socialism.[17] Newman found comparing reading lists a meaningful way to forge connections; it gave her something to talk about when she met someone for the first time. That in turn prompted her to think about how this trip was exposing her to all kinds of people from a variety of backgrounds.

One Sunday, after she delivered remarks, an audience member invited her to dinner. Before the meal, they chatted in the living room as a fire blazed in the hearth. Then the butler announced that dinner was ready to be served in the dining room. "For the first time I saw the silver and crystal and the China and the beautiful table cloth and vases—beautiful vases, you know. At that moment I didn't know what the hell I was doing there. The butler had probably never seen anything like me before," she wrote of the unexpected extravagance.[18]

Finally back in her room, Newman kicked off her black leather shoes, wiggled her toes, and slid a cigarette from her case. She allotted herself four a day. This was her third. She barely had time to take her first puff when someone rapped at the door. Upon opening it she was met with someone from the front desk, scolding her about smoking. A minor request, perhaps, but one Newman did not have the tolerance to accommodate. Remembering that one of her friend's sisters had extended an invitation to her, Newman packed her bag and checked out.[19]

A few days later, she was in Rochester, New York, checking into a boardinghouse whereupon she learned from ILGWU secretary-treasurer John Dyche that the shirtwaist workers had finalized their agreement with employers. They ended with the workers getting a 10 percent increase in wages, a fifty-four-hour workweek, and union recognition. "This last was of course the thing the strikes fought and bled for. This was the gain for which the girls endured hunger and cold and loneliness," she wrote.[20] Newman was flushed with pride. Although they didn't get 100 percent of what they wanted, it was okay, because "you never do, you compromise," Newman said.[21]

Upon leaving upstate New York, Newman felt she had made a lasting impression on the people she'd met: "There are 'unknown soldiers' in the army of labor too. Their names do not appear in our history books."[22] She felt satisfied that "women, rich and poor alike, now knew of the conditions under which the clothes they wore were made."[23]

During the all-day train ride back to Manhattan, Newman made mental notes of what went right and what went wrong in Buffalo. Just a little more than a year earlier she and Rose Schneiderman, Clara Lemlich, and

Fannia Cohn were attending lectures at the Socialist Literary Society. She remembered the hours they spent discussing Thomas Hood's "Song of the Shirt" and Percy Bysshe Shelley's "The Masque of Anarchy": "The last two stanzas I will never forget. To us they represented all the women during the shirt waist worker's strike: 'And these words, shall then become Like Oppression's thundered doom Ringing through each heart and brain Heard again—again—again!"[24] Once again, Newman wrote, the women proved they were the tip of the spear in the fight to pierce unfair working conditions.

With the success of the shirtwaist strike, the Local 25, the WTUL, and the ILGWU proved that young women weren't "flippy, flighty little things, working for pin money."[25] They showed that women could be as interested in fair workplace conditions as they were in the style of hairdressing for the coming season. Yet, the ILGWU's strength did not reside in the purses of the wealthy alone. It was primarily due to the sheer number of members, many of whom were immigrants, who struggled against autocracy and exploitation. They were "imbued with a hatred for all oppression in whatever form—social, economic, political, religious—they brought with them a thorough going social idealism and fighting spirit which was to serve them well in their first struggles against their new exploiters, the garment manufacturers," Cohn wrote in her unpublished history of the ILGWU.[26]

Not long after the Cleveland cloak maker strike, Newman attended a Labor Day parade in which thousands of women marched. "The world does Move!" she was quoted as saying. "For not so very long ago it was very difficult to get the American working woman to parade, or to take part in any public demonstration; she considered it a man's job, the man thought that it was not womanly to parade through the streets . . . Times, however, have changed."[27] They marched not only to show they wanted better working conditions but also to show they were here and they were staying.

Decades before New York State governor Nelson Rockefeller's wife, Mary, threaded a sewing machine and sewed a union label onto a day dress at a New York factory, Newman traveled to Boston to persuade manufacturers and department stores to do just that: use the union label.[28] It was 1910, and while union membership in the ILGWU and the WTUL kept increasing in New York City, Boston's numbers lagged. The WTUL decided a more personal touch was needed to persuade the city's women wage earners to join. With ILGWU approval, Mary Dreier, the WTUL president, dispatched Newman to New England. She wanted Pauline to repeat her Buffalo performance by raising money and increasing enrollment.

Newman consulted her leather-bound daybook; a picture of Faneuil Hall was embossed on the burgundy cover. She always looked forward to buying a new one each year and using it as a sort of journal; she found something hopeful in opening it and seeing all the blank pages waiting to be filled. Newman recorded that she was to meet with Abraham Lincoln Filene, a noted "liberal and humanitarian."[29] On the morning of the meeting, she arose earlier than usual and donned what was now her signature style: white shirt, black tie, jacket, and black skirt. Filene gestured her to a seat in front of his desk. It didn't take long for Newman to convince the businessman to buy only goods that bore the ILGWU label. "My interview with Mr. Filene was a great satisfaction. He was kind and attentive and promised to comply," she said.[30] The small union label was a little personal message to each buyer. It said, Think about who made this garment and under what conditions they did so.

Before Filene died in 1957 at the age of ninety-two, he had built a $600-million-a-year empire. His path began in 1901 when he and his brother Edward inherited a piece-goods clothing store. Over time, they transformed the conservative, old-fashioned dry goods business into a pioneering enterprise. To start, they decided they would not hire any girl under the age of sixteen, and they would hire only those who had graduated with credit from grammar school.[31]

Filene and Newman discussed how paying higher wages, allowing employees to set the terms of their own employment, and encouraging them to get an education would benefit the business as much as the employee.[32] They spoke about the profit-sharing plan he had introduced in 1903 as well as the way he pioneered a minimum wage for women.

In 1912, two years after President William Howard Taft declared that employers ought to give American workers between two and three months of vacation a year so that they might refresh and continue working with *a renewed energy and effectiveness,* Filene announced his store would close on Saturdays as well as during the summer closings. Eventually, Filene would introduce paid winter and summer vacation. Doing so showed an understanding that a healthy employee meant a productive employee, as he also fully staffed a twenty-five-bed infirmary across the street from the store. Additionally, the Filene brothers would go on to institute a company union and a credit union for employees along with an employee-elected arbitration board and codes for fair business dealings. But for now, it was enough that he was going to use the union label.

By the end of their meeting, Newman's head was teeming with ideas. She thought about all the things that should be, but weren't, in workers' contracts and how in an industry where women made up more than 80 percent of the workforce, the ILGWU leadership ought to reflect that. Newman knew she had accomplished a great deal in upstate New York and was making significant headway in Boston. Still, she was getting annoyed. The ILGWU leadership, which was predominantly male, seemed to be subtly undermining her and other women at every turn, particularly because leadership positions remained closed to women organizers.

From Newman's perspective, it was outrageous that Samuel Gompers, who was himself an immigrant, openly decried the idea of including women in labor unions. He complained that women in certain positions depressed wages for men and, worse, that men were the primary breadwinners, so they deserved to earn more than women.[33] Nevertheless, Newman felt that Gompers's position was slightly demeaning. He espoused dusty ideas; women in leadership, or in any previously male-dominated space, would ultimately lead to the degradation of society. "Women would unsex themselves, said the critics; they would lose their feminine charms, homes would be neglected, and manners would be roughened . . . It was [a] 'sign of untold evils to come on the race.'"[34] But as Newman proved, women were becoming public speakers and labor organizers. They were fund-raising and they were pushing for the vote. They were not going to go back. *She* was not going to go back.

It was a scorching afternoon in July 1910 when the Cloak Makers' Union, under the leadership of Abraham Rosenberg, launched a general strike. At the time of the strike, about one hundred garment shops were working under union conditions, enough to make a difference when the call for the strike came. Several days earlier, union officials had told the employees to be on the lookout for a red circular.[35]

Though women accounted for only about 20 percent of the workforce in this sector, they led the charge. Like the 1909 shirtwaist makers' strike, workers' demands were similar: a reduction in hours, double-time pay for overtime, and the right to unionize. However, unlike the 1909 shirtwaist makers' strike, this one was well thought out and better executed. The idea had taken root in June after hundreds of union members traveled to Boston for the ILGWU's tenth annual convention. This time there was no hemming and hawing; the executive board planned to call for a general strike. Twelve days later, on June 22, a public meeting at Madison Square Garden "was filled to overflowing" with members ready to strike.[36] Ten days later, union members voted: 18,771 in favor and 615 against. The strike began on July 7.

That day, scores of workers walked out of their factories, stopped traffic, and trooped to the union halls carrying the tools of their trade: scissors, needles, spools of thread. "In my mind I could only picture myself such a scene taking place when the Jews were led out of Egypt," Cohn said.[37] On Friday nights, some protesters came to the WTUL to sing. The WTUL thought it would be a nice touch to have a trained chorus to sing labor songs, "with its music to sooth[e] the savage breast of any force that may oppose it."[38] The time when women knew little about the union and strikes was over. "The East Side woman of today is an enthusiastic unionist without belonging to a union and when her husband goes on strike she is with him heart and soul," Newman wrote.[39]

Throughout this time, Newman skillfully wielded her words, penning columns for various union publications, including *Life and Labor*, *Justice*, and *The Suffragist*, the official magazine of the National Woman's Party. Her typewriter became an extension of her voice, whether it was talking about how industries controlled "the destinies of its hundreds of thousands of men and women whose jobs and livelihood they own," and "the exploitation of these men and women, and especially of the women," in a June 1921 issue of *Life and Labor*,[40] or persuading female union members to fight for the right to vote so that they might establish a six-hour day in spring, eight hours in the winter, and *none* in the summer: "Of course one [of] you could never bring it about, but all of you could, and in a comparatively short time at that. All you need is to get together into an organization on the economic field, and in a few years you will have power on the political field."[41]

So comfortable was Newman with the written word, she sometimes preferred it to speaking: "I am so tired of speaking that my ambition is now to write."[42] That feeling never lasted long, and before she knew it, she was back at work. Having read a letter to the editor from one worker that made an impassioned plea for "stories that tell of struggle, and that tell of people who want justice passionately," Newman responded with several articles that she thought would reach the readership.[43] Aside from *Life and Labor*, which was a union publication, Newman, the WTUL, and the ILGWU sought to amplify their message in the Jewish press. The Orthodox newspaper *Yidishes Tageblatt* supported the workers, frequently giving front-page coverage to the big garment strikes and reporting on challenges Jewish women and men faced in the workplace as they tried to eke out a decent standard of living.

Two days before the walkout, the strike committee presented management with their demands, which were unmet. Rather than sit down with the committee, management formed a defensive association known as the Cloak, Suit, and Skirt Manufacturers' Protective Association. Every member of the association vowed they would never "join in any agreement whatsoever with any organization which shall directly or indirectly involve the surrender of the control and management of his factory or subfactories to any set or group of men whether calling themselves a union or anything else."[44]

Days later the State Board of Mediation and Arbitration sent officials to meet with both sides. After a week of talking, they were stuck on the same points. Then on July 18 the Union Settlement Committee chair sent a note to the manufacturers' association chair. The talks moved ahead, albeit in snail-like fashion. The main sticking point was whether shops would be open or closed. Abraham Lincoln Filene, a member of the Civic Federation of New England, tried to mediate along with Meyer Bloomfield, a New York City–based attorney. Unable to make any progress, he enlisted the help of future Supreme Court Justice Louis D. Brandeis.

Three days before Labor Day, an agreement was reached. The "Protocol of Peace" abolished inside subcontracting, charges for power, and contracts for individual workers. It also established ten legal holidays with full pay for weekly workers, a regular weekly payday, payment of wages in each fifty-hour workweek, and double pay for overtime.[45] By the time the agreement was reached, Newman was on board a Chicago-bound train.

Newman sat on another hard wooden chair at another desk in another hotel she couldn't remember the name of. She pulled out a sheet of Ladies' Shirt Waist Makers Union Local 15 letterhead and began a letter to Schneiderman, whom she missed terribly. "If there ever was a time that I wanted you—that time was last night," she wrote.[46] "O but how I wanted you. All evening I kept on saying 'if only Rose were here.' . . . Rose dear you will have to come here in the very near future, I may arrange a meeting and have you as a speaker."

In the quiet between speeches and meetings, between standing in front of factories passing out leaflets, Newman was struggling with feelings of loneliness. It was October 1910 and by now she had been hopscotching across the country for several weeks giving strike assistance to workers, encouraging them, paraphrasing Percy Bysshe Shelley in his ode "The Masque of Anarchy," to "rise from their slumber."[47] She visited textile mills in Massachusetts and department stores in Buffalo. There were talks with silk weavers in New Jersey and marble quarry workers in Vermont.[48] In Huntsville, Alabama, laundry workers were organizing, and in Kansas City yarn workers, telegraphers, and bookbinders were heading toward a strike—unless they secured substantial pay increases. In Chicago, Newman helped domestic workers and hosiery workers organize; she also convinced them to join the WTUL, which was now offering classes in everything from pottery and piano to voice lessons and leadership.

She longed for her New York City. More specifically, she longed for Schneiderman, with whom she could comfortably bare her most private thoughts. The two had met as young teens in the first years of the WTUL. Schneiderman was Newman's first friend and, as their letters from this time period show, her first love, as shown in their salutations: "My dearest rose," "dearest Paul," and "I am yours forever or never."[49] But for now, a forlorn Newman was growing increasingly attached to her friendship with Schneiderman. Their letters were heartfelt and sentimental, and, more important, they helped sustain Newman as she navigated the ever-evolving balance between work and politics.

Pauline Newman did not, and would never, identify as a lesbian. There is nothing unusual in that; neither did the many who lived with and loved other women in this period identify as lesbians. This was true even though several lived with and loved other women. As historians like Dorothy Sue Cobble and Lillian Faderman have pointed out, some of that can be explained in part because in the first half of the 1900s the term "lesbian" was used to describe "other" women: working-class, masculine-presenting women. If someone wanted to not only be accepted in society but to also succeed in society, then one would likely deny one's sexual orientation.

Indeed, heterosexuality was an inescapable part of Newman's world from the time she was a child. Girls talked about dating, dated, read romance novels; sisters married; and mothers and fathers arranged marriages. Most of the women she knew from the Triangle Shirtwaist Factory used to chat about how excited they were to stop working once they tossed the wedding bouquet. Newman didn't know many women who both rejected marriage and managed to avoid social condemnation or stigma. Much of this was because of how traditional gender roles were perceived at the time and the fact that marriage was viewed through a heteronormative lens. As such, heterosexual activity and relationships were considered essential to developing a healthy self.[50] Nevertheless, letters from this time period show that Newman and Schneiderman wrote almost weekly. Even that was sometimes not enough for Newman: "Why don't you write more? I know that you have no time to write often, but when you do write, write a lot!"[51] Or "I want you to show that you forgive me, for not writing to you sooner, and by the quickness of your answer shall I know it."[52]

Instead of cake and candles on her birthday, Newman visited two factories followed by an afternoon of bowling for the sake of exercise. The rest of the day was spent alone in her room preparing another speech. This would be one of the first she would deliver on the subject of health care.

Newman tried not to breathe through her nose. The filthy lavatories combined with the rancid stench of the gas jets threatened to overpower her. A roach skittered across her boot. She shrugged. Mice and roaches were as much a part of the workshop floor as were the sewing machines and worktables. It was the third kimono and wrapper shop she had visited in as many days. This one, Levisin Brother & Nevins in Brooklyn, was not paying its workers the minimum weekly wage of ten dollars that union members demanded. It was also not meeting sanitary conditions.

After the cloak makers' strike ended, Newman began visiting kimono and wrapper shops across the city. She also started turning her attention to health care. For decades, piecework was the backbone of New York City's garment industry. Most of it was done in sweatshops; consequently, the same diseases that afflicted those living in close-quarter tenements spread to consumers across the city. As such, the National Consumers League got involved in housing reform and anti-tuberculosis campaigns. Newman was, of course, interested in this work.[53] Having spent the better part of two years visiting factories and speaking with workers, it was abundantly clear to her and others in the ILGWU that deficient workplace conditions in the garment industry were inextricably linked to poor health. As New York State labor legislation had so far failed to improve conditions, the Joint Board of Sanitary Control was established in 1910. The tripartite body was comprised of the ILGWU; the Cloak, Suit, and Skirt Makers Union; and the Manufacturers Protective Association. For the "first time in the history of the labor movement in America an additional clause was added to the demands of the union and that additional case was for a sanitary shop—sanitary conditions, better lighting, regular chairs, instead of sitting on boxes, better ventilation," Newman said.[54]

The job called for her to visit factories, both sweatshops and larger, more established ones like the Triangle Shirtwaist Factory. She would be working closely with Dr. George Moses Price. Born in Poltava, Russia (now Ukraine), Price left for the United States when he was eighteen. Like Newman, Schneiderman, and so many of the men and women he would work with, he left because of the pervasive, violent anti-Semitism. He was anxious to leave Russia, a place he described as his "backward homeland." He thought no one except other Jewish people could relate to the way he felt, writing in his diary:

> A person forsaking his homeland and his place of birth is usually depressed. He bids farewell to everything that is dear to him. While in his mind's eye he parts with every nook and corner, he harbors hope that someday he will return to see familiar places again. Not so with the Russian Jew . . . The Russian Jew witnesses his being deprived of inalienable rights, and how he is considered a worthless being deserving of no consideration.[55]

After nearly twenty days of waves buffeting the ship on which he was traveling, Price was relieved to reach "the magnificent shores of

America."[56] He soon discovered that those shores held numerous obstacles and challenges for immigrants, especially for those consigned to work in factories. These challenges and inequities were very much on his mind when he graduated from New York University Medical School in 1895 and again when he was appointed to be inspector of the New York Health Department. Later Price would become the chairman of the executive committee of the Joint Board of Sanitary Control in the Cloak and Suit Industry of New York. It was from this perch that Price realized negotiations between labor and management overlooked health-related issues. Like Newman, he wanted to remedy the situation. Too many shops were still located in cellars or attics. Far too many businesses still lacked fire escapes and blocked or locked fire exits. Many didn't have tin-lined fireproof bins, and those that had tin-lined bins didn't have covers. Staircases were treacherous. There were no separate bathrooms for men and women nor water-supplied wash basins.[57] From their point of view, the garment industry was a multimillion-dollar health disaster.

As Newman noted, most employees went their whole life without seeing a doctor or a dentist, not because they were in perfect health but because they couldn't afford the fee or the time it took to make and keep an appointment. They couldn't afford to purchase proper food. Many were frequently ill. It was an issue of cost and access, Price agreed. In his view there was "a tremendous amount of preventable physical pain and mental anguish, needless deaths and economic efficiency and social waste." Even garment workers who were now protected by unions didn't earn enough to "secure competent and adequate health service from private practitioners."

As Price was editing the joint board's most recent report, Newman settled into her train seat. She was headed back to Philadelphia, finally putting her suitcase down in early November. But the City of Brotherly Love was proving to be a city of corruption and discontent as far as garment factories were concerned. She was there at the behest of the ILGWU to set things right.

Sitting inside the ILGWU offices, glad to be inside while hail and rain lashed the building, she heard a light knock on the door. In walked a young woman. *A Russian immigrant,* Newman thought to herself, recognizing in her the girl she herself had been not so long ago. "You're not going out tonight. I wouldn't send a dog out in weather like this," Newman said, tilting her head at the window. The young woman ignored Newman and grabbed a stack of pamphlets and left. "She had the faith and will to help build the organization. She was really one of the unknown soldiers."[58]

6

The Triangle Fire

When the young women of the Triangle Shirtwaist Factory sat down in front of their Singer sewing machines on Saturday, March 25, 1911, they didn't know their lives were about to be extinguished by a lit cigarette. It was nearly 4:40 p.m. The cutters were just about finished for the day and one of them flicked a still-smoldering cigarette butt into a pail filled with paper patterns and remnants. It sparked. Noticing the flames, the cutter threw a bucket of water on it—to no avail. The flames leaped to the spare fabric and shirts hanging from the ceiling. Seconds after that, the fire spread to the upper floors. Five minutes after that, around 4:45 p.m., someone on the eighth floor pulled the fire alarm. The building vibrated with the bell.

"In less time than I can tell it all became confusion at the ninth floor," Katie Weiner said.[1] As the women crowded the elevator, Weiner rushed to find her sister. Out of the corner of her eye, she saw her sister near the window. Flames shot up into the room. "I started to run toward her, but the smoke was so dense that it choked me. I could not reach her." Meanwhile, an elevator door opened and several workers leaped for the cables. A few managed to grab hold and shimmy down. The rest tumbled down the shaft and died on impact.[2]

By the time the horse-drawn Engine Company 72 trotted the six blocks from the firehouse to the corner of Greene Street and Washington Place, forked flames licked the sky and plumes of black smoke rolled over rooftops. Next came the Company 18 pump engine, drawn by three horses. A hook and ladder truck from Company 20 came up Mercer Street so fast it nearly missed the turn onto Washington Place. Tragically, not one of those ladders could extend higher than six stories. These were the first of about thirty-five pieces of firefighting apparatus to arrive.

Meanwhile, thirty-one-year-old Frances Perkins was sitting down to tea at her friend's townhouse at 26 North Washington Square. Suddenly the air filled with the screech of fire whistles. Rushing outside, the two women saw a sky turned black with smoke. Clutching her skirt in one hand, Perkins sprinted across Washington Square Park. "We got there just as they started to jump," said the newly appointed head of the New York office of the National Consumer League. "I shall never forget the frozen horror which came over us as we stood with our hands on our throats watching that horrible sight, knowing that there was no help. The firemen kept shouting for them not to jump. But they had no choice; the flames were right behind them, for by this time the fire was far gone."[3]

Dr. D. C. Winterbottom, they city's coroner, happened to glance out the window of his brownstone. Located at 63 Washington Square South, virtually around the corner from the Triangle Shirtwaist Factory, he couldn't see the building but he could smell the smoke. The telephone rang. Winterbottom grabbed his leather doctor's bag and arrived ten minutes later.

Ambulances, following close behind the fire trucks, skidded to a halt in front of the corner building. The drivers jumped out, ready to assist the firefighters and to treat the injured workers. They were not prepared for the scene that unfolded before them. Young women were bunched on the ninth-story windowsills, some with hair aflame. Some smoothed their skirts before stepping into the sky. Some held hands. Some closed their eyes. Those below watched helplessly as the women tumbled through the air and thudded onto the sidewalks, some crashing through glass cellar lights. "One woman fell so close to the ambulance that I thought if we drove it up to the curb it would be possible for some persons to strike the top of the ambulance and so break their falls," recounted one physician who worked a few blocks away at St. Vincent's Hospital.[4]

Meanwhile, Captain Howard Ruch of Company 18 and his crew struggled to maneuver the heavy rubber hoses away from the falling bodies. He ordered the men to spread life nets, hoping they might save some lives. Instead, the tumbling bodies tore through the nets, some knocking firemen off their booted feet. The filaments of the nets sliced through the men's calloused hands.[5] The carnage so terrified the firemen's horses that they tried to break away. A few horses were too slow to avoid being crushed by the weight of workers desperate to flee the flames. Throughout this chaos, firemen trained ten hose lines on the ten-story building. The heavy spray of water gushed from the windows in what the *New York Times* described as a "miniature Niagara."[6] Eighteen minutes later, the inferno was under control. Eighteen minutes too late for the 146 women who now lay dead.

Pauline Newman, twenty-one, almost didn't stop at her hotel's front desk in Philadelphia. She was running late for her morning meeting. The serious expression on the clerk's face changed her mind. She took the phone. Upon hearing the news, she shoved her belongings into her suitcase and rushed out the door. "I couldn't get the train to go fast enough," she said of her mad dash to the Thirtieth Street Station.[7] Newman had spent nearly eight years working at the Triangle Shirtwaist Factory, so she knew many of the victims and many of the victims' families.

Back in Manhattan, she raced to Greene Street, where she met up with some of the union people. "You don't forget a day like that. It was awful, especially when the parents came. I can't forget, but I don't want to think about it too much," she said.[8] Newman was sliding into a depression; figuring out a way to prevent something like the Triangle Shirtwaist Factory fire from happening again was her way of climbing out.

Bronzed from basking in the Florida sunshine, Joseph J. Asch, the building's owner, stood before a bevy of reporters in the Hotel Belmont on Park Avenue and Forty-Second Street. The white-mustachioed fifty-year-old was traveling with his wife from St. Augustine, Florida, to his home in Saugatuck, Connecticut. Having first learned of the fire upon opening the Sunday paper, he now insisted that his 135-foot high, four-hundred-thousand-dollar building was fireproof. But, as an investigation would soon show, a better firetrap could not have been designed.

The issues that caused the fire were wired into the building from the moment New York City approved architect John Wooley's building plans on July 13, 1900. In time, it would become apparent that the architect had cut innumerable corners and exploited multiple loopholes during the permitting process. At 135 feet tall, the building was allowed to have wooden trim, wooden window frames, and wooden floors. Had it been 15 feet higher, the builders would have been required to use metal, stone, or concrete. The staircases and doors were also not up to code. At the time, New York law stipulated that a structure like the Asch Building, with an interior area of 10,000 square feet per floor, should have had three staircases. There were only two. That's because Wooley asked for, and was allowed, an exception. City officials had decided that the fire escape leading to an inner courtyard could be counted as a third staircase. Other hazards included the fact that both staircases were only 33 inches wide, considerably less than the natural arm span of a woman of average height; thus, one had to ascend or descend only in single file. Lastly, a 6-foot iron rail fence topped with 4-inch spikes surrounded the skylight, making a rooftop exit futile.[9]

Then there were the doors. The stairways were so narrow that the doors could not swing safely outward, as required by the building code. Again a loophole in the language of the building code made an exception possible. The law mandated that exit doors swing outward "wherever practicable." Well, Wooley told city officials, it wasn't "practicable" for exit doors to swing outward because the last step of each stairway was flush against the door itself. The exception was granted, even though an inward-swinging door was a fire hazard—if too many people squeezed into a stairwell while trying to flee a fire, there would be no room for the door to open.

At the time of the fire, the union members and families of victims didn't know any of this. Most would first learn of it during the ensuing weeks and months as bits of the subsequent official report were made public. Ultimately, it would not be until November 1911, when the first trial over the Triangle Shirtwaist Factory fire began, that they would learn the complete story.

The ILGWU and the Local 25 did not need to wait for the report. The tragedy alone galvanized them. Like Newman and Cohn, Perkins and Lemlich, many of the women's close friends and acquaintances perished in the fire. The four women became single-minded in their work to organize garment workers nationwide. In their view, 146 lives had been sacrificed on the altar of profits. Newman decided it was past time to arouse the public and government and secure the workplace protection working women and men deserved.[10] "If this tragedy could make New York stop to think whether it were not allowing men to go too madly and disastrously and selfishly in pursuit of money, then these crowded workers would not have died in vain," the Rev. Dr. Charles L. Slattery said.[11]

Six months before the fire, the Joint Board of Sanitary Control, of which Newman was a part, found that a majority of the city's garment factories were firetraps. Nine days before the fire, on March 16, the New York *Call* published excerpts from the board's report that showed fire prevention facilities were "very much below even the most indispensable precautions necessary."[12] More precisely, the board's investigators ascertained that 99 percent of all shops in New York City were unsafe. Fourteen lacked fire escapes, 101 had poorly functioning drop ladders, 491 had only one exit, 23 factories locked their doors during the day, 58 had dark hallways, and 94 percent of them had exit doors that swung inward. At the Triangle Shirtwaist Factory, Max Blanck and Isaac Harris maintained they locked the doors only to prevent theft, despite a New York State law that said doors "shall not be locked, bolted, or fastened" during working hours. Yet, just as with child labor laws, enforcement was lacking. In this case, resources were scarce and the will even scarcer.[13]

As the acting superintendent of buildings would soon testify, there were fewer than fifty inspectors to look at the 50,000 buildings in New York City. In February 1911, just a month before the blaze, the fire department said 13,603 of those were dangerous. Yet, inspectors visited only 2,051 of them.[14] As for fire sprinklers, Fire Commissioner Rhinelander Waldo issued an order to every factory to install fire sprinklers. The Protective League of Property Owners accused him of meddling and of trying to force businesses to purchase expensive and unwieldy apparatus. Sprinklers were not installed.

Indeed, the 1911 fire was not the first one inside the Asch Building. Four small nighttime fires of unknown origin had taken place. In each case, firefighters extinguished the blaze before substantial damage occurred. In each case, Blanck and Harris had introduced no measures to improve fire safety. The first one occurred in April 1902. At the time, the company collected $19,102 for a fire with "cause unknown." Seven months later, Triangle collected $12,905 in insurance for another fire with "cause unknown." Three years later, in April 1905, the Shirtwaist Kings collected an undisclosed amount from insurance. In April 1907 the Diamond Waist Company, which Triangle owned and operated, collected an unspecified amount, and in April 1910 it received $17,000 in insurance.[15] On the morning of March 25, the Triangle Shirtwaist Company held $199,750 in insurance. While that might look suspicious, the situation wasn't unique to the Triangle Shirtwaist Company. Although officials were generous regarding insurance, they were stingy with fire prevention.

Jewish custom stipulates that burial happens within twenty-four hours of a person's death. Although the majority of the young women killed were Jewish, this timeline would prove to be impossible, as it would take time to identify the dead. So two days after the fire, three hundred men and women gathered in predawn darkness on the East Twenty-Sixth Street pier. The sun did not rise until 5:50 a.m. that morning, but the families were already standing outside, impatient to enter the improvised morgue.[16] Inside the covered pier, men had arranged dozens of wooden coffins into neat rows.[17] The police department requested one hundred coffins from the city morgue the night before; only sixty-five were available. Wagons and ambulances brought additional coffins, some of which came from Blackwell's Island, where some of the dead once served a sentence for striking. Now, as the first light glinted off the East River, sixty policemen, under command of a Captain Martens, arrived from the Fifty-Sixth Street Station and formed two double rows. Once the families were allowed inside, the identifications could begin.

Burned beyond recognition, some of the girls could only be identified by a scrap of cloth or a scuff mark on the outside of a shoe. One mother and father stood over their daughter. Her limbs had been burned off; her face looked untouched. Those who were not severely burned were shrouded and their faces left uncovered. "Men and women wept. Many were outraged," Newman wrote.[18] So the day unfolded, scores of people coming to the pier hoping to identify a loved one.

Ten days after firemen extinguished the fire's last embers, the rains came down. The deluge didn't stop a silent mourning procession on April 5 to honor the seven remaining unidentified victims. It took six hours for one hundred thousand mourners and several net-draped horses to pass the three hundred thousand people garbed in black who wanted to pay their respects. As Newman recalled, "It seemed that the entire city was on the march. It was raining, but nobody cared, everybody went anyhow . . . I don't think we will ever forget it. Thousands of people stood in the rain, watching. It looked like the entire city of NY was at the parade, if you'll call it a parade."[19] Because many of the victims were poor immigrants, their families couldn't afford the funeral expenses. The Hebrew Free Burial Association helped people who could not afford to buy a cemetery plot. They provided space in Staten Island for both Italian and Jewish victims since there were not yet enough Italian organizations with the means to help.

The first protests erupted two days after the fire. Representatives of at least twenty labor and civic organizations congregated outside the WTUL headquarters. Mary Dreier, the league president, presided. One of the first to address the crowd was Rabbi Stephen S. Wise of the four-year-old Free Synagogue. Born in 1874 in Budapest, Wise had immigrated to the United States when he was a child. While working as a rabbi in Portland, Oregon, he got involved in the introduction of new child labor laws. Eventually he worked closely with Louis D. Brandeis and became an ardent supporter of suffrage and workers' rights. Wise called for the creation of a citizens' fact-finding committee of no fewer than twenty-five people. "We don't want an outburst of charity for those who have suffered only to have the whole thing forgotten," he said.[20] "Instead of having safety appliances in a museum, however laudable its purpose, we ought to put in a museum any man who is unwilling to utilize every possible industrial appliance for the safety and security of the toilers."[21]

A few blocks away, the ILGWU Local 25 draped its Clinton Street headquarters in black. The pleated fabric extended from the roof all the way to the sidewalk. Relatives stopped in at all hours of the day and night hoping to learn something, anything, about how their loved one died and about what financial assistance they might receive going forward.

Schneiderman, Newman, Lemlich, and several other women from the WTUL spent days traversing the Lower East Side searching for victims' families so that they might pay their respects. It wasn't difficult; they only had to look for funeral wreaths nailed to the doors of tenements like blazes on a trail or to follow the wailing in the streets of relatives and friends. "But sometimes you climbed floor after floor up an old tenement, went down the long, dark hall, knocked on the door and after it was opened found them sitting there—a father and his children or an old mother who had lost her daughter—sitting there silent, crushed," Schneiderman said.[22] "This wasn't the first time men and women have been burned to death. The life of men and women is so cheap, property is so sacred, there are so many of us to every job, that it matters little if a hundred and fort[y]-five die," Schneiderman said about the fire.[23] In what was New York City's first large-scale disaster operation, representatives from the Joint Relief Committee of the Ladies' Waistmakers' Union, the Red Cross, and the WTUL started going door-to-door to visit with victims' families.

The morning after the fire, Robert W. de Forest, the Red Cross Emergency Relief Committee chair, pressed Mayor William J. Gaynor to issue a citywide appeal for donations. Contributions came from old and young alike, from those with means and those without. One person wrote, "My littel cousin Beatrice and I are sending you five dollars a piece from our savings bank to help them out of trubbel please give it to the right one to use it for sombody whose littel girl jumped out of a window i wouldent like to jump out of a high window myself."[24] Andrew Carnegie promised five thousand dollars. Later, questions would arise as to how the money was disbursed. Hundreds of complaints poured in to the Women's Trade Union League, but complaints were rarely investigated. The families also pushed the union officials to get the Red Cross to account for one hundred thousand dollars collected for the benefit of the families of the fire victims but not yet paid to them.

A little over a month after the acclaimed Irish tenor John McCormack made his Carnegie Hall debut, New York City's union leaders, politicians, philanthropists, and clergy passed through the same three sets of heavy doors. They were gathered for a memorial service to raise money for the victims' families; the death of a sister, daughter, or wife meant the end of vital income. Many of the dead young women were the breadwinners, as their earnings supported their fathers and mothers, some here and some abroad. Others were helping support younger siblings, sending brothers to school. According to a 1911 US Bureau of Labor study, about one-third of households in which there was no father depended on the income of their working daughters.[25] Knowing this, the mood inside the music hall was somber with underlying notes of cynicism and rage. "This is not the first time girls have been burned alive in the city. Every week I must learn of the untimely death of one of my sister workers . . . I can't talk fellowship to you who are gathered here. Too much blood has been spilled. I know from experience it is up to the working people to save themselves," Schneiderman said at the memorial organized by Anne Morgan.[26]

A more organized protest followed about two weeks later when Morgan rented the Metropolitan Opera House for an interfaith service. Jacob H. Schiff, a Wall Street financier and philanthropist, opened the meeting. After his remarks, District Attorney Eugene A. Philbin stepped up and told the assembly that Gaynor's appeal was working and that contributions so far totaled seventy-five thousand dollars, or what he described as "the public's conscience money."[27] The speakers did not try to soften their message. They did not care if they made the audience of mostly upper-class people squirm uncomfortably in their plush velvet seats. Roman Catholic Diocese Brooklyn Monsignor William White admonished the crowd for elevating property rights above life. Next, Bishop David B. Greer of the Episcopal Church of New York pleaded with the audience to think about how the tragedy had resulted in differences being forgotten for a little while as the "whole community rises to one common brotherhood." However, he reminded them, "One thing is sure. Hereafter the law as to fire protection must be enforced not for a few weeks or for a few months but for all times, faithfully, conscientiously, and effectively. If this is not done, the responsibility—the sin—is on the public, on us."[28]

Mindful that the majority of the dead were Jewish, Morgan also invited Rabbi Wise to speak. Wise implored the audience to realize that people, not God, were responsible for the tragedy:

> The disaster was not the deed of God but the greed of man. This was no inevitable disaster which could not be foreseen . . . When we go before the legislature let us not allow them to put us off forever with the old answer, "We have no money." If we have no money for the necessary enforcement of the laws which safeguard the lives of workers it is because so much of our money is wasted and squandered and stolen.[29]

They were elegant words, painful words. But, thought Schneiderman, they missed the heart of the matter. So, just as Clara Lemlich had interrupted the proceedings in Cooper Union back in 1909, Rose Schneiderman strode to the podium. Here was someone who knew the experience of the Triangle workers. In a halting voice barely above a whisper, she spoke:

> I would be a traitor to those poor burned bodies if I were to come here to talk good fellowship. We have tried you good people of the public, and we have found you wanting . . . Every time the workers come out in the

> only way the[y] know to protest against conditions which are unbearable, the strong hand of the law is allowed to press heavily down upon us . . . The strong hand of the law beats us back when we rise—back into the conditions that made life unbearable . . . I can't talk fellowship to you who are gathered here.[30]

Needed in Philadelphia to organize striking workers, Newman was gutted that she could not join her colleagues and closest friends. She was paralyzed to do anything other than closely follow the proceedings. "I could not write; I could not do anything for the last two or three weeks. The Triangle tragedy had a terrible effect on me," she said.[31] The shadow of the day would nonetheless follow her the rest of her days. At the same time, she also read Schneiderman's speech. She was so proud of her friend: "You really gave them hell, [and I] am glad of it . . . I wonder how Miss Morgan felt after you got through."[32]

While reading her friend's speech for the second time, she again wondered about her role with the ILGWU. Perhaps she would be more effective if she worked full-time with the WTUL. She submitted her first of what would be many resignations from the organization. John Dyche, the ILGWU secretary with whom she had argued on more than one occasion, refused her letter. Schneiderman beseeched Newman to reconsider, telling her friend she was needed in the movement. Thus Newman stayed, her sense of duty prevailing. "Rose put them right. She said that would be treason to the dead if we stopped at this point. And out of this meeting came the legislation for fire protection in buildings, and Frances Perkins had a hand in that, and so did Al Smith," said Newman, who couldn't attend the memorial. She was needed in Philadelphia.[33]

Somehow, amid all the darkness of the past months, a sliver of light managed to reach Newman. For it was here, in this city on the banks of the Schuylkill River, that she first met Frieda Miller. Newman was immediately struck by this "very vivacious, cheerful, knowledgeable, kindly person. She was a person who loved life. She was concerned with people, loved music . . . literature . . . the country . . . nature . . . loved all that is enjoyable and knowledgeable."[34] As the two began spending time together, Newman learned of Miller's background; her home in La Crosse, Wisconsin; and her family's summer home at Devil's Lake, with its quartzite bluffs. Miller learned of Kovno and sledding, of Cossacks and how Newman pleaded with her father to go to school. She learned about what it was like for Newman to trudge up dark staircases to jobs. The more they talked, the more Newman fell for this woman, who was in so many ways her opposite. Miller was formally educated, while Newman was not. Miller came from some means, while Newman did not. Miller was at ease in social settings, while Newman was less confident in her ability to charm.[35]

After the initial shock of the Triangle Shirtwaist fire faded, the families of the victims, survivors, and union leadership set out to make concrete changes. Newman, Price, and Perkins were among those hired to the state Factory Investigating Commission. Of the commission's nine members, five were lawmakers. The first hearing was on October 14, 1911, and there would be public hearings in New York City, Buffalo, Rochester, Syracuse, and Troy. As Perkins would later recall in a 1964 lecture at Cornell University, it was vital that the New York State legislature, rather than the governor, appoint the commission. That way the legislature would be more likely to follow the findings. Sitting on the commission were two civilians, Abraham Elkus and Mary Dreier, as well as an equal number of Democrats and Republicans. In the end the commission would call more than 220 witnesses, and field inspectors would visit more than 1,800 businesses. It would also produce seven extensive volumes relating to the fire. Over time, the commission expanded its work and reported on several issues, including sanitary conditions, overwork, safety issues, and child labor.[36]

The new commission was tasked with finding out what caused the blaze, but more importantly, it was on a mission to develop, and enforce, stricter safety standards. Mary Dreier was the only female on the commission. After months of reporting, the commission issued a lengthy list of recommendations, which they delivered to the New York State legislature. Among their recommendations were the following: Cellars could no longer house factories, and any factory that stood more than two stories high required a fire escape. Managers could not lock doors during working hours. Every staircase needed handrails. Smoking was forbidden and shops needed to be aired out frequently. Windows needed to be cleaned and waste disposed of regularly. Lastly, and in the board's view one of the most important requirements, was that there be regular fire drills. It was essential that the joint board hire more factory inspectors and that a new fire prevention bureau be created.

Commission members understood that any proposed rules were hollow without sufficient means of enforcement. Aside from asking for a budget increase so that regular inspections and enforcement could be instituted, they also came up with a new notification system. A notice would be given to owners and management after the first failed inspection. Failure to pass a second inspection meant the commission would meet personally with the owner or management. If owners remained uncompliant, the management and owner would be referred to the union.[37]

"Murderers! Kill the murderers!" shouted the families and friends of victims as Max Blanck and Isaac Harris, who had been arrested and charged with first- and second-degree manslaughter, were led into court.[38] On the stand, survivor after survivor recounted their experience and the frantic search for exits. "I saw smoke pouring up the stairs and started toward the Green[e] Street entrance when I noticed that there was a crowd of excited persons standing there," Yetta Lublitz testified.[39] She told the court how no one could open the door to the stairwell on her floor, how she saw young women with flames where their hair should have been, and how she wrapped a cloth around her head to protect it from the flames.

Despite more than one hundred witnesses, the joint board, firefighters, and the workers themselves testifying about the factory conditions and the lack of safety, Blanck and Harris were acquitted. The outcome didn't surprise courtroom watchers, given Judge Thomas C. Crain's charge to the jury:

> You must first be satisfied before you can find these defendants guilty of the crime of manslaughter in the first degree not merely because the door was locked—if it was locked—but that it was locked during the period mentioned under circumstances bringing knowledge of that fact to these defendants . . . But it is not sufficient that the evidence should establish that the door was locked—if it was locked—during such a period, nor yet that the defendants knew that it was locked during such a period—if it was locked.[40]

About six months later, in December 1911, Juror 11, H. Huerston Hiers, told reporters from the *New York Times* that he couldn't see "that anyone was responsible for the loss of life and it seems to me that it was an act of God."[41] However, Juror 10, Victor Steinmen, told reporters how he tossed and turned all night. He was confused. He knew the public wanted punishment and he believed the door was locked, but the charge left room for doubt to creep in as to whether Blanck and Harris knew the door was locked.[42] On December 27, 1911, he too voted to acquit.

Newman couldn't attend the trial; she had been called out of town once again on union business. Even so, thoughts of the tragedy consumed her. She would write and speak about the incident for the rest of her life. In 1980, more than a half a century after the fire, Newman wrote "A Worker Recalls Her Time at the Triangle Shirt Waist Factory" for *Labor History* magazine. In the piece, she described in detail how unsafe she felt being locked inside the factory by day, unable to take breaks, but how necessary it was to earn money to help support her family. Her article prompted Ernest Deutch, of Brooklyn, New York, to write a letter to the *New York*

Times: "I think I can add confirmation to her claims. At the time I was an office boy in a small real estate firm whose owner was on the jury trying the case. In a discussion in the office with a visitor he [the owner] was asked 'why was the door to the fire-escape locked?' The answer was 'to keep those bitches from stealing.'"[43]

Three years later, on March 11, 1914, Harris and Blanck settled twenty-three individual civil suits; paying seventy-five dollars for each life lost in the fire.

7

Hopscotching

The first leaves unfurled like tiny green flags outside the Philadelphia branch of the WTUL, where Newman was helping organize Jewish and Italian waistmakers. On loan from the ILGWU, Newman missed New York City, especially her friends, but she reminded herself that she was doing essential work. Although when John Dyche, the ILGWU president, requested that she head to Cleveland, Ohio, she welcomed the interruption. A strike was brewing, and Dyche knew if a protest was taking place, it was Newman who would be wanted on site.

Answering Dyche's call to action, Newman packed a bag and uprooted herself again. Catching wind of the strike, the city's largest newspaper, the *Cleveland Plain Dealer*, ran a banner headline on June 6: "Big Strike Looms in Garment Trade." About six thousand cloak makers, including at least two thousand women, toiled in thirty-three shops across the city.[1] With an output of about $250 million annually, the sector nipped at the heels of New York City in productivity. Like their New York City counterparts, they too made demands. And as in New York City, the negotiations fell apart. They wanted a maximum fifty-hour workweek with half days on Saturdays. They wanted double pay for overtime and the observance of legal holidays such as Independence Day and Thanksgiving Day. More important, they wanted an end to the practice of inside contracting, which kept people from job promotion and, more to the point, took money out of their pockets. They could no longer abide digging into their savings to buy needles and thread, electricity and sewing machines. But unlike the shirtwaist strike, the ILGWU General Executive Board in New York sanctioned the Cleveland locals' call to strike. Additionally, this time the locals would also enjoy support from other unions.

Perhaps it was the change of venue, perhaps it was the literal distance from New York City, but Newman felt herself cutting through the fog of depression that had enveloped her since the Triangle Shirtwaist Factory fire. It also helped that this trip was more challenging than the work she did on the East Coast in cities like Rochester and Boston. For example, unlike New York City, in Cleveland she faced a medley of religions and ethnicities and she, a Jewish immigrant, needed to figure out how to relate to all of the women. More than two decades after stepping onto Ellis Island, Newman, who had shed any last vestiges of religious observance, was nonetheless keenly aware that her English was not country club smooth. No matter how hard she worked to polish her pronunciation, a Yiddish accent clung to her vowels.

During her first week in Cleveland, Dyche did something that infuriated Newman. He told her he planned to send a male union organizer to work with her. That alone might not have been so bad. What caused her to fume was that the organizer would be paid more for the same work. From Newman's perspective, it was a flagrant show of how the ILGWU leadership did not take issues of gender inequality seriously; in her view, it seemed as if leadership believed she was unable to perform the job as well as a man and therefore didn't deserve to be paid the same. As she wrote to Schneiderman, "You, Rose, know that the seven dollars [difference in pay] does not bother me but there is a principle involved and for that I am ready to fight. It was an insult and it hurts an awful lot."[2] To start, the union owed her nearly one thousand dollars in back pay.[3] The idea that they would pay a male organizer more than she was earning was exasperating at best. On top of the pay difference, Dyche continued to harass her, from comments about what she wore to expressing his "love" for her. However, as angry as Newman was, she said nothing to Dyche. In fact, she told only Schneiderman, because she knew the all-male general executive board would not support her.[4] She also knew that if she showed the slightest weakness, the board could take this job away from her.

Aggravated, Newman told Schneiderman that she just might quit the ILGWU and embark on a new career, perhaps as a freelance writer at a newspaper. But when her eruption was over, she softened her stance and threw herself back into the work. On June 8, Locals 27 and 29 led a phalanx from the heart of the Cleveland business district to the factory district. Women marched. Men marched. The wives of strikers marched and so did their children. They held signs: "Our Fathers and Mothers Are Striking to Give Us a Better Education." They carried banners: "Our daddies are fighting to give us a better education," and "Our manufacturers claim to be philanthropists, but we demand fair wages, not charity."[5] They sang songs. Gray-haired women, some ramrod straight and others gnarled like oak-hickory trees, marched beside young girls wearing white frocks, ribbons, and flowers in their hair.

Although the mood of the strike resembled the 1909 shirtwaist strike, it lacked the same cross-class solidarity. That was a point of contention for social worker and national WTUL organizer Gertrude Barnum, who said, "I AM simply amazed to learn that the society women, club women and church societies sat passively through the Cleveland strike while the employers refused to arbitrate and insisted upon settling issues by the force of starvation and false arrests and intimidation by hired thugs and sluggers."[6]

Their absence was not a failure of Newman to act. She met with strikers' mothers. She wrote opinion pieces for several publications, including the New York *Call*, the *Ladies' Garment Worker*, *Life and Labor*, and *The Progressive Woman*. In her June 1913 article "The Child Labor Law" for *The Progressive Woman*, Newman wrote about how the child labor law, which, while not perfect, signified a step forward for the working class as it meant thousands of children would be able to sit behind a desk rather than stand behind a loom.[7] However, she cautioned, the working class had to make sure the law was enforced. Her spirited speeches reminded people that it was the duty of every woman who believes in fair play and justice to unreservedly support the WTUL. Nothing worked. That they didn't participate revealed a crack in the foundation of the national WTUL over the best method to bridge what appeared to be a widening class divide.

The stalemate continued. A week later, on July 14, 1911, Newman sat inside her hotel room and slit open an envelope containing a rather wordy letter from Dreier. She explained that one of the strikers had asked her to send Schneiderman to Cleveland to help. Mindful of her friend Schneiderman's frenetic workload, Newman told Dreier to dismiss that idea. She also wrote to Schneiderman: "Mary wanted to hear my opinion of the matter for she hates to disturb your vacation. Knowing how badly you need to rest I have advised Mary not to ask you now, perhaps later on for the fight is a bitter one."[8]

Slowly Newman made her way through the small stack of mail. The next letter was from her sister Fanny, who was asking for money. Newman might not have been broke, but she had little savings. Still, she felt it was her duty to help her sisters. "And while they are not getting much of my money—their children get a lot of it. I spent $10 for the boy and also other few dollars for daily expenses, because I don't eat at my sisters; and am staying in Miss Emersons flat."[9]

Writing to Schneiderman reminded Newman how much she yearned for New York City. She missed sliding out a wooden chair to sit at a communal table at Child's and dig into a stack of syrup-drenched griddle cakes. She missed climbing to the balcony in the Metropolitan Opera to hear Caruso in the company of her friends. Yet, as much as she missed all that, she also found herself toying with the idea of moving to Chicago and trying her hand as a journalist. She had been offered a position at a newspaper. Whether she truly wanted to switch careers or was simply frustrated with her union work, she couldn't honestly say.

As soon as she finished writing to Schneiderman, she rushed to another meeting; apparently the manufacturers were poised to issue their response to union demands. In the end, the union won a wage settlement and secured assurances that hiring would be on a preferential basis. They did not get the hoped-for closed shop arrangement. However, they did win the right for collective bargaining and an invitation to standardize conditions in other manufacturing centers in an industry where markets were increasingly national in character. It wasn't the win Newman hoped for, but it was a feather in her cap nonetheless.

By October, Newman, now twenty-two, was back in New York City among the corbelled facades of her neighborhood: "My dear Rose I am almost a week here and it seems as though I have been away for months . . . Last night I went to a ball given by the waitresses union. Met several organizers who are also on the road and I had a very good time. Danced and drank wine so as to forget myself a little; and I did. I came home early this morning."[10] Then it was time to hang up her dress, pack her beaded dancing shoes away, and board another train. She was headed back to Chicago.

Somewhere in between New York and Chicago the familiar pangs of loneliness resurfaced. In a letter to Schneiderman, Newman said she was becoming resigned to the fact that although she led an interesting life, she felt profoundly lonely: "I have so many plans to carry out, so much work to do—work that shall live after I am gone—yet no one to help me, no one to advise me. Always alone. It is dreadful. Yet it seems that there is no way out of it—at least for the present. I am just thrown about like a wave. From one city to another. When will it end?"[11] Thus their epistolatory relationship continued.

Newman was disconsolate. Until now she never had a serious romantic attachment. She was not even certain she wanted to walk down the aisle on anyone's arm. As Charlotte Perkins Gilman wrote in her 1906 essay for *Harper's Bazaar* "The Passing of Matrimony," more women were choosing to remain single, in part so they wouldn't have to try to balance a professional life against a domestic one.[12] Newman had seen the limitations that marriage imposed on young women who wanted more outside the home. Conventional gender roles didn't suit her. However, she craved intimacy and companionship and hinted as much in her frequent letters to Schneiderman. So when she met Frank Bohn, a fellow labor organizer, she fell for him. Of course, Schneiderman was the first person she shared the news with. "I have so much to tell you! Among all other things—one thing happened never to be forgotten! Something that shall remain in my memory for ever and I will always look back to it with pleasure—yet with some regret," she wrote.[13]

A fellow socialist, Bohn was a distant colleague with whom she had traded several friendly letters before returning to Chicago. Now he was scheduled to be in Chicago for work. Unsure of how long he planned to stay in the Windy City, he wondered if they might spend a few evenings together. Until now Newman's feelings toward Bohn hovered between platonic and romantic, but she was feeling vulnerable and overwhelmed. Time seemed too short to accomplish all she wanted: "The thought that I may never be able to accomplish it is enough to make me feel miserable for the rest of my life!"[14] Enter Bohn. Older by a few years, he offered comfort and companionship. The two enjoyed discussing books and current events. He hinted that he could help her win a scholarship to the University of Wisconsin. While Newman found much to like about Bohn—he was in the labor movement, he cared about their work, he was interested in books—and tuition seemed like an attractive offer, it was more the way he lavished her with attention that led her to believe she might be besotted. "Well, you know that my feelings . . . gather strongly because of his kind and friendly letters and when I heard that his desire is to be with me—mine became ever stronger," she wrote Schneiderman.[15]

Their relationship plodded along. Now and again they shared a meal or took a walk. They corresponded. All the while, Newman continued confiding in Schneiderman, telling her friend that she didn't find much remarkable about Bohn's attitude as a whole. In short, he was "not worse or better than the average attitude of a Socialist man toward a woman." That didn't mean she relaxed fully around him, though. Perhaps it was because she was confused about her feelings toward Schneiderman; perhaps it was because she was confused about sex in general. "I am told lately that he believes in promiscuity and I am inclined to believe that he does . . . While I am free in everything, I am puritanical in sex and home questions and it just sickens me to think of anyone who is not a strict monogamist," she wrote.[16]

As prolific a letter writer as Newman was, she never wrote about whether she fantasized carrying a bridal bouquet or having to wake up in the middle of the night to rock a crying baby back to sleep. She never wrote about how she felt about not meeting the prevailing maternalistic views of the time.[17] She never confided whether she rejected Bohn because she didn't love him, because she thought staying single granted her more latitude to realize her professional goals, or whether she was able to stay working because she remained single. It is clear, however, that Newman, like many in her circle, did not pursue marriage.[18]

The winter of 1912 began as one of the most bitter in recent memory. Newman's clothes did little to counter Chicago's bitter winds. "They must have been inviting the wind, because the latter took full advantage of their invitation—only to make my stay there uncomfortable," she wrote in a piece for *Life and Labor*.[19] Lately she had found herself writing about topics that took readers beyond the factory walls. She used her articles to advocate for women—their role in the movement, their accomplishments, and how much they needed the vote. In her piece "The Workers of the World" for *The Progressive Woman*, she wrote about how a strike of thirty thousand laundry workers achieved victory, getting virtually all of their demands recognized. "Let us hope that the strike has taught the workers a lesson of self-reliance; not to beg, but demand; not to depend upon anybody's good will, but to USE THEIR OWN POWER for their own benefit!"[20] She wanted her readers to understand the importance of self-reliance.

As supportive as she was, her pieces were by no means valentines. She criticized the movement when and where she saw fit. In the former piece, she took strike leaders to task, not because she wanted to "'knock' some body" but because she wanted to "point out the terrible mistakes which have been made here on the expense of the poor girls, and that the same mistakes may not occur again."[21]

On a personal note, she still wasn't sure whether it was a mistake to see Bohn again, so she accepted his invitation to see *What Every Woman Knows*, J. M. Barrie's play about how men's accomplishments were the direct result of a woman's involvement. Dressing in her smartest skirt and blouse, Newman waited for Bohn to pick her up. After the play was over and the heavy velvet curtain came down, they strolled along the theater district. Bohn turned toward her and

> expressed his desire to go up somewhere, and rest. I consented to it and we went up to a hotel. I knew what would follow and I was determined that we would do nothing but rest. Rose did you ever experience to hold the hand of the man you love? If you did, you will understand how happy I was! Can you also imagine the big, tall, serious B. on his knees and kissing my fingertips? Oh Rose! How I wished that 12 o'clock should

> never come! (For that was the appointed hour to go home.) You can easily understand how I felt Rose."[22]

In the end, she did not sleep with Bohn; he left town and she ultimately lost track of him. Once he left, Newman broke off the relationship entirely and returned to Philadelphia. No sooner had she done so than she began to second-guess herself. Perhaps she had ended things too soon. Would she be sorry someday for not sleeping with him?

After Bohn came a man called Joe, about whom Newman also wrote to Schneiderman: "I have been thinking days and nights, and . . . I don't think I am in love with Joe . . . I doubt very much whether, he as such could satisfy me."[23]

It's unclear whether Newman felt deeply for either of these men. However, it is clear that she never intended to commit to any man. For now, as letters from this time period show, she remained committed to her feelings for Schneiderman: "I feel that there is not a person today whom I love more than I do you . . . I really don't know whether I could love to a greater extent than I—but you know it, enough said."[24] Whether Schneiderman shared her feelings is also not clear. In any event, Newman shelved those questions and got back on the road. The peripatetic organizer was due in Belleville, Illinois, thirty miles from the Missouri border.

The train pulled into the station early, leaving Newman time for a brisk walk downtown. She passed a small building from which she heard loud and unusual noises. Thinking people were fighting and crying, her curiosity got the better of her. She walked up the steps and, pressing her nose to the glass, saw people writhing on the floor and gesturing. Some abruptly stood only to fall down again:

> And I thought it was a madhouse. I really did. And when I told it to the miners, after they came, they said, "oh, you just heard the Holy Rollers." It was a poor, poor place. They had looked so poorly. And the picture of Christ was the one you used to get in the ten cent store, you know, and there they were rolling, Holy Rollers. But they weren't only rolling. They were shouting and crying. Oh, it was an awful night.[25]

Over the past decade Newman had chanced to meet many people from a variety of backgrounds. But for the young Jewish immigrant, meeting the "Holy Rollers," referring to members of an evangelical Christian group that expresses religious fervor through frenzied motions or trances, was something new entirely. It wasn't just the raucous sounds. The beliefs espoused by the Holy Rollers were vastly different from her own, which now leaned toward the secular.

She stood transfixed for a few moments and then remembered she was due at a union meeting to talk with coal miners. After the meeting, where she met with miners who earned about three dollars for a "very long and dangerous day," she was invited to a miner's home. They continued talking about the ways unionizing could offer job protection and better pay. It was an understatement to say the mining was dangerous work. Out of every thousand miners, more than three would die in the mines each year.[26]

Later that night, Newman sat at her polished desk in the New Hotel Saline and pulled out a sheet of hotel stationery. Uncapping her pen, she took a moment to inhale the quiet; it had been an extraordinarily frenzied day. She had spent the better part of it speaking about socialism and the right of miners to fair labor conditions. Naturally, she wanted to tell Schneiderman all about it. Every meeting drove home the disconnect between how multitudes of Americans worked and lived and how others remained oblivious to those conditions. In her letter she wrote:

> Rose, I have always wanted to study the lives of the miners and I am glad of having had that chance. It is not exaggerated when we say that through their labor the world is kept warm, the rail roads in operation . . . [Yet] most of them have not enough coal to keep their little shacks warm. Think of it! They who supply coal for all the people have no coal to warm their two or three little rooms![27]

Newman firmly believed she was making headway in helping the miners shape their demands. Nonetheless, she longed to once again be in New York City, where she could see Schneiderman and her friends face-to-face: "[I'm] just crazy to have a long talk with you! And I have so much to tell you! If you only knew! But will wait until I get your letter which I hope you have sent. I did not hear from you for so long!"[28]

Her letters were about more than business and longing. She did allow herself the odd moment to dream about less serious things, like whether she should buy a stylish new suit or a pert new hat. Or whether she'd someday buy a sliver of land and build a bungalow. "So that when I get tired—I could go to a place of my own. Don't you think that I ought to do it?" she wrote to Schneiderman. "Then I was thinking of saving another few dollars, give up work, and then to take a course in journalism. Now I know that I could not do all at once, but I do want to do something, and don't know what to do first. Well, let us wait and see what time will say."[29] It was a fun bit of daydreaming but that was all.

The unorganized have the poorest pay and are the most exploited, Newman wrote in an article titled "Difficulties with Sister." In the article she implored working women to fight for what was rightfully theirs: fair wages and hours: "And, why not concentrate all efforts to the organizing of the working woman? I'd rather you girls would organize and demand your own. Why not show these philanthropists that you can take care of your own interests?"[30] She also pushed these women to assert themselves rather than rely on middle-class and upper-class reformers. There was a bit of Newman as Pollyanna at play here; the reality was that wealthy allies would always exert influence.

Some of this was because many workers lacked education. It was also because employers heaped sophistries on their workers, telling them if they remained loyal, they would attain a career, or that hard work was "its own reward."[31] Setting aside the obvious paternalism, it was fiction, Newman insisted. Therefore, it was important to organize and push for the right to vote. It was also important to continue to nurture the partnership between wealthy women and working women because "rich ladies, ministers of various denominations, 'humane' employers, professors of universities are actively engaged in this movement," she wrote of the suffrage movement. And yet, "while I do not oppose this movement (I have more important things to do) I for one would rather see the working women mind their own business. For we must remember that to shorten the workday and raise wages is, or SHOULD BE, the business of the working woman herself. No one can or will do it better than she herself."[32] It wasn't that Newman thought suffrage as a side issue; yet, if she were pressed to rank the two, she would likely rank working conditions a bit higher on the scale. Crisscrossing the country, Newman realized that if women wanted an end to working in dirt- and dust-filled factories on faulty equipment, they needed to organize.[33]

8

"I Would Rather Be the Fighter"

The man thrust the sheaf of paper into Newman's hand moments after she stepped off the train in Kalamazoo, Michigan. He was gone before she caught a good glimpse him, and she set down her suitcase to look more closely at the papers. The twelve-page, single-spaced, typed injunction warned her that she risked a one-thousand-dollar fine and jail time if she so much as spoke with employees of the Kalamazoo Corset Company when they left work for the day. She faced legal jeopardy if she tried to convince anyone not to work for the company or if she tried to persuade anyone to quit. Lastly, she was barred from picketing outside the factory. In fact, she was not even allowed to speak with workers living in any neighborhood near the complainant's factory.[1]

Newman folded the document, shoved it into her pocket, and continued on her way. Upon entering the ILGWU Local 82, she was greeted with a standing ovation.[2] It was June 4, 1912, and the Kalamazoo Corset Workers Union was more than four months into a strike. Earlier that year, while she stepped up efforts to organize women workers in New York, "unrest had spread in the Middle West," Fannia Cohn remarked.[3] By Valentine's Day, hundreds of women in Kalamazoo called a strike after the Kalamazoo Corset Company refused to renew its labor agreement. Asking for a fifty-four-hour workweek and a minimum salary of $7 a week, which would still put them below the average annual salary of $750, was apparently pushing things too far for the managers. In addition, the company fired a dozen active union members for showing "disloyalty" to the company. The owners saw to it that strike leaders were arrested, and they intimidated the rest of the workforce with injunctions.

Originally, the Featherbone Corset Company, the company changed its name to the Kalamazoo Corset Company in 1894 after it moved more than seventy miles from Three Oaks, Michigan, to Kalamazoo. There it set up shop inside a four-story brick building at the corner of Church and Eleanor streets. The company made a name for itself when it started using turkey wing bones in its corsets rather than whalebones, which emitted a less than fragrant scent. Now, five months later, no resolution was on the horizon. Newman, now almost twenty-three, was there to help break the impasse—hence the meeting at the union headquarters. Only after the meeting ended did she have a chance to unpack her belongings at the Berghoff Hotel. She wrote to Schneiderman after a long soak in the tiled tub: "As for me, well, this work is a little pleasanter, because it is more like MY work, to be the fighter, is more natural to me, than to be the diplomat after all. But the situation here, is rather discouraging." Of her meeting with managers, she said, "After a conference held between me and the 'goody-goody' people, they declared that I am not so dangerous after all, and told me that they are almost sure that we could settle the strike in a few days." Wishful thinking on their part, wrote Newman. Once described as someone one could smoke a cigar with, Newman was not about to cave.[4]

She had arrived in Kalamazoo on a warm morning in June, at the end of a twenty-four-hour train trip. Insofar as she pictured her destination—between fighting to keep her eyes open and reviewing her notes—she had envisioned a city not too dissimilar from New York. As it happened, Kalamazoo in 1912 was a very different American town from what this immigrant from Lithuania had imagined. It lacked the noise and the crowds, the trolleys and the tenement houses. But, she reminded herself, those were surface differences. The fact was that corset workers in Kalamazoo aspired to the same thing as shirtwaist workers on the Lower East Side: They wanted to be treated fairly and humanely.

She joined Josephine Casey, an organizer for the ILGWU and leader of the strike. Casey had already served time in jail after being arrested for picketing. During the trial, one of her lawyers told the court, "Miss JC is fighting for a principle. This woman has made the cause of labor her life work. If she must be charged with conspiracy for carrying on this lifework for the betterment of the working classes, then I say it is better that all courts be abolished."[5]

The union had already gone on strike in 1911, at the end of which they'd signed a one-year contract with the corset manufacturers. When it came time to renew the contract, management refused. "The corset manufacturers seem to forget that trade unions are not organized for one year only, but that they are here to stay just as long as present-day conditions prevail. They evidently forgot that even women are learning to regard the union as the only weapon with which to obtain a living wage and better conditions in general," chastised Newman in her article "The Workers of the World" for *The Progressive Woman*.[6] Impressed with her writing, the Chicago chapter of the national Women's Trade Union League invited her to pen a monthly column. Eager to have another outlet, Newman readily accepted the offer.

To launch the campaign for its "American Beauty" line, James Hatfield, the head of Kalamazoo Corset Company, hired Edward and Harry Zickel. Known as the Zickel Brothers, they chiefly published sheet music but also composed promotional songs and marches for the corset company like the "American Beauty March and Two-Step," "My American Beauty Rose," and "My American Beauty Girl." Yet, as up-tempo as the songs were, they could not mask the deplorable working conditions inside the area's largest employer. Of the 1,000 people who worked there, 835 were women. Every single one of them walked out to join the strike.

The last time Newman had done this amount of organizing was when she led the 1907 rent strike, so she was momentarily surprised now by how much she missed it. In the WTUL magazine *Life and Labor*, she described the way manufacturers like Hatfield hired security to harass people in the neighborhoods where striking employees lived. She wrote about how some of the protests turned violent. In one instance, guards shot a woman who disobeyed their orders not to enter a strikebreaker's house and then threatened another woman who rushed to her aid. Shaken, Newman described how the women remained unbowed and how she "never shall forget the heroism of the women." With the situation rushing to a standstill, Newman knew what to do. "I am sending out girls on the road to boycott the Corsets manufactured by the Kalamazoo Corset Co. That is about all that can be done now," she wrote to Schneiderman.[7] Though later, in her column for *On the Battle Front*, she wrote, "We did not call it a boycott, but that is what it was."[8]

As the boycott was taking place, the pesky matter of the injunction, which stipulated that organizers not speak directly with workers, remained. To circumvent the order, Casey devised a plan. Every morning, she led groups of strikers in "picket prayers" in front of the factory. Standing shoulder to shoulder, they recited the following prayer:

> Oh God, our Father . . . our employer who has plenty has denied our request. He has misused the law to help him crush us . . . Thou who didn't save Noah and his family, may it please Thee to save the girls now

> on strike from the wicked city of Sodom. Oh, help us to get a living wage . . . Grant that we may win the strike . . . so that we may not need to cry often, "Lord, deliver us from temptation."[9]

The plan proved ingenious. The press, which until now was following the strike only somewhat sporadically, now covered it with the attention Newman thought it deserved. She and Casey were keen to sit down for interviews with the press. Speaking to reporters from the *Detroit Times* and Kalamazoo, Newman and Casey emphasized their reasons for the strike: dirty air, lack of overtime pay, and fear of being fired on a whim. Casey also talked about the ever-present sexual harassment female workers faced. She expressly called for the company to fire each and every foreman who insulted female employees and who had a hand in "dragging the girls down to ruin." Both insisted that the "tyranny of the foreman" needed to end. Not a factory existed "where the same immoral conditions does [*sic*] not exist!"[10]

From the moment women left their homes and entered the workplace, they faced the possibility of workplace sexual harassment and assault. *The Voice of Industry*, a worker-run newspaper published in Lowell, Massachusetts, between 1845 and 1848, detailed working conditions, including harassment. The workers, mostly women, pleaded not for protection but, rather, for offending men to be held accountable. "It may be," wrote one woman, "that most women are so dwarfed and weakened that they believe that dressing, cooking and loving make up the whole of life. You boast of the protection you afford to women. Protection from what? From the rude and disorderly of your own sex? Reform men, and women will no longer need the protection you make such a parade of giving."[11] It was an argument that would frequently surface during debates about the merits of protective labor legislation.[12] For example, the Massachusetts Supreme Judicial Court used the issue to justify limiting a women's work hours as the best way to increase her chances of being protected.

No stranger to factory life, Newman knew what it was like to work in a factory where "the forman [*sic*] and superintendents will flirt with the girls, and it is nothing new for those who know that this exists today everywhere."[13] Yet, beyond that, Newman was reluctant to say more. Not because she didn't think it worthy of attention. She did. But she was concerned that the issue could distract from what she believed were the strike's main goals: reduced hours and higher pay. Additionally, Newman worried that taking a more public stance would bolster those who opposed women in the workplace. In her view, educating young women was a better strategy than tying the issue to the strike.

Although the strike engendered support from Kalamazoo's newly elected progressive mayor, Charles B. Hays, like many strikes in recent years, it sputtered to an end. Management wouldn't negotiate beyond a few of the points and the ILGWU leadership in New York didn't push. The union and management agreed to new measures, including a reduction in hours. However, there was no way to hold management accountable. In fact, just a few years after the strike the factory resumed its former practices. In the end, Newman was disappointed with the outcome in Kalamazoo but not dissuaded. As she told a reporter from the *Kalamazoo Telegraph*, the work appealed to her combative nature: "I am supposed to play the part of the diplomat when I would rather be the fighter. It's more natural to fight than to be diplomatic. Being diplomatic makes you a hypocrite. You say yes when you mean no, and smile when you feel like frowning. But you do it because you think some good may come of it."[14]

Two months after the young Serbian patriot Gavrilo Princip fatally shot Archduke Franz Ferdinand and his wife on Sunday, June 28, 1914, lighting the match that set Europe ablaze, women wearing white dresses and fanciful hats paraded from New York City's Fifth Avenue to the Washington Square Arch. Many held banners edged in yellow and blue bunting, the color of the WTUL. Though World War I had begun, the women felt moved to rejoice.

Just a few months earlier, on June 15, the Sixty-Third Congress had passed the Clayton Antitrust Act by an overwhelming majority. A supplement to the Sherman Act of 1890, the Clayton Antitrust Act aimed to curb the growing number of trusts and monopolies. Considered the most essential legislation passed on behalf of working men and women, the act defined unethical business practices like price fixing and monopolies and various labor rights. For labor leaders, it was particularly important because it also declared strikes, boycotts, and labor unions legal under federal law. Unemployment, which danced just below 8 percent when the act passed, fell to 1.4 percent in part because of new manufacturing jobs. It seemed labor held the upper hand, ever so slightly. By April 6, 1917, the US Army would boast a standing army of 127,500 officers and soldiers. As such, unions saw an opportunity to improve their working conditions in the early years of the war. For example, in 1915 the International Association of Machinists and the International Association of Structural Iron Workers, both based in Bridgeport, Connecticut, would strike to secure better working hours in the munitions factories. In so doing, they went from a ten-hour day to an eight-hour day.

Although hammering out deals similar to the one agreed upon in Bridgeport became easier for Newman after more than a decade into the work, she still found it challenging to recruit new union members. There were many different ways to attract new members, from standing outside factories and passing out leaflets to holding meetings where she and her colleagues answered questions about the reasons to form a union. However, there was one method in particular that grated on Newman. Those were what she and some of her colleagues derisively nicknamed the "chocolate cake parties." Usually a well-meaning socialite hosted a party in her house. Aside from too much cake and too much weak tea, they shone too strong a light on the cultural and economic differences between the wealthier supporters and the Russian, Italian, Jewish, and Irish workers, which caused more embarrassment than empathy. Newman wasn't the only one who despised the sugar-fueled affairs. Mary Dreier thought they were positively useless, albeit for different reasons than Newman. Simply put, she felt they didn't attract the right kind of young women. Rather, they attracted "giggly girls whose sole interest in life was boys and how to attract them, . . . oversexed and unwholesome, and I don't like them."[15]

Newman's portfolio continued expanding. By now she had been working as an inspector with New York's Joint Board of Sanitary Control for four years. The work was demanding, she told her readers in "An Inspector's Point of View":

> We remember the dark and dingy shops, the unshaded lights, or, worse still,—the gas jets (which impaired many people's eyesight). We remember the lavatories in the yards and those located in the shops and full of filth . . . We still have employers who have never made the acquaintance of modern principles of health and cleanliness.[16]

It could be tiresome and tedious and, of course, Newman lacked legal power. She approached each visit with the eye of someone who knew what it was like to toil in unsanitary and unsafe conditions. She knew where to look for violations, whether it was windows sealed shut or gas jets leaking (which impaired many people's eyesight). She knew where to look for rodent droppings, which signified an infestation, and whether the washrooms were clean enough. This was exactly what she was doing when she showed up in Connecticut to inspect the Wauregan Mills. Notebook in hand, eyeglasses perched on her nose, she went to work.

Named for a Mohegan word meaning "Pleasant Valley," Wauregan's history as an industrial village reached back more than half a century. In 1850, nearly a century before Newman visited, Amos D. Lockwood bought the water privileges and surrounding land at Wauregan. The Connecticut legislature approved the Wauregan Mills Company charter in 1853, and over time the mill became known for its woven cotton goods, especially its flannel and cotton sheeting. Trivial, perhaps, but knowing those details led Newman to reevaluate her lack of formal schooling. She realized that what she lacked in formal education she made up for in practical experience. In "An Inspector's Point of View" she wrote:

> I started life in the College of the Triangle Waist Company . . . at the age of 13. I graduated from there with honors, and proceeded at once to the University of the Reliance Waist Company . . . Got my M.A. from the Ladies' Garment Workers' Union when I delivered an oration on "Shall we submit to the exploitation of Dean Low Wages and Professor Long Hours, or shall we organize in a school of our own?" With this diploma I toured for the ILGWU for many years. My post graduate work I took in the university of a cotton mill in Wauregan, Con. Got my Ph.D. from the Women's Trade Union League of New York. Having been very desirous of obtaining a Doctor's [i.e., doctorate] degree for it means a great deal these days; it established a status for one without much difficulty—I began work with the joint Board of Sanitary Control as inspector as well as lecturer and publicity agent.[17]

After investigating complaints about the conditions in several garment shops, Newman returned to the picket line in the early part of 1915. On January 5 thousands of tailors and waistmakers gathered outside the New York Hippodrome. Together, acting like a human battering ram, they broke down the doors of the enormous theater. Inside the hall that could seat more than five thousand people, a small group of ILGWU members were voting on whether to strike. The violent display came after John Dyche and Abraham Rosenberg told the workers they would not be permitted to vote on a general strike. Now faced with a potential riot, the crowd was allowed inside to cast their ballots. In the end, the strike came to an underwhelming finish, in part because it had been fixed from the start. The union agreed they would strike for a few days at most if management agreed to implement minimum wage standards. Management readily agreed; they too wanted a quick end to the matter.

A few weeks later a taxicab parked in front of 49 Henry Street in New York City. Out popped the monopoly-busting, handle-bar-mustached president Theodore Roosevelt. Inside the hall he met with nearly six hundred striking kimono workers. "Now young ladies, I want to know all about your lives; how you work and how you manage to be cheerful. Just gather around me and tell me your stories," he said.[18] His remarks were translated into Spanish, Italian, Greek, Yiddish, and Turkish, the languages of many of the striking workers. He lamented the factory conditions as "crushing the future motherhood of the country," and his eyebrows shot up when he learned they weren't allowed to sing at work. A fine sentiment, but to Newman, who as part of the joint board was involved in helping organize the strike, it missed the point.

Kimonos were part of the white goods trade, a sector of the garment industry that included robes and underwear. Getting the workers, most of whom were younger than fifteen, to unionize turned out to be tougher than expected. First, the businesses were spread across the city—some in sweatshops, some in lofts. Second, most of the workers couldn't chat with one another since they didn't speak the same languages. Furthermore, inspections organized by Newman revealed the deplorable conditions in which employees labored. This wasn't the first time that kimono workers took up signs and walked off the job. In 1910, Fannia Cohn, who previously worked in the industry, tried to lead a strike. However, when the ILGWU didn't lend its support, the strike failed.

Three months later, in March, Boston cloak makers walked off the job and succeeded in getting the employer's association to sign a "protocol of peace." Four months after that, again with Newman's involvement in organizing, between four thousand and eight thousand cloak makers in Philadelphia went on strike, demanding similar reforms that the shirtwaist strikers had won in New York in 1910. However, the Philadelphia cloak makers weren't successful. It was a "bitter and violent conflict" that lasted for twenty-six weeks, cost the union more than $250,000, and in the end was called off.[19] Each of these strikes came about because of the work Newman and her fellow organizers did in recruiting union members and educating them about their right to require employers provide fair working conditions.

Part of the reason most of these strikes were not fully resolved in labor's favor was because of mounting tensions between the joint board and ILGWU, Cohn said—tension that Dyche caused. Although he took a conciliatory attitude toward the employers, he was uncompromising with the workers who engaged in what he decided were "illegal stoppages."[20] In some cases Dyche also pushed to replace workers, a stance that incurred their enmity. Taking a position similar to the one it took during the 1909 shirtwaist strike, the ILGWU argued that the current strike was neither strategically viable nor clear in its aims. The union also worried that a strike failure would jeopardize the gains they had already made in the garment industry.[21]

All of this was going on as the fourth anniversary of the Triangle Shirtwaist Factory fire approached. Newman dreaded the occasion; still she helped put together the Joint Board of Sanitary Control's book

Memento Mori. Between the pages, the commission remembered the dead but also warned of complacency. It reminded the public that "the road to safety too often seems to lie through disaster."[22] Now, four years later, it appeared that few of the recommended measures had been implemented. "After the Asch Building disaster, the public demanded that buildings should be made safe for their occupancy in case of fire. Has that been done? My answer is NO," wrote H.F.H. Porter, C.E., in an article titled "Safety of Factory Buildings."[23] The height of loft buildings remained unregulated and unlimited. Stairways in new buildings were not sufficient and most old buildings had no new stairways. Decrepit and useless fire escapes were allowed to remain. Above all, the fire drill law was not enforced. Many manufacturers considered it a suggestion, not a requirement.

The Bear Mountain Inn looked inviting. Apple trees dotted the lush green property and there was a lake upon which the women could row. Inside, the scattered area rugs and new wicker furniture created a welcoming space. A Victrola, a piano, and a well-stocked library rounded out the amenities. Perched above the Hudson River, the inn offered expansive views from arched porches. Newman decided it would be the perfect setting from which to execute her next project: education. It was an issue she felt she had neglected for far too long. She envisioned several such places across the country, called Unity Houses. The Bear Mountain Inn would be one of the places.

Many parents plucked their children out of school as soon as the law allowed, leaving the children undereducated and their teachers racing to cram as much learning in as possible. Both parents and teachers were expected to "accomplish so large a task as 'preparation for life' in so brief a period as lies between babyhood and the fourteenth birthday."[24] Although it was illegal in New York State for children under fourteen to work, the law wasn't enforced. Teenagers between fourteen and sixteen years old were supposed to provide certificates that indicated they had completed the requisite schooling, but no one checked.

While Newman couldn't change the school system, she could at least offer an opportunity for working women. To that end she envisioned a cooperative-run workers' resort that would also offer educational programs. For a registration fee of one dollar, the women would be able to enjoy the equipment, furniture, beds, linen, and dishes as well as classes in English, literature, and American history.[25] In Newman's view, Unity Houses would fit seamlessly with the work she, Schneiderman, and O'Reilly had started back in 1914, when they founded the industrial section of the New York Woman Suffrage Party, or WSP. The overall party, which had been founded in 1909, would last only one more year. After the New York State suffrage amendment failed, the party would disintegrate. Even so, the Unity Houses would remain one of its legacies.

Mostly located in working-class neighborhoods, Unity Houses were places where activists could meet and collaborate on everything from suffrage to working conditions. Aside from hosting social events and educational programs, they also offered child care, job training, and legal assistance. Free from spouses or supervisors, working-class women could speak more freely here. Similar to the cross-class work Newman and others did for labor reform, there was going to be a delicate dance between socialists and monied suffragists. Newman concentrated her grassroots organizing and mobilizing to establish suffrage leagues in working-class neighborhoods.[26] Although suffrage had been a secondary concern for Newman for so many years, she increasingly saw it as equally important as working conditions.

Indeed, as twenty-six-year-old Newman tucked her newly bobbed hair behind her ears, it would have crossed her mind that trying to secure things like maternity insurance (what we call maternity leave) for women would be easier if women could vote. In just a few moments she would make her debut before the New York State Legislature to testify about maternity insurance. The committee assembled and the hearing was called to order. "New York may be up to the minute in a number of things, but it has been decidedly behind the times as far as maternity insurance is concerned," Newman wrote in a piece for *The American Hebrew and Jewish Messenger*.[27] However, it didn't have to be that way, she explained to the committee. In fact, the legislature would have a chance to pass maternity insurance when it next convened. If it did, it would do what five European countries, including Germany, Austria, Hungary, Serbia, Switzerland, Great Britain, Australia, and "even Russia," have long since done, she said.

Indeed, in 1908 Professor Paul Mayet of Berlin addressed the International Congress on Social Insurance in Rome. In his remarks he spoke about how one ought to think of maternity insurance as more beneficial for the child than the mother: "The physiological needs of the mother and of the child are fundamental at the threshold of the infant's life. If they are not observed, both mother and infant suffer; sickness and death are punishment for neglect."[28] That's what Newman was trying to impress on lawmakers today. That was the essence of the language she pushed to get included in the American Association for Labor Legislation's draft of a health insurance bill. That afternoon she needed to convince the legislators that the bill was worth moving out of committee.

Critics said that neither unmarried women workers nor the public should have to subsidize maternity insurance. Newman did not countenance what she considered the same tired arguments people trotted out regarding funding public schools and libraries. "Why should the Smiths be taxed for the new high school when they send their children to boarding school? Why must people pay taxes for municipal railways when they always ride limousines? One might as well object to paying taxes for health insurance in general on the ground that one has never been sick and does not expect to be," she wrote.[29] She remained calm but adamant and reiterated her belief that passage was necessary so that insured men and women would get the necessary medical, surgical, and obstetrical aid, materials, and appliances. Beneficiaries would get the money for eight weeks and could not engage in "gainful employment" during that period. Commanding the legislators' attention, Newman took advantage and pushed the idea of a maximum eight-hour day for women. She explained that passage of the maternity insurance bill would benefit not only women; it would also benefit society as a whole. A barrage of questions ensued. Opponents argued that men would send their wives to work in the factories just to get the benefit. Newman easily poked a hole in that line of argument. Women would need to be insured for six months before becoming eligible for the benefit.

After the hearing Newman made her way to Washington Irving High School. Inside the beautiful auditorium she took her seat alongside union representatives from Philadelphia, Baltimore, New Jersey, Connecticut, and New York. Seated before them were men and women, young and old, organized and non-organized. It was the first time they were hearing about unionism and labor legislation. Those on the dais told "the old, old story of over work and under pay; of how they are effected by the 'long day' and what a blessing it would be to have a few hours a week for themselves."[30] The audience listened as the speakers spoke not out of theory but from experience. As Newman wrote, "They knew what they were about. They were ready to do everything that would bring them and their sisters a shorter work day and a freer life."[31]

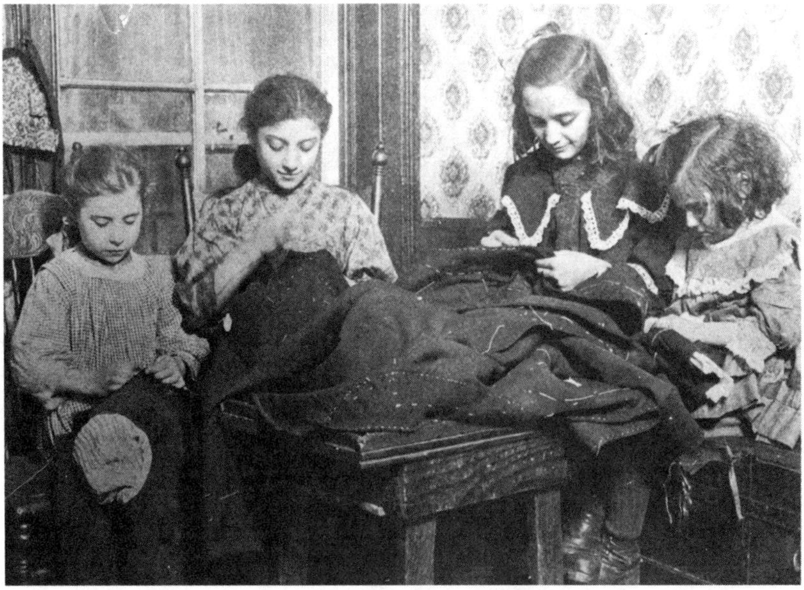

Children as young as three or four years old worked into the night trimming threads and pulling basting stitches. Photographer: Lewis Hine, ca. 1900. (Kheel Center for Labor-Management Documentation and Archives)

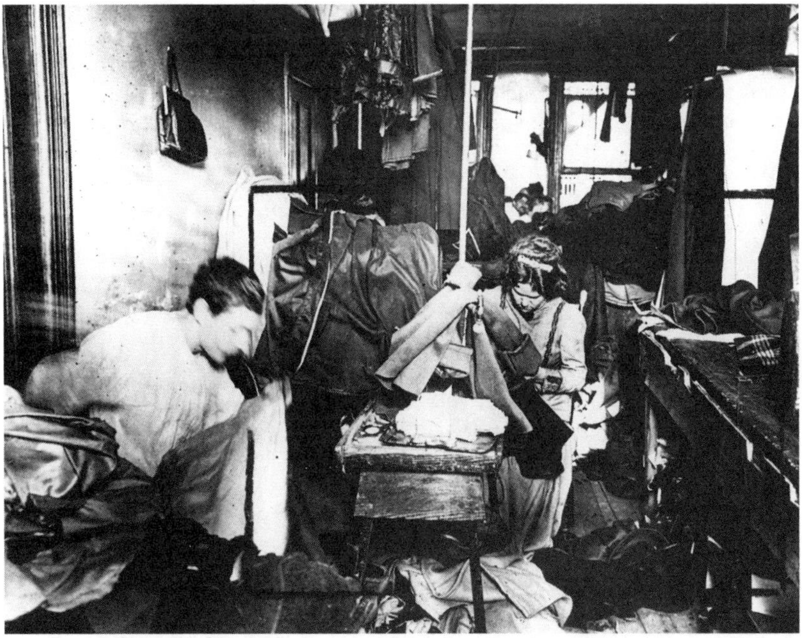

Dark, cramped shops made exhausting work still more difficult and dangerous. Children hired in violation of child labor laws were helped to hide in large boxes of cloth on the rare occasion when inspectors checked working conditions. Photographer: unknown, ca. 1900. (Kheel Center for Labor-Management Documentation and Archives)

The Women's Trade Union League was formed in 1903 to support women's participation in unions and to better their living and working conditions by improving wages, access to education, ending night work for women, and eliminating child labor. Photographer: Byron, 1909. (Kheel Center for Labor-Management Documentation and Archives)

Clara Lemlich portrait. Photographer: unknown, 1909. (Kheel Center for Labor-Management Documentation and Archives)

A mass meeting of shirtwaist strikers and their supporters at Rutgers Square, New York City, December 4, 1909. Photographer: unknown, 1909. (Kheel Center for Labor-Management Documentation and Archives)

Unprincipled owners hired scabs, police, thugs, and prostitutes to disrupt orderly picketing. Arrested strikers were taken to New York City's Jefferson Market Prison for booking. Photographer: unknown, ca. 1910. (Kheel Center for Labor-Management Documentation and Archives)

Women who were arrested on the picket lines and sent to Blackwell's Island wear "Workhouse Prisoner" signs, claiming their service with pride, and were cheered by other strikers and supporters. Photographer: unknown, ca 1910. (Kheel Center for Labor-Management Documentation and Archives)

Pauline Newman, a Russian immigrant, began working at the Triangle Shirtwaist Factory in 1903 when she was thirteen years old. Finding that many of her coworkers could not read, she organized an evening study group where they also discussed labor issues and politics. Newman was active in the shirtwaist strike and the Women's Trade Union League. She became a union organizer for the International Ladies' Garment Workers' Union and director of the ILGWU Health Center. (Kheel Center for Labor-Management Documentation and Archives)

An illustration of Pauline Newman depicting her in 1906. (Schlesinger Library, Radcliffe Institute, Harvard University)

The silent procession of 100,000 mourners. Photographer: unknown, 1911. (Kheel Center for Labor-Management Documentation and Archives)

"Triangle Shirt Waist Manufacturers Listening to Testimony Against Them." Max Blanck and Isaac Harris. Artist: unknown, 1911. (Kheel Center for Labor-Management Documentation and Archives)

As a garment worker and member of the New York Women's Trade Union League (WTUL) Executive Board, Rose Schneiderman worked to focus wealthy women's attention on labor issues during the shirtwaist strike. Photographer: unknown, ca. 1905. (Kheel Center for Labor-Management Documentation and Archives)

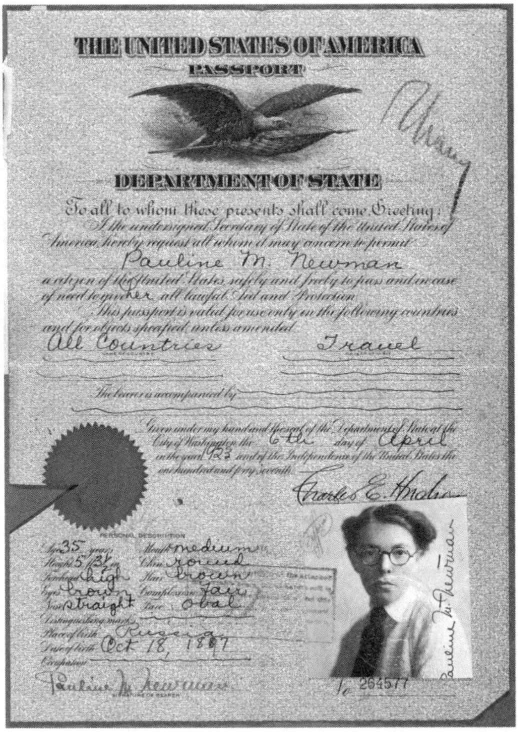

THE UNITED STATES OF AMERICA
PASSPORT
DEPARTMENT OF STATE
To all to whom these presents shall come, Greeting:
I the undersigned Secretary of State of the United States of America, hereby request all whom it may concern to permit
Pauline M. Newman
a citizen of the United States, safely and freely to pass and in case of need to give her all lawful Aid and Protection.
This passport is valid for use only in the following countries and for objects specified, unless amended.
All Countries Travel
The bearer is accompanied by
Given under my hand and the seal of the Department of State at the City of Washington the 6th day of April in the year 1923 and of the Independence of the United States the one hundred and forty seventh.
Charles E. Hughes
PERSONAL DESCRIPTION
Age 35 years Mouth medium
Height 5 ft 3½ in. Chin round
Forehead high Hair brown
Eyes brown Complexion fair
Nose straight Face oval
Distinguishing marks
Place of birth Russia
Date of birth Oct 18, 1887
Occupation
Pauline M. Newman
SIGNATURE OF BEARER
264577

Pauline Newman's travel document from 1923. (Schlesinger Library, Harvard Radcliffe Institute)

Pauline Newman and Frieda Miller in Philadelphia, date unknown. (Owen Family Archive, courtesy Michael Owen)

Pauline Newman poses in Stonehenge during Newman and Miller's trip to Europe in 1923. (Schlesinger Library, Harvard Radcliffe Institute)

A pregnant Frieda S. Miller seated on a ferry boat, 1923. (Schlesinger Library, Harvard Radcliffe Institute)

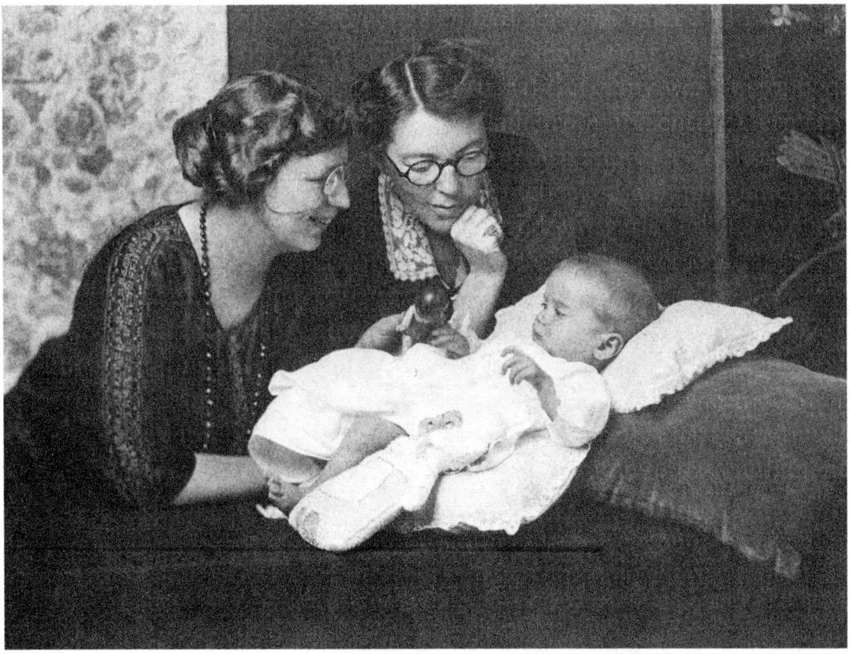

Frieda S. Miller and Pauline Newman looking at newborn Elisabeth, 1923. (Schlesinger Library, Harvard Radcliffe Institute)

Frieda S. Miller on horseback with her daughter, Elisabeth, who was an avid equestrian. (Schlesinger Library, Harvard Radcliffe Institute)

Elisabeth (Miller) Burger washing her dog, Nickie, 1933. (Schlesinger Library, Harvard Radcliffe Institute)

A portrait of Elisabeth taken while she was studying at Vassar College, 1943. (Schlesinger Library, Harvard Radcliffe Institute)

Pauline Newman and Frieda Miller pose with Elisabeth and her husband, Sir David Owen, on their wedding day. (Schlesinger Library, Harvard Radcliffe Institute)

Pauline Newman was a doting grandmother to Hugh and Michael Owen. Here she is with Michael in Coffeetown, Pennsylvania. (Schlesinger Library, Harvard Radcliffe Institute)

Poster for Pauline Newman's congressional campaign, 1918. (Schlesinger Library, Harvard Radcliff Institute)

9

Finding Frieda

Newman read the letter on her desk for a second time, more slowly than the first. Dated September 11, 1918, it was from Frieda Miller asking her once again to reconsider her offer. She wanted Newman to come to Philadelphia and helm the WTUL's organizing efforts. Signing it "Fraternally yours," Miller told Newman that she knew from their previous discussions what the work would involve and how badly she was needed.[1] Once Newman took the job, the details were quickly agreed upon. The executive board unanimously voted that Newman would receive a salary of forty dollars a week. They also urged her to come posthaste. Newman wouldn't be getting used to New York City after all; instead, she would pack her bags and find a hotel in Philadelphia to call home.

Newman and Miller, who were rooming at the College Club, began running the office as a team in no time. Newman, the more brash and outspoken of the two, would become the voice of the Philadelphia WTUL. More standoffish by nature, Miller would become the logistics manager and policy developer. In time, and with the help of Frances Perkins, Miller would rise to high positions in state and federal government. She and Newman had grown quite close to Perkins, the future US secretary of labor, when they worked together on safety issues after the Triangle Shirtwaist Factory fire.

As Newman remembered it, the attraction between her and Miller was swift. Their personalities complemented each other. Miller's refined appearance and mannerisms appealed to Newman, who was forever mindful of her lack of formal education. From Miller's perspective, Newman's openness and yearning for a family appealed. Although Elisabeth, Frieda Miller's daughter, came to appreciate their relationship as a deeply emotional one, she would never describe it as sexual.[2] As American historians have pointed out, this was not unusual; during this time period the term "lesbian" was not common parlance. It's also important to note that one ought not view Newman and Miller's relationship through a contemporary lens, as at the time, same-sex relationships were often thought of as immoral or deviant. Additionally, given societal expectations for women then, Newman and Miller would have likely found it challenging to openly acknowledge their relationship.[3]

Miller hailed from an established family in the heartland—La Crosse, Wisconsin, to be precise. Her grandfather, a mill owner, immigrated to the middle of America with his wife in 1848. Of the seven children they raised, one was Miller's father. When Miller was just out of toddlerhood, her mother, Erna, died. Overwhelmed, Miller's father, James, sent her and her sister, Elsie, to live with her grandparents, Charles and Augusta Segelke. Although Miller never wanted for anything materially, the lack of emotional security that had once filled her house left a jagged hole that could not be smoothed. She grew to hold her emotions close, never quite learning to confide in anyone. Instead she poured her energies into intellectual matters.

Miller pursued her studies with vigor. In 1911 she graduated from Milwaukee-Downer College, a small women's college in Wisconsin. The college counted the elder sister of Harriet Beecher Stowe, Catharine Beecher, among its alumnae. Beecher created "The Beecher Plan," which zeroed in on four professions most inclined to hire women: teaching, child care, nursing, and "conservation of the domestic state." While Miller would pursue teaching for a time, neither she nor anyone in the labor movement would deign to think women should be consigned to only those four professions. Upon graduation Miller traded Wisconsin for Illinois.

Taking up residence in Green Hall at the University of Chicago, Miller studied French and German, sociology, political economy, and political science. She was regarded as "a delightful person in a group of that kind." Earning mostly A's, the PhD candidate never completed her degree, and the suicide of one of Miller's professors, Robert Franklin Hoxie, "is undoubtedly the explanation of her never having completed her dissertation and taken her examination in her major subject."[4] It was not all academics all the time. According to an account of her time at the university, Miller nearly led a strike against the dining hall in 1917. Like many college students, she and fellow classmates were not fond of the offerings and so seriously considered staging a protest.[5]

Whether she left after Hoxie's death or because she was eager to get on with work, Miller accepted a position as an instructor of economics at Bryn

Mawr College. There she discovered she could combine economics with social reform, the latter being something she was inspired to because she had seen her grandfather treat his employees fairly when she was a child. Located in the bucolic suburbs of Philadelphia, Bryn Mawr encouraged young women to work at settlement houses. The trend, which began in the late 1800s, saw college women flock to various charitable associations where they could marry their academic interests to societal reforms.

The settlement house movement was a piece of the Progressive Movement puzzle, which sought to address challenges of industrialization, urbanization, and inequality. As such, women's colleges were ideally situated since it gave their students a hands-on chance to apply their particular skill set to help address urban poverty, poor living conditions, public health, and suffrage. Even so, Miller found working at Bryn Mawr only moderately satisfying and soon decided she "wanted to do something more socially beneficial than writing an academic dissertation," so she agreed to become executive secretary of the WTUL's Philadelphia chapter. A few years into that job, she realized she needed more help—hence her repeated appeals to Newman to come work with her.

The two women also complemented each other professionally. "They met in a context where, she [Miller] was the one who was more the college-educated and all that but Pauline knew the nitty-gritty. So it wasn't so much class, but it was that they each could learn from each other. It was interesting to know someone who had had the practical experiences," Elisabeth, Frieda's daughter, would later recall.[6] Whereas Newman was an outstanding organizer, Miller lacked experience with "real live people on the picket lines."[7]

Thousands of miles away from the Philadelphia WTUL, American men were living in miles of trenches etched across France and Belgium. The Wilson administration, which had made staying out of the war a key campaign issue, had pivoted. It argued that if Germany wasn't stopped, autocracy would spread across Europe. Aside from presenting Germany as an existential menace, the administration also appealed to those who argued that if Germany were allowed to go unchecked, shipping lanes and trade routes would continue to be endangered. By war's end, 4.8 million men would serve in the US Army, 2.8 million of them overseas. Of those, 116,516 would die.[8]

As socialists, Newman and Miller opposed the war. The party believed that by becoming involved in the war, the United States was playing at imperialism. From its perspective, America had joined the war to further empower the capitalist class. Nevertheless, as the Socialist Party's national executive committee announced, it did "not presume to pass judgment upon the conduct of our brother parties in Europe. We realize that they are the victims of the present vicious industrial, political and military system and that they did the best they could under the circumstances."[9]

Yet, Newman was also a realist and she understood what the consequences would be if the United States stayed out of the war: "To say that we like it, or were terribly enthusiastic about it, I would say no. I think that was the mood . . . I think we did what we were told to do; we sold bonds and bought bonds and we spoke wherever we were wanted to. We wanted Germany not to win, and if we didn't want Germany to win, we had to do our share."[10] Once the United States entered the war, socialists like Newman and trade unionists like AFL president Samuel Gompers, a strong supporter of Woodrow Wilson, grew ever more leery of international efforts involving Germany, Italy, Bulgaria, and the Ottoman Empire.[11]

Additionally, Newman saw the war as an opportunity to further women in the workplace; they would find jobs as anything from stenographers to radio operators, bankers to barbers. In that sense, she diverged from the prevailing attitude of many unions, including the Coast Seamen, the Locomotive Firemen, the United Mine Workers, and the Railway Conductors, who declared greed and capitalism drove the war.[12] After the war Newman and other female labor activists would push Wilson to name a woman to the US delegation to the International Labor Organization's founding. The body would be responsible for drafting labor standards for the world's workers.

In the late spring of 1918, John F. Hart, president of Amalgamated Meat Cutters and Butcher Workmen, strode to the podium of the Garden Theater in New York City to address the third biennale. As far as he was concerned, women might have the right to participate on the picket lines but ought to be wary of getting too comfortable in the jobs they stepped into. Speaking in a sonorous voice, he proclaimed that while Uncle Sam was shipping its young men across the Atlantic in transport ships, the federal government was simultaneously trying to install women in positions once held by men, from working in slaughterhouses to plowing fields: "The women are doing the work and doing it equally as men ever performed, and are unfortunately doing it for a much lower wage," he told the room.[13] Neither Hart nor the union men were pleased that women were willing to work for a lower wage.

Meanwhile, the WTUL and the ILGWU, which opposed the war from a philosophical standpoint, could not deny the opportunity it presented. Women would find new avenues of employment in industries that once locked them out. They would finally have a chance to work in sectors deemed essential to national interests. Beyond that, they might have the chance to force the issue of wage equality.

Much of the outspoken resistance and disdain for the increasing number of women in the workforce came to the surface during the American Federation of Labor's thirty-eighth annual convention in Pittsburgh, Pennsylvania, that November. Hart relished whipping up such sentiment, warning men that if they weren't careful, women would replace them at work. Although Hart said they would, of course, insist on women receiving the same wage for the same work that men received, they would "leave that for the locals and the membership to think over, assuring them that it is an important question" and one that would "greatly impact [their] future interests."[14] Reading between the lines, union leaders and management knew they could refuse.

During the convention, the AFL, with Gompers at the helm, voted to pass Resolution No. 92, which included the clause: "WHEREAS, The American Federation of Labor stands for equal pay for equal work, believing that these women should receive the same wages as those received by the men whose places they have taken in order to help the prosecution of this war and the elimination of the hun [*sic*]."[15] Newman wasn't fooled. On the surface it appeared the AFL was supporting women, but Gompers was wishy-washy back in 1909 and he was wishy-washy now. He favored keeping women out of certain sectors of the workforce and he didn't try to hide it. Just so no one would misunderstand him, he wrote a lengthy piece titled "Don't Sacrifice Womanhood" for the 1917 summer issue of *American Federationist*. In it, he insisted that labor oppose burdening women with tasks they would be unable to perform because of their biological sex.[16] Gompers dressed his misogyny as care for the well-being of women and concern for American motherhood. He maintained that he was merely suggesting that women be required to get a physician's approval before being allowed to do men's work. He was merely concerned about a woman's "fragile nature" and was only trying to prevent "the dilution of skilled labor by unskilled" labor.[17] Although he was adamant that he was only looking out for everyone's best interests, he insisted the secretary of every local union of women wage earners nationwide should receive his "Don't Sacrifice Womanhood" message.

Newman was irate. At every turn, Gompers seemed to be holding women back. Yet, rather than confront him directly, she took her anger public. Her column "An Old Problem—To be Faced Anew" was about more than the Socialist Party; it was also a thinly veiled jab at the labor unions. "Experience, observations and life have taught me another story. It has taught me that, while no one will question the equality of sexes existing in the Socialist Party, it remains a men's party just the same," she wrote, adding that men were hired solely on the basis of their gender.[18]

Nevertheless, as tens of thousands of women entered the workforce—lacing up steel-toed boots, oiling tractor gears, heaving boxes onto trucks, filing lawsuits, and making sense of companies' accounts—women's magazines ran articles and advertisements highlighting their contribution to the war effort. Women could remain feminine while plowing fields or making munitions.

Since Newman had sent her first articles to *The Forward* more than a decade earlier, her writing had matured. A lot of that came from the careful editorial guidance she received from Sarah Cory Rippey. As the managing editor of *Life and Labor*, Rippey constantly encouraged Newman to keep sending work, even if the magazine wasn't always able to publish it in a timely manner. "The little verses you were good enough to send are carefully put away in the file, awaiting an appropriate time and place for their publication. And even though tardily, may I extend to you my hearty congratulations upon your splendid piece of work on the Canadian Congress story," Rippey wrote.[19] Newman also counted on Josephine Conger Kaneko, editor of the Socialist Party magazine *The Progressive Woman* to help hone her writing. Such encouragement prompted Newman to pen "Lest We Forget" seven years after the Triangle Shirtwaist fire. The piece was as powerful as it was poignant: "In the moaning of the March winds I seem to hear the voices of the Triangle victims. And as the day of the catastrophy [*sic*] approaches these voices become louder and louder. They will not leave me. They insist that I who listened to them before, must not turn from them now."[20]

While such sobering thoughts underpinned her writing at this time, Newman gave herself permission to waltz toward the possibility of love. Until Newman met Miller, the possibility of a fulfilling relationship seemed out of reach for her. Of her original study group from the Socialist Literary Society days, Newman was the only one still without a partner.[21] This marked the first time Newman found herself in a serious and loving relationship. Her relationship with Bohn had lacked depth, although when she reread his letters to her, she realized he was the expected choice. She was thankful that her mother and sisters were not there to pester her about marriage. Women were taught to believe that marriage and children would be their greatest triumph.[22] Yet, Newman also knew there were advantages in living alone, or at least remaining unmarried.

Though she and Miller were growing closer, Newman worked hard to retain the agency to do as she wished, able to spend her money in the way she thought best. She and Miller kept their finances separate. According to the 1892 book *Thoughts of Busy Girls*:

> For one thing, a single woman preserves more independence of action and more self-reliance of character. One can say, "Yes, I will do so or so," or, "no, I will not do so or so," instead of, "Well, you know, I can't say until I hear what my husband says . . . A single woman, who earns her own living, let it be ever so scanty, has the comfort of expending the amount she earns as she thinks best.[23]

The relationship with Miller started as Newman was feeling more fulfilled professionally. Always outspoken at work, she felt herself becoming more confident in using her clothes as an expression of herself. She cut her hair somewhat shorter than the short bob fashion of the time. She had developed a taste for tweeds and ties. She didn't really take much stock in what others thought of her—except perhaps her closest friends.

Her friends were her family. And although they lived in Chicago, Newman had spent little time with her sisters, Fanny and Sarah, in recent years. Her brothers were now virtual strangers and her mother no longer lived in New York. In fact, years later Newman would talk about how she didn't know her nieces and nephews. She had spent so much time alone that she almost didn't recognize how quickly she was taken with Miller. "It was natural to be friendly. We had the same work to do. We had a lot in common. She was immensely interested in social questions; she was deeply interested in literature and poetry and music," Newman said.[24]

Though Miller tended to guard her feelings, she could be jolly, and it was that side of her personality that Newman loved to tease out. So it was that they donned costumes and masks and made their way to WTUL headquarters on Halloween. Inside, paper skeletons twirled and carved pumpkins sat on tables next to bowls of candy corn. Rose Schneiderman organized the fête. Miller and Newman circulated among the seventy-five people packed into two rooms. As Schneiderman reported, "We had a lovely Hallowe'en decorations and Zamford of the International Bakery and Confectionary Workers' Union, donated two wonderful Hallowe'en cakes. There were games and dancing."[25]

As they grew more intimate, the line between Miller and Newman's romantic and professional partnership blurred. Their budding romance was illustrative of the way working-class and privileged women had joined forces to achieve change.[26] For now, their relationship was able to float above their very real class and money differences, their very real ethnic and schooling differences.[27]

During those early days when they were getting to know each other, Miller and Newman enjoyed several celebrations, from a quiet New Year's Eve to a Socialist Party masked ball. They frequented the cinema and were especially excited to get tickets, courtesy of Schneiderman, to see the 1917 drama *Redemption*. Inside the George M. Cohan Theatre, on West Forty-Third and Broadway, they sat in red velvet chairs, entranced as the silent film flickered across the screen. Starring Evelyn Nesbit, Russell Thaw, and Charles Wellesley, the film was loosely based on Nesbit's life. The actress and model was one point in a love triangle that involved Harry Kendall Thaw, a railroad baron, and the renowned architect Stanford White. The imbroglio reached a deadly crescendo when Thaw murdered White thirty-two stories aboveground on Madison Square Garden's rooftop theater. It was ironic given that White had designed the building, which, as newspapers pointed out at the time, was the second tallest in New York. Nesbit's performance "managed to convey a sense of courageous womanhood grappling with an unjust foe that was not without its appeal," read the *New York Times* review.[28]

Miller and Newman joined Schneiderman for dinner after the show. It was a grand spring evening, their joy tempered only by the headlines about the war and the people they knew whose husbands and sons were living and fighting in trenches overseas. The trio helped supply garments for soldiers and made scarves and sweaters. Some worked with the Red Cross. "Nobody refused anything. Even if they were opposed to the war, they did what they could to help those who were still alive," Newman said.[29]

On March 11, 1918, one of the first cases of the influenza virus was recorded at Fort Riley in Kansas. One week later, 522 soldiers lay confined to narrow iron-framed beds in the camp hospital, each one sick with the same severe respiratory virus. The first mention of it would be in April, in a weekly public health report. No one was immune. People felt flushed and clammy in the morning and were dead by nightfall. Others struggled to breathe as bone-shaking chills wracked their bodies. Six months later, 3 million were dead worldwide. When it ended, there would be an estimated 675,000 dead in the United States and 50 million dead worldwide.[30]

Regarded as the world's deadliest plague since the Black Death, the flu pandemic showed the need for new public health measures. The New York City Board of Health issued a 4:00 p.m. closing for all stores, except food and pharmacies. US public health officials called on people to wear masks on the subways and elevated trains. In New York City, calls to care for upward of 2,000 children orphaned by the flu went out from the Hebrew National Orphan House.[31] Hence, when Miller returned to her room flushed and clammy one October afternoon, Newman knew the contagion had crossed her doorstep.[32] That month, an estimated 195,000 Americans would die from the virus.

Newman, who didn't fall ill, nursed Miller for weeks. Miller's fever was so high, her respiratory distress so great, she nearly died. Newman decided against sending her to a hospital. It was a good choice. Because so many professional nurses were being dispatched to military camps across the continental United States and overseas, and hospitals refused to use trained African American nurses, there was a severe nursing shortage. Miller's doctor agreed, telling Newman that not only were the hospitals overflowing, but "there's nothing to be done anyway. Give her an eggnog once a day or something, and keep in touch with me," so Newman nursed Miller back to health.[33]

Then one morning the illness lifted. On Armistice Day, Miller was strong enough to sit up. "We moved the chair over to the window; we could see that the war ended. See the people dancing in the street for joy. The war was over," Newman said.[34] Bells rang. People crowded into the streets waving flags and passing out smiles. Strangers embraced. Churches and synagogues filled with the thankful. People blew horns and rang cowbells. Factories closed and stores shuttered. It was a time of jubilation. "Thursday of last week cannot be described. I have never seen a demonstration of its kind before," Schneiderman wrote to Newman.[35] As their close friend and colleague Lorena O'Reilly put it, "Suppose we did go mad for a minute—but What did the madness prove. Peace, peace and more peace is the heart's desire of human kind."[36]

The war was over; nevertheless, questions remained. "This making the world safe for Democracy is a large order. But since the order has been given America will deliver the good—it may however travel by way of Social Industrial Democracy rather than political Democracy," O'Reilly wrote to Newman.[37] In short, the women of the ILGWU and WTUL were ready for a postwar sensibility that included women. After all, President Woodrow Wilson would go on to establish the United States Women's Bureau in the US Labor Department in 1920 as a way to help women protect the gains they had made during the war years. Miller would go to work in the bureau under Mary Anderson, a member of the Chicago WTUL.

Ecstatic about the war's end, Newman was also proud that the Socialist Party nominated her to run for the Eleventh Congressional District in New York. The irony of being the first woman to run for Congress on the party's ticket was not lost on her. While women won the right to vote in New York in 1917—it was the first Eastern state to do so—they didn't yet have the right nationally. A fierce campaigner, Newman proudly stayed on message—namely, promoting labor rights and suffrage. Posters featuring a serious Newman in a sensible hat and wire-rimmed glasses plastered the walls of meeting halls and emblazoned pamphlets. "I was a good campaigner, had a good voice and always managed to set and to hold the attention of the crowd—I always had a crowd . . . I had a good voice—strong and clear. My vote for congress exceeded that of the party—which was a personal tribute, I do think," she later recalled.[38]

She was adamant that it was time to stop "making women a near divinity and of man a mere side issue." It was her belief that the political insubordination of women hurt modern society. In short, suffrage and labor rights were intertwined, the former "only a means to an end. A weapon to achieve our ultimate goal . . . to regulate and finally abolish the evils from which the working class suffers."[39] Newman knew that once women realized that the ballot meant power, they would use it to further their interests in the workplace and on the home front.

She also knew how to take a jab at her political adversaries—especially when it came to the issue of temperance:

> The paramount issue advanced by both of them [the candidates] is whether or not the people of America are to be "dry" and drink within the law or outside of it! And the American people accept this bunk, this confusion as an issue. They seem to let it becloud their minds. A strange campaign indeed! As the drink could take place of food, clothing and shelter. As tho it could give the American working men and women economic security; as tho it could solve our problem of labor, social insurance, the cost of living, water power, housing, education, civil liberties and many another problem confronting the men and women who work for a living![40]

It was ludicrous, she said. But there it was. The only thing people should be talking about was job security. She wanted to know what would happen when men returned from the front expecting to get their old jobs back. Surely they earned the right to work. Surely they deserved decent conditions and fair pay. But, she wondered, should women have to "meekly give up those places and return to the miserable underpaid jobs from which many of them came?"[41]

While campaigning in Albany, Newman stayed with Gertrude Tome, chair of the Women's Suffrage Party of New York. It was certainly more comfortable than staying at the YWCA. In a nod to her days on the soapbox,

Newman would sometimes engage people on the corner. Saturday nights often drew more of a crowd. Because so few women spoke on streetcorners in those days, she was something of a novelty. As always, a few hecklers joined those who had sincerely stopped to listen: "Their heckles were not questions, but rather: 'Why don't you go home and wash the dishes?' and things like that. You know, they weren't intelligent questions. It was just amusing, because what could you say to that? I said 'the dishes were done before I left the house.' I said 'are you satisfied now?'" she recalled.[42] Garnering only 14.2 percent of the vote, she ultimately lost her bid for Congress to Democrat John F. Carew.

One year later, in 1919, Newman met Eleanor Roosevelt at the first International Conference of Working Women. The late October meeting saw labor feminists gather from around the world, including Canada, Poland, Serbia, and England. Together they discussed and deliberated a host of topics, including motherhood and wage labor. Having recently become involved in the New York WTUL, Eleanor Roosevelt would come to be one of the strongest advocates and financial supporters for the organization. During the conference, Newman reconnected with Frances Perkins. Although Newman was still engaging in rank-and-file organizing, she was becoming more engaged in lobbying for legislation that would protect workers. In some ways it was the end of the beginning for Newman, as she was now transitioning toward work issues, such as minimum wage, maximum hours, and safety standards: issues, that affected workers as a whole rather than leading organizing and strike efforts on a case-by-case basis.

When Newman became a member of the New York State Minimum Wage Board, she would often testify before the New York State Legislature. When she did, she did not hold back, as was the case when she gave the legislators an earful about how the hotel and restaurant industry had effectively evaded labor laws for more than thirty years: "I think the time has come to speak frankly and to tell the 'honorable' gentlemen of the opposition that no thinking person believes in their outworn song of the 'industry can't afford' this, or that. This song has lost its charm. It has lost its meaning. We have heard it lo, these many years, and some of us are tired of its sound!"[43]

In the midst of tackling these thorny issues and upsetting political incidents, Newman snatched time for the arts, whether literature or music. It was something she took pleasure in doing ever since buying a copy of *Great Expectations* off a pushcart in the Lower East Side. As she wrote to Schneiderman, it was vital to her "to engage with the world outside the trade union movement, a world with books and art, and the beauty of nature, a world which invited me to get to know it, to admire and to love it."[44] This was a lighter thought, given that on the same day she wrote those words Newman was heading to Union Square to protest the death sentence of labor leader and socialist Thomas Mooney, who was sentenced to death for his role in the San Francisco Preparedness Day Bombing of 1916. The bombing, which killed ten and wounded forty, took place during a parade that supported American entry into World War I. Along with Mooney, Warren K. Billings had been convicted and sentenced to life in prison. Mooney's sentence was commuted to life in prison, and the two men were released in 1939 after it was shown that their convictions were based on false testimony.

When Christmas came that year, Newman and Miller should have been celebrating good health and peace together. Instead, Miller traveled home to Wisconsin: "Christmas greetings got here last evening in time for all festivities everything unchanged left Elsa feeling well as there is no word today everything must be all right leave at noon tomorrow take night train out of Chicago arriving Philadelphia nine thirty-five Saturday evening sorry too late for concert best I can manage, love Frieda."[45] The Western Union telegram, with its red and green beribboned wreath, was no replacement for Miller, but it would have to do.

10

Working Mothers

Miller threw up. Again. She couldn't keep her food down; she was zapped of all energy. She didn't need to take a test. She knew she was pregnant and she knew what she needed to do. First, she needed to end her relationship with Charles Kutz, a fellow labor activist and president of the machinists' union. No matter how many times Kutz, a devout Catholic and father of several children, told his "wonderful sweetheart" how he pined for his "dearest my dearest" and how he "could no more be happy nor content without you, than I could live without food or air," she knew he was never going to divorce his wife.[1] Second, Miller had to tell her "Paul." Third, she needed a plan—one she hoped would involve Pauline Newman.

There were few options for women in this realm in 1923. True, with the ratification of the Nineteenth Amendment on August 18, 1920, women now had the right to vote. But there remained many areas of public and private life where they lacked control. Abortion had been illegal throughout the United States since the 1880s, except when imperative to save a woman's life. Generally, if a woman wanted to end her pregnancy, she needed to find a doctor who would perform one in secret, or she could perform one herself, which was potentially deadly. A woman could also give the baby up for adoption. Or, as Miller wished, she could raise it with Newman. So she told Newman.

Reeling from the news, Newman, now thirty, did her best to overlook Miller's affair with Kutz. She believed Miller when she promised it was the first and only time she had ever strayed. She needed to believe that Miller would be as devoted to her as she was to Miller. Together they invented a story about Miller's baby. Ever since Newman had nursed Miller back to health from the flu, the two were almost inseparable. Having cared for

Miller left Newman feeling inclined to anticipate and acquiesce to Miller's needs. However, Miller did not return Newman's devotion with equal measure. How this dynamic might one day play out was not something she cared to entertain.

The two women told their close friends and acquaintances that Miller planned to adopt an orphan in Europe. They left out the details of where and why; the hazier the story, the better. The deception was never about their living arrangements. After all, several of their friends, like Schneiderman and Maud Swartz, president of the WTUL, were in same-sex relationships, living together in what some described as a "Boston marriage." The New England term was coined in the late nineteenth and early twentieth century after Henry James's novel *The Bostonians*, in which the deeply passionate bond shared between the two main characters Verena Tarrant and Olive Chancellor—while not explicitly sexual—pushed against traditional gender roles and societal expectations of women. Mary Dreier lived with Frances Kellor, and Helen Marot lived with Caroline Pratt, head of the City and Country School. These women felt deception was necessary because even in their social circle, there was always the chance of being stigmatized over having a child out of wedlock, particularly because of Miller and Kutz's adulterous affair.

After telling their friends, Miller and Newman resigned from their Philadelphia WTUL posts and embarked on an extended trip to Europe. Starting in London and ending in Italy, the trip would allow Miller to conceal her pregnancy. In August, during the middle of the trip, before she was too far along, the two women would attend the International Congress of Working Women in Vienna, Austria. Upon returning stateside, Miller intended to legally adopt the baby. This would give further cover to the lie. Lastly, the two women agreed the baby would never be told the truth: that Miller was her biological mother.

They left New York and traveled back across the ocean that once carried Newman here, this time in a decidedly more comfortable setting. Newman and Miller arrived in London and checked into the Raglan Hotel, located off Russell Square in Bloomsbury. The couple looked forward to a spell of quiet time, punctuated with some work. Newman had already corresponded with several women in England's labor movement ahead of their visit, including Ada Broughton, secretary of the Bermondsey Labour Party. Broughton was delighted to meet Newman and keen to talk with her about how the labor movement worked in England. So it was that on a Sunday afternoon, while Miller rested, Newman found herself sitting on the No. 68 bus to the Surrey Docks in southeast London. That afternoon, the "deal porters"—dockers who carried deal, or timber, across their shoulders at these commercial docks—were expected to demonstrate in nearby Southwark Park in advance of their planned strike.[2]

The pair also looked forward to meeting Margaret G. Bondfield, secretary of the women workers' section of the National Union of General Workers. In anticipation of Newman's visit, Bondfield wrote early in January, advising Newman not to "expect to take London in a jump of about 24 hours." Bondfield offered to be her guide.[3] She showed her Buckingham Palace and Westminster Abbey, Big Ben and Hampstead Heath. During the afternoon, their meandering conversation covered everything from work to negotiations for German reparations. It appeared that France and Great Britain were not in agreement, a rupture that Bondfield thought "may mean more strife, misery and bloodshed and more suffering and horror for the German people. It is indeed a bad moment."[4] In these first weeks of the trip, Miller and Newman settled into a routine. The two would catch up on correspondence, take meetings with labor activists, and, in the case of Miller, occasionally rest.

From England, the couple crossed the English Channel, spent time in Germany, and then it was on to Vienna on August 14, 1923, for the Third Congress of the International Federation of Working Women. Hailing from fourteen countries, the delegates lodged in Schönbrunn Castle, the summer home of the Habsburgs, where a six-year-old Wolfgang Mozart once played the violin. After the congress, which focused on unions in international labor law, Newman and Miller traveled by train to Como, Italy. There the couple spent a few nights on the shores of Lake Maggiore before heading south to Naples, where they checked into Macpherson's Hotel Britannique. Overlooking the Gulf of Naples, the picturesque hotel had welcomed many illustrious guests since it opened in 1870, including the Irish playwright and political activist Bernard Shaw, with whom they had spent a delightful moment a few weeks earlier.

Their sundrenched mornings and chilly evenings were interrupted on December 7. Miller's contractions were coming closer and closer—too close to make it to a hospital. Newman called down to the desk and asked them to call a doctor, who in turn sent a message posthaste: "Dear Sister, I was called this morning to see an American lady—who is in labour . . . no preparation—come at once."[5] A Miss Macdonald, a certified medical surgical fever and maternity nurse, knocked on the door.

Attended by only the doctor and the nurse, with Newman nearby for support, Miller safely delivered a baby girl on December 7, 1923, at 11:30 a.m. When she reported the birth to the American consulate, Miller listed Elisabeth's father as James Miller and her mother's name as Frieda Strong.[6] However, the official, November 22, 1935, adoption certificate lists

Miller as the mother; there is no father listed. Dorothy Kenyon, a 1917 graduate of New York University Law School, feminist, and civil liberties supporter, stepped in as the witness.[7] It's unknown how Newman, who co-parented Elisabeth, felt about being officially excluded. She never mentioned it in her daybooks or notebooks.

Over time, Elisabeth came to think it was the circumstances of her birth and the secret pact her mother and Newman struck that lay at the root of why the two women stayed together all those years: "And so that in a way, from my point of view I think the relationship between my mother and P, although not always terrific, was clearly formed by this venture. And, of course, bringing me up and all that can't have been all bad, I mean it was kind of a bond, and maybe a nice one."[8]

Once Elisabeth was old enough to travel, the couple sailed back to the United States. Miller filled a dark brown leather notebook with handwritten notes about how to care for her newborn daughter, including general baby tips like no soap on her face, olive oil on scalp if she were to get dandruff, how to stop her breasts from producing milk, nursing her, and also what she ought to pack for the crossing—figs, magnesia, and washcloths. She also jotted down recipes for chestnut soup, barley broth, and pudding.[9]

Any tension and apprehension that the couple felt before they left for their "tour of the continent" had dissipated by the time they returned stateside. While they both had jobs waiting for them, Miller with the New York State Labor Board and Newman with the Joint Board of Sanitary Control, their hearts now beat around baby Elisabeth. The little family moved into a fourth-floor apartment on the edge of New York City's Greenwich Village. The apartment was ideally situated for the couple as the neighborhood was a longtime haven for artists, writers, and union activists; even political organizations with whom they aligned, including the Socialist Party of America, the Communist Party of the United States, and the Anarchist Workers of America, had offices there.

The bedroom faced gardens; the living room looked out over a schoolyard and warehouse. Light suffused the back rooms. Because Miller was an early riser who would awaken frequently at night, she slept on a daybed in the spacious living room. Both women's desks stood in the corner of the dining room, and during Christmastime they installed a small tree in the dumbwaiter they normally used to bring up groceries.

The apartment's location also allowed Newman to more easily balance working with Dr. George Moses Price of the Joint Board of Sanitary Control to build the Union Health Center while shouldering most of Elisabeth's daily care. Born in Poltava, Russia (now Ukraine), Price left for the United

States when he was eighteen. Like Newman, Schneiderman, and so many of the men and women Price would work with, he left because of pervasive, violent anti-Semitism. Soon after graduating from New York University Medical School in 1895, he was appointed to be inspector of the New York Health Department. Later Price would become the chairman of the executive committee of the Joint Board of Sanitary Control in the cloak and suit industry of New York.

As such, the health center fast became one of Newman's pet projects. As she knew from her visits with the joint board, too many workers could ill afford the cost of private medical care or take time off to apply for and receive public charity since most venues were open only during working hours.[10] Poor health was linked with other manifestations of social disorganization, such as unemployment, low income, poor housing, and inadequate food.[11] In Newman's view, workers' rights were one thing, but what value did those rights have if you were too sick to enjoy them? So she and Price decided the best course was for Newman to go door-to-door and educate people about the center. "I went to the shops and talked to the workers, and of course, our publication helped. We had the printed matter in three languages: Jewish, English, and Italian. That of course told them about the union health center," she recalled about the health center's educational literature.[12]

When the Union Health Center opened at 31 Union Square, it was the jewel in the crown of Newman's accomplishments. Physicals, x-rays, electrocardiographs, basic eye exams, and ear, nose, and throat services were available. The onsite pharmacy filled workers' prescriptions. A dental center, which would be open six days a week, soon followed. Outfitted with modern equipment, everything was white and sparkling, from the chairs to the cabinets, to the floors and the paint on the walls.[13] Newman wasn't shy about demonstrating how the medical equipment worked. Early x-ray machines were "large, loud, sparking, smelly and ostentatious devices, prone to mishap and injury."[14] To prove that x-ray machines were safe, Newman invited the workers to watch her being x-rayed. After the technician x-rayed her chest, she turned toward the group and said, "See it didn't hurt me; didn't bother me and all we know now is what's inside of me, that's all."[15]

Like so many of the union's endeavors, a lack of funding was a persistent problem. One afternoon while Newman pored over paperwork, Price knocked on her office door. He apologized for the interruption. He was distressed and said he could "no longer ask the physicians to work without remuneration, [or] the clerks, nurses and others without pay."[16] He couldn't even pay his phone bill. She calmed him down, reassuring him that she knew people in the ILGWU and the WTUL who could help. She obtained twenty thousand dollars from the Rosenwald Foundation, which granted funds to support education, and several more thousands from the Garland Foundation, officially recognized as the American fund for public service.[17]

During this time, Miller was spending more time upstate in her job with the New York State Labor Board, which meant Miller often left Elisabeth in the care of nurses and Newman. Pleased for Miller, Newman wrote in her journals about resenting her partner's rise in prominence, even if it came as she herself was receiving less public attention than during the early days of her work. Miller discovered that her education and background afforded her more professional opportunities than those enjoyed by the self-taught Newman. Moreover, friendships like the one she had with Frances Perkins, which dated to the latter's post as industrial commissioner of New York, helped open doors. Indeed, by 1929 Miller would be wearing the title of head of the Bureau of Women in Industry for the New York State Labor Department.[18] Newman safely tucked away any feelings of jealousy she might have had. For now, the pair busied themselves with raising Elisabeth.

One of Elisabeth's earliest memories was walking to nearby Washington Square holding Newman's hand. Another lasting memory was when they took her to see Eva Le Gallienne as Peter Pan in a performance in which the *New York Times* described her as "a gallant, buoyant, clean-cut figure, and gave Peter plenty of élan and boyish grace."[19]

When work separated Miller and Newman, they wrote to each other frequently, just like Newman and Schneiderman once did. A postcard with blue gentians here, a card with two penguins, heads and necks entwined to form a heart there. Miller wrote long letters in forest green ink, while Newman favored black. The letters included a mix of work and family, centering on the goings-on of little Elisabeth:

> Sunday evening, Pruney dear— Here we are, at the end of the day again and it seems as tho it just began. Your letter came early this morning, and of course Elisabeth claimed it instantly. This evening when I put her to bed there was the usual—"I want to go to bed" but then she added—"I want Paul to go to bed too, right away!" However, she went to sleep very placidly for we kept her moving sufficiently so that she was tired.

Newman signed the letter with a soft word for Miller, reminding her that "Liz and I miss you 'wewy much' but we hope you're making the most of it, Paul."[20]

After Elisabeth turned four, Miller and Newman enrolled her in the City and Country School, which was then located at 165 West Twelfth Street. Run as a teachers' cooperative with Caroline Pratt as the principal, the school instilled in its students the concept that one learned by doing. The girls went around in cotton dresses and blue jeans before anyone else did, and "if you saw a really messy kid coming down the street, it probably went to our school," Elisabeth later wrote.[21]

Miller chose not to slow down the pace of her business travel. This left Newman responsible for the majority of child care. Newman loved Elisabeth dearly and cherished their time together, as her journals and correspondence show. By this time, Newman had cropped her hair and wore what was then considered more masculine clothing. Sometimes when she picked up Elisabeth from school, the girl's classmates would ask her, "Who is that person?" because of Newman's dress.[22] Although none of the adults raised an eyebrow that two women were raising Elisabeth or that she was adopted, Elisabeth felt unsettled when her friends and other students spoke about their fathers. Not having a father in the home and not having been told anything about her father proved trying. It became a lifelong trial that ultimately informed her relationship with Newman.[23] As Elisabeth later wrote:

> I mean I felt that she was family in as much as she was always there and I didn't say "What's she doing here?" On the other hand I felt my mother was the most important person in the set-up. I knew more about my mother's strengths than Pauline's strengths, shall we say. I knew that Pauline didn't have as good a command of English, for instance. Well, I knew that Pauline had been born somewhere else and had learned English as a second language. But I don't think I had much appreciation of what Pauline had accomplished . . . But I thought that my mother did everything right and was a handsome, good-looking woman, and dressed nicely. I admired her.[24]

For all their apprehension about how they would have been perceived back in 1923, Miller and Newman's friends, who shared their political and social beliefs, accepted this unconventional family. Sometimes they held union meetings at home, and sometimes they just got together for poker and dinner with their close friends in the neighborhood: Nancy Cook and Marion Dickerman, Mary Dewson and Mary Porter, and Leonora O'Reilly and Frances Kellor.

Throughout their life, Newman's and Miller's friends and colleagues accepted the trio, including Elisabeth, as a family. It just "was." Newman and Miller might not have been comfortable with the label "lesbian"; in fact, Elisabeth would later describe Newman as "quite simply my mother's best friend." Her insistence on describing their lifelong relationship could also speak more to an era when one's personal life truly was personal.

Elisabeth grew to regard these women as her extended family. "I accepted that our society was a group of women who had a kind of collegial spirit, although they were doing different things," she recounted many years later. "They treated me like a family mascot. And I thought of them as friends rather than just adults. I enjoyed them and thought they were nice women because they took an interest in me."[25]

And yet, the relationship between Newman and Miller involved both personal love and everyday logistical companionship, the same as any serious, long-term partnership. Their friends recognized them as partners and family. Much of the correspondence between these women—Newman and Schneiderman, Newman and Miller, Schneiderman and Dreier—was signed with love to each other, love "from both of us to both of you," or "love to you all." Whenever they went on conferences or vacations, there was no question that they would share a room with their partner. They were viewed as a unit just as two people in a heterosexual marriage or partnership.[26]

Thus, life in their Greenwich Village apartment was stamped with all the hallmarks of a family; Newman helped raise Elisabeth, acting just as a mother would. Yet, at various times throughout their lives, they would go out of their way to insist that she was neither the girl's mother nor her grandmother. This was evident in the way Elisabeth addressed the two women. Miller was always "Mummy" and Newman would forever be "Pauline." Not only did Miller and Elisabeth emphasize bloodlines, but Newman was equally obdurate in this matter. She never once described herself as Elisabeth's "mother." Indeed, in 1976 she took offense to descriptions of her as a mother.[27] Regardless, it was an exuberant household filled with the bedlam that comes from having a young child and two professional women engaged in consequential policy reform.

Four years after women won the right to vote, arguments over the Equal Rights Amendment (ERA) and the best way for women to achieve equal footing in the workplace exploded. These arguments exposed further cracks in the labor movement. In one camp stood those like Alice Paul, the militant feminist leader who was one of the primary leaders of the women's suffrage movement during World War I. Together with Crystal Eastman, the socialist labor lawyer and suffragist, Paul introduced the amendment in 1923 on the seventy-fifth anniversary of the 1848 Seneca Falls Convention in New York. Also known as the Lucretia Mott Amendment, the ERA would guarantee equal rights to women: *"Men and women shall have equal rights throughout the United States and every place subject to its jurisdiction."*[28]

In the other camp stood those like Newman, Miller, Schneiderman, and Roosevelt, who stipulated that protective legislation was the best way to safeguard a woman's health and welfare. In 1867 Wisconsin became the first state to pass such legislation, though it was the Massachusetts law passed in 1902 that provided the rest of the country with a template. The law decreed that women could not be employed more than a total of fifty-eight hours a week. Across the country employers challenged the legislation until it ended up in the US Supreme Court. It was a vociferous and sometimes vituperative debate.

For social justice feminists like Newman, passage of the ERA might mean the Court would likely overturn any or all woman-specific laws and policies, some of which had been on the books for more than two decades. Those laws included ones that regulated working conditions in low-paid service, industrial, and agricultural jobs. The WTUL counted the passage of these laws as some of its greatest victories. As historians have pointed out, these laws were the bedrock upon which more expansive rights—for women and men—were built.[29] On the opposite side were the conservative women's groups like the Daughters of the American Revolution. They attacked progressive women's peace and internationalist endeavors as profoundly un-American, going so far as to insinuate that Margaret Dreier Robins was fomenting insurrection.[30]

When the Supreme Court held that Oregon's ten-hour law, or "The Oregon Standard," was constitutional, the WTUL considered it a major win. The decision safeguarded protective laws, which limited the number of hours that a woman or child could work in certain jobs and guaranteed them a minimum wage. It meant the laws in twenty states, or almost all the states where women work in factories, would hold—for now.

For some, the ERA was the next logical step following the ratification of the Nineteenth Amendment. To them, enshrining the principle of gender equality in the Constitution would lift women from second-class citizenship. Neither Newman, Miller, Perkins, Roosevelt, nor Schneiderman agreed. To a woman they vehemently opposed the amendment. From their vantage point, the only way to guarantee an equal footing for women in the workplace was through protective legislation.

Neither Newman nor Miller, nor any of the ERA opponents, considered their opposition as conservative or backward—quite the contrary. They felt it provided a safety net of minimum wages and maximum hours and believed collective bargaining was the best way for a worker to negotiate their own wages and working conditions.[31] But in the 1920s and 1930s, it was the Progressive Movement that sought to thwart the ERA. So determined were the opponents to the ERA that they launched the Campaign Committee Against the Equal Rights Amendment and the National Committee to Defeat the Unequal Rights Amendment. Twenty-seven organizations signed on to the campaign as well as labor movement notables like Frances Perkins, Catherine Catt, Freida Miller, and Rose Schneiderman. Year after year they lobbied against its passage, arguing that the ERA would unleash hazardous working conditions and long hours. Year after year they blanketed the House Judiciary Committee with letters attesting to their point of view. Jane Addams also decried the ERA as an impediment to women's growth. The mother of the Settlement Movement maintained that American women had made significant strides and that its passage would only impede other legislation from getting passed.

Newman also saw the ERA as a class issue. She took aim at wealthier women who supported the ERA, saying their wealth blinded them:

> The leadership of that party is [in] the hands of those whose wealth permits them to commute from New York or Paris and preach the gospel of an unrestricted working day. I claim that not until Mrs. Broun, Mrs. Belmont, and other "champions" of "equality" have worked ten and more hours a day in a laundry or foundry have they any right to oppose the forty-eight hour week for women workers. Not until Mrs. Hooker and Miss Hale (Mrs. Haywood Broun) have had to scrub floors at thirty cents an hour have they any right to oppose minimum wage legislation. Not until they have spent several years in a Southern textile mill have they any right to oppose special legislation for working women. Until they have done that they had better leave the question of industrial legislation to industrial women.[32]

There were, however, unintended consequences. Protective legislation laws effectively closed women out of certain jobs, such as meatpackers and forklift operators, metal polishers and telephone line repairers. It was a small concession as far as Newman was concerned.

At the same time, the fight for a minimum wage was gaining traction. It had been an issue ever since the WTUL included it in its 1909 legislative platform. At the time, Newman, Schneiderman, and others supported it. Those in opposition, like the US Chamber of Commerce, argued that if a minimum wage law passed, then employers would turn it into a maximum wage, thus preventing unions the chance to negotiate for salary increases.

There had already been a flurry of lawsuits challenging the constitutionality of minimum wage laws. Opponents said minimum wage laws violated the liberty-of-contract doctrine. The courts interpreted the doctrine to mean that workers could make contracts without arbitrary government meddling. Then *Adkins v. Children's Hospital* reached the US Supreme Court, which ruled the law unconstitutional. Fourteen years later, however, the court reversed its decision and held that a law concerning the minimum wage for women in the state of Washington was constitutional.

Even if the minimum wage problem were solved, wage disparities would not evaporate. Far ahead of her time, Newman pointed out that most women worked all day and then went home to do their own sewing, washing, and cleaning for no pay. "That is 'woman's work,' and on the whole, the working woman fulfills her 'natural' duties without protest. Neither the employer nor the community expects a working man to do these things," she wrote. "Woman's work," or work in the home, was work for which women did not receive compensation.[33]

Inside Newman's office at the ILGWU Health Center, a portrait of then–New York State governor Franklin Delano Roosevelt hung on the wall, and a photo of Elisabeth sat on her desk. Sometimes Newman brought Elisabeth with her to work, where the young girl whirled in the office chair and made paper clip chains. "Just as Pauline was a pioneer in her role as an organizer of women in sweatshops and factories . . . the home that I grew up in was in some respects a harbinger of things to come—a female-headed household made up of two employed women and a child," Elisabeth said.[34]

Sometimes Newman played hooky from a union meeting to stay home with Elisabeth or to read a book. She felt a little guilty when she did this, so she told few people. Those she did tell understood. Many of them wished for children but were afraid to take that step as single women or as women in same-sex relationships. One of Newman's friends wrote:

> I quite understand and so would I often go home if I had Elizabeth . . . I am interested in Elizabeth. You must love her and so should I. Of course I will get her and you gloves if you will tell me the sizes. So she goes to school now. I wonder what you will do with her later on. It must be interesting to watch her growth in mind and body. Do send me a snap when you take another. I should love to see her and you ask me when I am coming.[35]

With a double income and jobs close to home, Newman and Miller settled into a comfortable rhythm. Newman's daybooks are chock full of doctor's appointments, social occasions, and meetings; the two women hired an English nurse named Jessie, who provided an extra pair of hands. Jessie was soon replaced by Clara Fischer, who commuted from her home in the Bronx, where she lived with her husband and mother. She arrived promptly at 8:30 every morning and stayed all day, leaving just after she cooked dinner for the family of three. She was a "very sweet person. She wasn't particularly educated, I'm sure, but she was kind to me and my bull dog, and did everything with us," Elisabeth remembered.[36]

As in any relationship, each partner possessed traits that both delighted and irritated the other. Newman's blunt demeanor could rub Miller the wrong way, and Miller's reserved, standoffish manner could irritate Newman. But in those early years, Miller tended to find Newman's combative nature endearing. Elisabeth later recalled:

> Pauline was kind of like a—well, she became heavy in mid- and later age, but she had many of the characteristics of a bantam rooster . . . There were all sorts of stories which in my youth were good fun and everybody enjoyed them. One of the classics was a story about Mother and Pauline having ordered a coffee pot from Macy's. There was something very wrong with it when it came, and so Pauline took it back. And as far as I know she probably ended up discussing it in no uncertain terms with the president of Macy's. One of her specialties was "giving them hell." She never pulled her punches and she gave it to them straight. And they all gave in in the end because it was much easier than combatting her.[37]

Miller knew whenever she had a problem that needed "giving them hell," she only had to call Newman.

Sometime in 1925, Miller and Newman decided to purchase a house outside of the city, where they could have sunshine and fresh air, green and quiet. They settled on West Redding, Connecticut, "which wasn't so fashionable in those days as it is now."[38] Mary Dreier's younger sister Katherine owned a home near there as well. Located about sixty miles from Manhattan, the property was idyllic. A lilac hedge bordered a small garden where Elisabeth, Miller, and Newman planted flowers and vegetables. They planted four-inch-high birch trees on the north side of the porch and couldn't imagine that someday the trees would be taller than the house itself. There was an outdoor fireplace on the hilltop where they could roast marshmallows near apple trees and berry bushes. It was a slice of tranquility. Here they could sleep, enjoy misty mornings, and decompress.

Typically they would spend weekends there during the year. Come summer, they would base themselves there. Miller would commute by train daily; Newman, who loathed getting up early in the morning, sometimes stayed in the city during the week and took the train out on weekends. There Elisabeth played with other children, two of whom lived just across the country lane. This was a welcome change since she was often the only child in a group of adults.

If ever a retreat like West Redding was needed to decompress, it was during the boiling summer of August 1927. Two years after they bought the house, Newman was bereft. Italian immigrant anarchists Nicola Sacco and Bartolomeo Vanzetti, who were convicted of robbery and murder in July 1921, were executed at midnight on Wednesday, August 24, 1927. "There is no place for sunshine today," Newman wrote to Miller. "The rain, and the slight wind, the clouded and somber sky is more to my liking to-day. It somehow fits in with an aching heart and a very weary mind!"[39] The incident became a cause célèbre among the immigrant, working-class, and labor communities who also identified as outsiders. Coming during a period of intense labor unrest in the country, the trial, conviction, and impending execution of the two men meant they too could be denied their rights and cast aside.

Earlier that morning, Newman had dropped Elisabeth off in Connecticut and then driven to Bethel, where, before boarding the local train to New York City, she found herself in want of a newspaper. She couldn't find one. She tried again in South Norwalk when she changed trains. The newsstand was closed. Then "on entering the train, however," she saw a man sleeping with a newspaper spread out beside him. She was so desperate to know the news that she picked up the paper "and there I saw that there is no hope left."[40]

The paper reprinted the letter Sacco wrote to his son Dante. Reading it, Newman could no longer control herself "and wept all the way into the City." From Grand Central Station she headed to the community church. It turned into a "death watch" meeting, so she left. Before getting to the league headquarters, she got a cup of coffee with a colleague. Someone asked her to speak to the group now assembled. Newman said yes but worried she wouldn't get through it without crying. A delegation of ILGWU members from Boston soon arrived. One look at the faces of those already gathered told them everything. Edna St. Vincent Millay's plea to the judge didn't help. There was to be no reprieve: "A grown [*sic*] from all of us, sobbing, tears, men, big men weeping and standing silently with heads down . . . It was the saddest meeting I have ever lived through."[41]

Afterward the group walked from Fifth Avenue to Union Square, where they watched a squad of police break up a small protest. From there "an old group of men and women I knew when hope was in my heart that a better, more just day is ahead of us" went to Child's and sipped coffee and tea and waited.[42] The friends tried their best to comfort each other. But what Newman really wanted was Miller:

> My dear girl—I am sorry you were not with me last evening. I wanted, tho it be only sorrow—to share it with you. I am terribly up-set, and the nervous strain is hard to bear . . . And as I said last night, "their agony

> is over, but the shame, the grief, the suffering of the great wrong, the disgrace of our laws and courts—are ours to endure!" It is still raining, and the heart is heavy while the spirit wanders toward you—where it might find some peace; Pauline.[43]

Fifty years after the execution, Massachusetts governor Michael Dukakis declared that the two men had not received a fair trial and proclaimed August 23 as Sacco and Vanzetti Memorial Day.

Two years had passed since that dreadful day in August. Now Newman and Miller climbed aboard a boat, looking forward to a leisurely ride up the Hudson River. It was June 8, 1929, and the Roosevelts had invited three hundred New York WTUL members to Hyde Park to celebrate the twenty-fifth anniversary of the organization's founding. More than eighty-one miles separated Lower Manhattan from Hyde Park. In the former, people still lived cheek to jowl inside dark tenements. The latter boasted fifteen rooms where ancestral portraits hung on the walls and one counted Frederick and Louise Vanderbilt as neighbors.

Although Eleanor did not join the WTUL until 1923, she had long been involved in its mission, as well as that of the League of Women Voters. While her husband was governor, she chaired the New York league's finance and education committee. A few years later, she launched the nonprofit furniture factory Val-Kill Industries, with her friends Nancy Cook, Marion Dickerman, and Caroline O'Day. Franklin, former assistant secretary of the US Navy and now governor of New York, would soon be nursing a defeat from an unsuccessful run for the vice presidency on a ticket headed by Ohio governor James Cox.

When they arrived that late spring afternoon, Newman, now nearly thirty-three, and Miller, nearly thirty, gathered with the other women, some familiar like Frances Perkins. Tables covered with white linens dotted the lawn of the 110-acre estate. The picturesque setting allowed Franklin and Eleanor, who had developed a keen political sense, to make clear that they stood on the side of labor reform, social reform, and women's issues.

Schneiderman, wearing a drapey white linen dress, sat at a small round table with a smiling Franklin Roosevelt, his trademark cigar in hand. The former cap maker had risen through the ranks and was now a fund-raiser and administrator. She now counted the Roosevelts among her friends. When the WTUL had convened the International Congress of Working Women in Washington, DC, earlier that year, Eleanor had extended a lunch invitation to the US delegation, of which Newman was a member. Soon after, the trade union women were attending frequent Sunday dinners at the Roosevelts' Sixty-Fifth Street brownstone in New York City. Over cold drinks and light fare they discussed wages, collective bargaining, union membership, and working conditions. These dining room table discussions helped to shape policy as it became clearer that organizing wasn't enough. Legislation was needed.

At the end of the day, Roosevelt handed Schneiderman a check for thirty thousand dollars to pay off the mortgage on the New York WTUL building. The afternoon closed with league members doing a song and dance pageant that Mary Dreier had written—a sober subject for a celebratory day: reenacting the 1909 Triangle Shirtwaist Factory fire.

As Newman headed back to New York City, she decided that she agreed with Schneiderman: Hyde Park was a respite indeed. Here they had the illusion of being cloistered from the grind of politics.

Newman's mouth tasted of copper; she had several broken teeth, and livid bruises covered her left leg and hand. Some months after that bright afternoon in Hyde Park, Newman was in a serious car accident. The timing was terrible. She was running for sheriff and was now in no shape to campaign. The Socialist Party had nominated her once again—this time for what has traditionally been a "man's job."[44] She had enthusiastically accepted the nomination, only to be derailed by the accident. She was quite irritated, but the campaign would have to continue without her.[45] Friends wrote, offering words of support, telling her she would have made a better sheriff than any other candidate.[46] Her failed run for sheriff was the last time she sought elected office. She would turn her attention to matters of women's rights and health, the ERA, and changing male-dominated leadership.

A year later Newman would put all thoughts of campaigning to rest as she again worked for a minimum wage. She reminded people that thirty years earlier, home production had moved from the fireside to the factory, and young girls were sent into the factories not only untrained but also without any bargaining power or any knowledge of how to organize: "We were ignorant as we were cheap. We accepted what was given us. We needed the jobs, so we did not ask any questions." As a result, women not only unknowingly became the undercutters of men's wages, but they were also kept below the level of subsistence.[47] That had to change. Further stressing her point, Newman wrote a letter to the editor of the *New York Times*. In it she suggested that opponents of a minimum wage bill switch places "with the girls, let us say in a cannery at the rate of 8 cents an hour? Or in an upstate garment shop at the rate of 37 cents a day?"[48]

Through the next several years, Miller would continue to ascend. By 1935 she would head the New York State Labor Department. As an alumna of University of Chicago later wrote, Miller's appointment was a testament to "the liberality of Mr. Roosevelt and perhaps in Al Smith. I am not sure how long Miss Miller has been with the Department but the great point about Mr. Roosevelt is that, and that was the oldest argument of the Suffragists, he really appoints the best person he can find for the job and if she happens to wear petticoats that fact does not blind him to her professional qualifications."[49] It was a position that required Miller to often be away from home. Feeling left behind, Newman would be excited to open their letter box and discover Miller's signature forest green ink on the outside of an envelope.[50]

While Miller was spending the holiday season in South America, Newman was helping Roosevelt and the WTUL mark the holiday season. Even six years after the October 29, 1929, stock market crash triggered the Great Depression, the members of the WTUL made sure to celebrate holidays. Since 1923, Eleanor Roosevelt had made it a tradition to host a Christmas party for the poor children of the WTUL, both at Hyde Park and at its headquarters. Sara Roosevelt held the door open for a gaggle of children and their mothers. It was Christmastime and Hyde Park was festooned with decorations. Inside, a fire crackled; ornaments bobbed from pine branches. Beneath the Christmas tree lay gifts wrapped in red paper, one for each child. The children gave a holiday performance written by Mary Dreier. At headquarters each child would receive a toy, an article of clothing, an orange, an apple, and a box of candy. There was always ice cream and cake. After the last gift was opened and the treats were boxed up, the league ladies, including Newman and the First Lady, went over to the Henry Street Settlement at 99 Park Avenue for tea.[51] It wouldn't be long before Newman again saw the First Lady.

11

Eight Days in the White House

"A waitress, a stenographer, and a dress maker from New York, and a textile worker from Alabama have unpacked their bags in the Lincoln Room of the White House," where, for the next eight days "they would sleep between governmental sheets and breakfast upon Federal fare."[1] Newman pinched herself. She stretched her arms and legs and wiggled her toes. Here she was about to go to sleep inside the White House. The icebox in the kitchen would be left unlocked—in case anyone wanted a midnight snack.

It was May 1936, and the White House was hosting a delegation of labor activists for the first time. And not just for an afternoon but for an entire week. The invitation marked how closely aligned the Roosevelts were with the mission and people of the ILGWU and the WTUL, as well as the degree to which those on the political left saw a renewed chance for change.[2] Two years earlier, Sister Margaret De Maggio, a rank-and-file member of the ILGWU, attended the White House to present plaques to First Lady Eleanor Roosevelt and President Franklin Roosevelt to honor their work and to commemorate the first anniversary of the New Deal.[3] A new era had begun.

When Roosevelt took the oath of office on March 4, 1933, while placing his hand on the leather-bound, Dutch-language Bible that held centuries of Roosevelt family names, he had an idea of the scope of the social programs he would seek to pass. As the Great Depression continued and unemployment remained in the double digits, the labor unions increased their pressure on the government to deal with what they saw as widespread economic injustice.[4] Five days after being sworn in, Roosevelt sent the Emergency Banking Act to Congress. Drafted by former president

Herbert Hoover's top advisors, it was a means of reopening banks under US Treasury supervision. The administration established several agencies designed to protect workers' rights and stabilize the economy. By July 1933 the US Employment Service counted 192 offices in 120 cities and 23 states. By June 1943 it would register 12.5 million people.[5] A year after Roosevelt was inaugurated, the National Housing Act passed. Essentially the act meant that private lenders could loan money for home purchases knowing that if a borrower didn't repay them, the government would.

The impact of these actions on labor and working women was mixed.[6] On the one hand, the National Labor Relations Act (NLRA) gave workers the right to organize and bargain collectively. The Social Security Act meant people would receive retirement benefits and unemployment insurance. On the other hand, the New Deal tended to reinforce traditional gender roles, thereby limiting the opportunities for working women. For example, the NLRA excluded domestic workers and agricultural workers from coverage because Southern Democrats opposed extending labor protections to both of these groups, who were overwhelmingly female and Black. Additionally, the Social Security Act provided benefits to married women based on their husbands' salaries rather than what they themselves earned. This not only discouraged women from working outside the home, but it also made it more difficult for them to gain any semblance of financial independence.

The First Lady was not there to welcome the group when they arrived at 1600 Pennsylvania Avenue. She was in New York City dining with her daughter, Anna, and two of Anna's friends.[7] Instead, President Roosevelt greeted the women and then a steward showed them to their rooms. Once they settled in, the president ushered them into a firelit parlor on the second-floor residence, where they ate a light supper. Afterward they retired to a sitting room, where, seated in an upholstered chair, the president was "chatty and nice." He told the women that his wife would take them on a tour of the staterooms and gardens in the morning after breakfast.[8] Then it was off to bed. Newman opened her valise and pulled out her pajamas from between her carefully pressed and folded suit. She washed her face and slipped into bed. Pulling the covers up, she "exclaimed over the proportions of Lincoln's bed, estimating it as 6 foot wide by 8 feet long, and the first time my toes didn't touch the end."[9]

Knowing meetings filled their schedule the next day, Newman acted as the "authoritarian older sister," warning the two other women they could count on being sent home if they overslept.[10] Outside the mullioned window, a silver sliver of light was all that was left in the midnight blue sky. If Newman were to reflect on the many moments, large and small, that culminated in this visit, she might have allowed herself a bit of satisfaction for all she had accomplished, including the rent strike she organized when she was but a teen and the establishment of the Union Health Centers. In another piece, this one for *Life and Labor*, Newman marveled that Americans had the right to vote: "When I left the school, one thought dominated my mind, to wit: Men and women from the time of Roger Williams to Iwo Jima fought and bled and died in order that I be free to vote my conviction!"[11]

This moment in the White House came at a time of widening cracks within the labor movement between Newman, Schneiderman, Lemlich, Dreier, and the younger generation. Now in their forties and fifties, their priorities had shifted, and some of the league's newer members seemed to favor communism, which, as far as Newman was concerned, was a deal breaker. Whereas Newman and her fellow socialists wanted to achieve a just and equitable society by working within the system, communists essentially favored overthrowing the capitalist system. Moreover, and more to the point of Newman's White House sleepover, the Socialist Party of America supported the New Deal whereas the Communist Party of America initially opposed it.

Nationwide, the effort to root out communists continued unabated. Since the Russian Revolution of 1917, the xenophobic search for a fifth column, of those suspected of being German spies and sympathizers, continued to intensify. The Department of Justice had launched the Palmer Raids back in November 1919 and January 1920, which saw the capture, arrest, and deportation of scores of suspected socialists, anarchists, and communists. In the early 1950s, Miller would become the subject of an FBI investigation while serving in the US Women's Bureau, which put her in a position to help continue to further shape many of the New Deal's programs. She spent much of her time away from Greenwich Village, zigzagging between Albany and Washington, DC, working on legislation surrounding minimum wage laws.

So it was that allegations of Miller's communist sympathies would dog her and temporarily restrict her access to government jobs.[12] She would eventually be cleared of the accusations. Newman didn't write about this episode in her datebooks, which she sometimes used as diaries. Still it's not difficult to imagine that the investigation tested their relationship, which in the confines of their apartment was not on equal footing, because as Miller rose through the ranks, Newman largely stayed home, trying to find a balance between work and taking care of Elisabeth and their apartment.

She felt Miller's absence most when spending weekends in West Redding. She found release in writing poems:

> For each star-lit night
> hall again whisper words of hope
> And the zephyrs shall again bring
> Dreams—old and new.
> And companionless as the moon
> I shall wander to places
> Long cherished and unforgotten.
> And though now alone
> I shall be the happier
> For the past.[13]

Nevertheless, now, in 1938, conservatives increased their efforts to root out public service officials they suspected of trying to infiltrate the government. And it was with this in mind that Mary Dreier wrote to Newman about how important it was for the WTUL to maintain a "rank conservative" appearance.[14] Newman resented being put in a position where she would have to appear to be more closely aligned with Republicans. After all, she had once led the largest rent strike in New York City. She had stood on the front lines of the 1909 Triangle Shirtwaist Factory fire strike. But she conceded the point. Maybe it was an age thing. Maybe, she kidded Dreier, she was getting too old: "Of course, I can understand, how our young members may be caught in a net of fine phrases, how high-sounding motives may thrill them . . . Personally, I would much rather see the League go out of existence than have it co-operate with Communist agencies. Conservative / Be it so."[15] It was Newman at her pragmatic best.

On a more upbeat note, it had been one year since the Wagner Act passed, birthing the National Labor Relations Act. The act set a minimum wage, gave employees the right to join unions, and obligated employers to bargain collectively with unions. The Wagner Act, named for Senator Robert Wagner of New York, came about because of numerous violent strikes. For example, on September 2, 1934, a gunfight erupted at the Trion Cotton Mill in Georgia, leaving two textile strikers dead and fifteen wounded.[16] Getting the act passed was a slog since it would mandate employers to either negotiate with unions in collective bargaining or face legal penalties. Critics, including men in the labor movement, argued it would rob men of much-needed jobs.[17] Republicans and business leaders, too, opposed the act, and the US Supreme Court also had a pattern of overturning state laws that regulated the workplace. Thus, Newman considered its passage a substantial victory. After all, the WTUL had spent decades pushing for a federal law that would set wage floors and hour ceilings as well as limit child labor.

The act came just a couple of years after New York State passed a statewide minimum wage law. It took the WTUL years to see the legislation pass, years of educating the public and lawmakers alike to see the need. "This law like other laws will serve its purpose only, when properly enforced," Newman wrote.[18] The way she saw it, minimum wage laws allowed people to enjoy financial independence and pursue their aspirations without becoming a "burden" to the state.

The hands of the clock ticked toward 7:00 a.m. Newman awoke before the alarm rang and roused the others. They traipsed downstairs to the family dining room, where, along with the First Lady, an abundant breakfast of fruit, scrambled eggs, bacon, and coffee awaited. "That's all, but plenty of it. Mrs. R is just as nice as she can be," Newman reflected.[19] Between sips of coffee and bites of toast, the New York delegation for the WTUL reviewed the agenda for the day's convention.

Many of the convention's sessions addressed the changing role of the ILGWU. A shift was happening in large part because mass production was gaining steam. As skills like cutting and pressing were not as highly in demand, union membership became predominantly female. At the same time, the leadership remained predominantly male and calcified in its outlook. On the ground, it was women like Schneiderman and Newman who were the tip of the spear. It was they who had called sixty thousand dressmakers to strike in 1933, three years earlier.

In afternoon and evening meetings during their week in the White House, Newman advised the First Lady and Secretary of Labor Frances Perkins how "unskilled, untrained girls are working now for low pay, just as we did 30 years ago. The word sweatshop today means long hours and low wages and does not carry the meaning of unsanitary conditions it used to have"; nevertheless, conditions were far from ideal. Newman let them know that even now some dress workers earned only 37 cents per day. Any silk dress selling for as low as $4.95 was a "sweatshop dress," she told them. She also told them about the "contraband" shops where management moved out before paying wages.[20]

Among the things Newman considered to be of the utmost importance was the inclusion of compulsory health insurance as part of a broader social safety net. She envisioned a tax-supported system of insurance that provided coverage for major illnesses and hospitalizations. Since the ILGWU Union Health Center had opened twenty-five years earlier, she saw firsthand the way illness wrecked the lives of too many men and women. She explained that she had met scores of people whose "homes were broken up because they could not meet the cost of needed medical care" and people who were either too proud or had too much inhibition to seek charity.[21]

However, as Newman explained to the Roosevelts and to Perkins, the free clinics were no longer enough to meet workers' needs. In her view, unions ought to be capable of providing affordable, preventive health care. Workers shouldn't have to pay between twenty and twenty-five dollars to see a specialist. The clinics were needed so that "diseases which could have been checked in their early stages are not allowed to eat into the system until they are beyond cure, families are left destitute and countless lives are lost."[22] The seeds for what would become President Harry S. Truman's plan for universal health care were planted. His 1945 proposal, which included federal financing and cost controls, represented an important step toward expanding access to health care in the United States. However, it ultimately failed to gain congressional support since the American Medical Association and conservative lawmakers vehemently opposed its passage.

A week later Newman was back in New York City, ensconced in her office, attending to correspondence. She penned a note to "dear Mrs. Roosevelt" thanking her for the privilege of being her guest. Newman wrote how much she enjoyed the informality and provocative discussion at breakfast. More important, the First Lady's "generous spirit, and above all, your *understanding* of our problems is something that I shall always remember with pleasure."[23]

After writing Roosevelt, Newman picked up a postcard from Miller again and reread it for what seemed like the umpteenth time. Miller was away again, this time in Lyon, France. At least she always remembered to write. This time Miller sent a card with lyrics to the song "Sur le pont, d'Avignon" on it. She told Newman to ask Elisabeth to sing the song, as she had learned it in school: "This is when I wish you and Elisabeth were with me. Much love, Fried."[24] This was the private Fried. In public the pair maintained a professional distance, using business language when working on projects together. Letters were signed, "Cordially yours, Fried S. Miller," or "Sincerely."[25]

After reading the card, Newman put it down and scooped up Elisabeth. It was errand day—time for a haircut and to buy new frames for her glasses. She had worn the same round style for decades and saw no reason to change now. She spent eight dollars on jodhpurs. Elisabeth adored riding and was becoming an accomplished rider, competing in Connecticut. And then she did "well[,] a million other little things to attend to and holding down a job besides—will convince you that the reason I did not write sooner was not because I did not wish to write. So that is that."[26] It was an outburst of frustration that reflected how it sometimes chafed her to be the one responsible for ticking off the seemingly never-ending list of mundane responsibilities while Miller was away—again. "I guess partly because my mother was responsible for me she occasionally tried to discipline me, whereas Pauline would—well, of course P was always serious about me, she'd never say oh, just go ahead and do whatever it is, but she always indulged me when she could, you know," Elisabeth recalled.[27]

After completing their errands, they drove to West Redding, where Newman spent a weekend taking off storm doors, "putting on the screens, unpacking, getting the meals (how do you like that? And we are still alive, too!)," she joked. Saturday ran into Sunday and then it was back to New York, where, between the constant interruptions of a ringing telephone and taking care of Elisabeth, she managed to write to Miller to complain about the ERA.[28]

Newman typed feverishly. Her diatribe repeated the refrain that the ERA would increase the exploitation of women workers and jeopardize protective legislation that she deemed essential for the health of mothers. "We oppose the so-called ERA because it disregards the fact that while men and women are equal in rights they are not identical in economic and social functions or in physical capacity," she wrote.[29] The issue had never gone away. Feeling pugnacious, Newman called the ERA proponents "selfish careerists," who were "economically unsound and intellectually confused" and didn't care one bit about low-income women.[30] On the flip side, those who supported the ERA slapped unions as being communist traitors to the American way of life.

The New York League of Women Voters also opposed the bill, arguing that its passage would result in the end of protective legislation. Newman still maintained the ERA was redundant because of "the idea of opening on something [we] already have . . . If a woman chooses to open a barber shop or a blacksmith shop, she has only to supply the equipment, open the doors and serve customers—if any come. If a railway tunnel is to be bored through a mountain, the law does not say that only men shall do it."[31] Once she finished, Newman pulled the letter from the typewriter and, before tucking it in an envelope, added a handwritten postscript. Having run out of steam, she told Miller, "My love to you is all I can say just now. Your Pauline."[32]

It had been years since Newman expounded from atop a soapbox, so long that Elisabeth, who was now almost the same age Newman had been when she led the rent strike, not only seemed to underappreciate Newman's workplace achievements; she also seemed to be perpetually comparing Miller and Newman. "As I grew up I realized I admired my mother more. Now, I'm talking as a child. My mother had more social graces, she was rather beautiful when she was young, and I identified with her. Now that doesn't mean I didn't love Pauline." But it wasn't until much later that Elisabeth had the chance to see Newman in her working role. "I sort of wish I had seen her talking to a picket line or something when I was about 12 or 13, I think that would have been impressive to me," Elisabeth said.[33]

Shortly before Valentine's Day 1938, Newman testified before the subcommittee of the Judiciary Committee on the proposed Equal Rights Amendment to the Constitution in 1938.[34] During her appearance she reminded the committee members of her stance: The ERA was bad policy. And she should know. As someone who went to work in a factory when she was just a child, as an organizer for her own union, and as an officer of the WTUL, she understood the issue in a way that not one of the committee members could. She explained how most working women believed the ERA would never end workplace discrimination since such discrimination is "based on deep rooted social prejudices rather than on legal differences. This amendment will not outlaw these prejudices. It cannot."[35] Specific legislation was needed, not a blanket amendment.

From Newman's perspective, passage of the ERA would undoubtedly result in chaos, confusion, and endless litigation. As Dorothy Straus, chair of the Campaign Committee against the Equal Rights Amendment, wrote, it would be foolish to compromise the solid gains women had made to improve their civil and legal status in return for "a vague promise of 'equality' which no one can explain?"[36] Quite simply, Newman said, it was a bad law and the committee ought to send it "where it rightfully belongs—the waste basket!"[37]

Also that February, a month before the Anschluss between Germany and Austria, and nine months before Orson Welles broadcast "The War of the Worlds," a Halloween episode of the radio series *The Mercury Theatre on the Air*, New York City was still mired in economic troubles. It was true that unemployment, once 25 percent in 1933, had fallen to 17 percent in 1938. It was true that the economy had steadied, thanks to the creation of the Securities and Exchange Commission and the Federal Deposit Insurance Corporation. It was also true that newly established agencies like the Civilian Conservation Corps and the Works Progress Administration meant people could work. Yet, as much as these programs strengthened the social safety net, many Americans were left out—like Black Americans, particularly Black women. Moreover, the New Deal increased the national debt by billions of dollars and, as some critics argued, handed too much power to the federal government.[38] Nevertheless, as Roosevelt continued to push his program, legislators on a subcommittee of the Senate Judiciary Committee were once again considering the ERA. It was the fifteenth time Congress would do so.[39]

Winter yielded to spring, spring to summer. All the while, the committee debated and Newman and her colleagues waited. That August she received an invitation from Mary Dreier inviting her, Miller, and Elisabeth to spend time at her home on Fernald Point in Southwest Harbor, Maine. As tempting as it was to accept an invitation to "eat haddock and go fishing" and to give Elisabeth a chance to spend time with girls her age, Newman declined.[40] Fighting the ERA was taking all of her time. Schneiderman wrote to Cordell Hull to explain that the phrase "equal rights" was vague and misleading. Moreover, it would not ensure equal opportunity for women.[41] The WTUL kept up the constant barrage of letters and opinion pieces. They enjoyed the support of Eleanor Roosevelt. But keeping the amendment "on ice in the committee" wouldn't work much longer. They must kill it.[42]

Although Newman, now fifty-two, no longer engaged in much grassroots organizing, she once again found herself on the road.[43] Newman traveled from Birmingham, Alabama, to Boston and points in between. In Vermont she lent strike assistance to marble workers. In Chicago she helped organize domestic workers and hosiery workers. In Huntsville, Alabama, she helped laundry workers, and in Kansas City she helped telegraphers and bookbinders to organize. Then it was off to Racine, Wisconsin, where she aided bakers and culinary workers.[44] The amount of travel was dizzying, and it also meant she and Miller were exchanging letters in lieu of having one-on-one time.

It was December 1940, just a few months after Roosevelt won another four years in the White House. Life inside the apartment on West Eleventh Street was far from tranquil. Newman and Miller's secret was about to unravel. Newly graduated from high school, Elisabeth was now seventeen. Miller took her on a cruise through Guatemala to celebrate the occasion. However, Miller seemed morose for much of the trip. One evening, before the band stopped playing, she returned to their cabin. Elisabeth followed, unsure of why her mother was so downcast. Her mother was never one to easily share her feelings.[45] But then she started crying. Shaken, Elisabeth asked her why she was so sad. "'I have to tell you—you're my real daughter,'" Elisabeth's son Michael Owen said when relaying the story decades later.[46] That Miller had successfully concealed this information for so long was in part because she put a lot of stock in the way others viewed her, regardless that she, Newman, and Elisabeth had always been accepted as family.

"My mother lived with her secret. Pauline abetted her in this. My mother was probably very glad she did give birth to me, but that does not mean that her life was easy or that my life as a young person was easy," Elisabeth wrote many decades later in her diary:

> My mother was a well-educated, healthy woman, in a better position than many to manage under difficult conditions. She did not manage to achieve a fully satisfactory life but she did lead a good and very respectable life. In my opinion she paid a high price and so did I. I was hurt by the lack of a father. How I felt that injustice! How I was tormented by it! How could I ever expect anyone to love me if I didn't know who my father was?[47]

Newman was just about to check out of the Hotel Metropolitano in Guayaquil, Ecuador, where she had attended a labor conference, when she heard someone shout her name. Mail awaited. She and Miller still wrote each other nearly every day, mostly about the mundane little things that stitch a life together, like a freezer that needed repairing or that Elisabeth was fighting a cold. In Quito, Peru, Newman wrote to "Fried and Elisabeth" to announce she was homeward bound. "I thank the gods for this since I am here and also—so far—I came near death, that being here seems a miracle," she said, adding that the trip couldn't end soon enough.[48]

The harrowing "near death" tale began when Newman and her group decided to do a little shopping. Nothing enticed her, so some of the passengers decided to fly back to Guayaquil. They urged Newman to join them. When Newman, who was afraid of heights, learned the plane would fly over the Andes, she decided to ride the six hours back by Jeep. She looked forward to seeing the highlands and its people. Newman was riding with a group of people when their Jeep careened and slid into a ditch. They wrestled their way out of the vehicle and slogged through the rain, the mud pulling at their feet. All was going rather well until a landslide almost buried the group.

Now she was safe, reclining on a lounge chair above deck as she traveled back to New York by ship. After her sun bath, she returned to her cabin for a shower. For someone who once traveled in steerage, she couldn't believe the luxury of the accommodations. She also wished for the company of Miller and Elisabeth: "As it is, I am always thinking, wondering whether all is well with you. At times I get no rest less that I wake myself. It's awful to be away from those you love—for me anyway . . . Much love to you both from Paul.[49]

Back on the deck, she filled out her customs forms. She wasn't sorry the trip was about to end, as she had been restless the last two days thinking about home. "This gnawing feeling can make [me] most unhappy, and I'll be glad to get home and hope that this feeling of something impending was nothing more than the longing for my loved ones," she wrote from the deck of the *Santa Clara*.[50] A brilliant sun was pinned to the deep blue sky and the tiniest whitecaps interrupted an otherwise calm sea.

A few months later, the tropical sun was but a faint memory as the skies in New York turned gunmetal gray. It was Elisabeth's eighteenth birthday and Miller and Newman were hosting her classmates for dinner. The celebration was interrupted by the news: Japanese airplanes had attacked Pearl Harbor. The United States was officially at war.

Three days later the board of the WTUL of America declared its full-fledged support in a letter to Roosevelt: "Knowing that our goal of ultimate good will not be achieved w/o safeguarding the four freedoms for which we are fighting, we urge that in these days of stress a program will be adopted that includes (a) the rest of a Council, with equal representation of government, industry and labor, to set the pattern of conduct for labor & industry; and (b) the abolition of discrimination against Negroes and other minority groups."[51]

When 353 Imperial Japanese aircraft attacked Pearl Harbor on December 7, 1941, an estimated 13 million women, or 28 percent, populated the American workforce; by the end of the war in 1945, about 34 percent women worked outside the home.[52] They fixed power lines, flew planes, and drove tractors. The made munitions, farmed, and helped manufacture uniforms. The war demanded this seismic shift in society, which would have great consequences for women on their personal lives, the lives of their families, and the way industry was organized. Women were working in all sectors of the economy once dominated by men, from manual jobs to office jobs.

Six months before Pearl Harbor, President Roosevelt signed Executive Order 8802, which helped eliminate discrimination in the US defense industry and led to the Fair Employment Practices Committee, which was tasked with monitoring hiring practices. In short, it declared that women who worked in wartime production should receive equal pay for their work. Even so, significant wage disparities existed. White women had more opportunity and higher wages compared with women of color.

Miller, one year into her job as head of the Division of Women in Industry at the New York State Department of Labor, was now spending a considerable amount of time in Albany. Perkins had referred her for the position, which called for her to formulate a plan to reintegrate women into the economic sector after the GIs returned home. Because Newman was traveling about the state, the two women were able to see each other. With Elisabeth now pursuing a degree in economics at Vassar College in Poughkeepsie, New York, Newman felt less of a pull toward home. When she did visit Miller, they dined with friends and, as Newman's daybooks show, the two frequently played penny-ante poker with their friends.

All told, Newman visited about 150 factories with government defense contracts. It quickly became apparent to her that the factories were not paying women the same wages that men received for the same work. Employers evaded paying the same wage because they could insist that men and women were actually doing different work. It was also virtually impossible to enforce Roosevelt's executive order. This further underscored her belief that a law was necessary to codify equal pay for equal work. In two years' time, Thomas Dewey, the state's Republican governor, would sign the Todd-Falk Bill, which outlawed pay discrimination in New York State on the basis of sex. Equal pay would not be attained on the federal level until 1963 when Congress passed the Equal Pay Protection Act.

In her travels about the state to see if women were earning the same as men, Newman learned that skilled female workers earned $31.21 a week compared to their male counterparts, who earned about $54.65 for similar work. As she collected this information, she had little time to absorb the news that Mary Dreier, her close friend for more than three decades, was ill. She paused to reflect on their friendship and how much of Dreier's "soul and indomitable spirit" was imprinted on the WTUL, from Halloween parties to picnics, from books they read and exchanged to the music they so enjoyed:[53]

> Let me see, how long is it since we first met—then, twenty, thirty—thirty five years, is it not? Years which your friendship has illuminated and made more enduring: years during which your association has given me cause to have faith in humanity; years that have obliterated differences of background and experiences—leaving a clear field for mutual interest and common understanding—the only basis on which real friendship must rest.[54]

Before Miller departed for England as special assistant for labor with Ambassador John Gilbert Winant, in 1943, she and Newman sat down for their one and only joint interview with a local New York radio station, in which Newman said:

> The slogan of equal pay for equal work is an old one. Women have continually fought to obtain the same rate of wages for themselves as is paid to men for the same work. This demand was based upon the

> principle of common equality and simple justice as well as the dictates of economic necessity. Today that demand is just as valid,—just as necessary—and for the same reason: But because it affects so many more women it is now increasingly important. However, the habits of employers of looking upon women as a cheaper labor supply has continued even where women have actually replaced men.[55]

After the interview, Newman saw her partner of twenty years off. Miller sailed across the Atlantic to a life of meetings, cocktail parties, weekends in Kent, and heated policy debates.[56]

As Newman curled up in an easy chair beneath the prints from Latin America, a pile of biographies and writings by Dickens and Chekov, at her feet later that night in their living room, she could not know that this was the beginning of the unraveling of their relationship. The letters between the two women would keep apace, but although they spoke mostly of work, legislation, and Elisabeth, Newman's simmering resentments about her seemingly never-ending quotidian chores sometimes surfaced.

As the trees dressed in russet and gold, signaling the arrival of autumn, Newman occupied herself with selling the West Redding house. The Connecticut property, encircled by the woods and close enough to New York City, had served them well, but now their eye was on a charming little place in Coffeetown, situated in Lehigh County, Pennsylvania. Still, as she signed the papers and started packing up the house, she felt like she was packing up one of the happiest periods of her life. "You, your mother and I will miss our home there. But you, I believe, will miss it even more. You were so very, very young, about two years old, I think when we bought the place. I can see you now toddling along, looking at every tree and flower," she wrote to Elisabeth, who was now twenty and finishing her education at Vassar College. "But, I shall remember those years always—years during which I was happy to see you grow and watch your beauty and sweetness. This and this alone gave meaning and a new purpose in life."[57]

Then it was almost Miller's birthday. Newman knew that Miller, whose fifty-third birthday approached, wanted photos and did not want to disappoint. However, as Elisabeth later recounted, Newman was never keen about having her picture taken and thought Miller could just imagine her with a few more gray strands, a tired look, or a line here and there.[58] Instead of sending a present, Newman wrote that she hoped Miller would be there in person to celebrate—before the invasion started.[59]

More to the point, Newman made clear her feelings that Miller should come home—if not for her, then for Elisabeth, who only wanted to spend time with her mother. Perhaps part of the reason she had never been completely open with Newman was because she resented her for being the one who was there all the time. Elisabeth's feelings for Miller were deeper, both because Miller was her biological mother and because in her eyes Miller was the more respectable of the two. Newman recognized the imbalance, and whatever hurt or slight she felt by that she kept to herself. Instead she constantly wrote to Miller, who was emotionally unavailable much of the time, saying that Elisabeth needed Miller, her advice, and her companionship. Moreover, she knew she was not, nor did she wish to be, a substitute for Miller.[60] Yet, she told Miller, Elisabeth was "entitled to have you to consult with about a job and perhaps other things. I feel very deeply about that and I only hope you will agree with me . . . Moreover, I think that the longer you stay away the harder it will be to re-establish connections—if you know what I mean. You have been out of the picture for some time."[61]

Newman felt untethered with Elisabeth away at Vassar College and Miller overseas in London. Of course, they wrote to each other; they never stopped writing to each other. Now more than ever, with the impending invasion and continued German blitz of London, fear of Miller trapped beneath the rubble kept her awake most nights, always sure something terrible had happened: "The moment the press reported the bombings, and the radios elaborated upon the events I cabled, and waited from the 19th of Feb. until the 29th before your cable arrived! It was awful!"[62] She didn't exhale until she heard directly from the State Department that all was okay. She couldn't arrive soon enough to suit her and Elisabeth.[63]

12

Miles of Ruins

Four years after Hitler committed suicide in a bunker on April 30, 1945, ending the war in Europe, and the Boeing B-29 Superfortress *Bockscar* dropped the 10,800-pound plutonium bomb "Fat Boy" on Nagasaki on August 6, 1945, ending the war with Japan, Newman picked her way through a rubble-strewn street in Germany. At sixty-two she no longer felt so agile. She had landed in West Germany in September 1949 at the behest of the US State Department to review factory conditions, lend her expertise to German trade unions, and help manage labor relations involving women workers. It was all part of America's ambitious postwar plan to export democracy and curb communism.

For ninety days Newman would zigzag across the country from Frankfurt to Munich, Nuremberg to Stuttgart, and points in between. Together with Sarah Southall, an expert in labor conditions, Newman would visit knitting and weaving factories, a foundry and a leather shop, and a factory that produced telephone parts. Along the way she would meet with industrialists, bankers, manufactures, and workers. Each meeting, each tour was intended to help rebuild the trade union movement that the Third Reich had so thoroughly destroyed.[1] Ironically, two years earlier Congress had overturned the veto of President Truman and enacted the Taft-Hartley Act, which regulates labor unions and what they can do in national emergencies. "Reaction is in the saddle again," Newman wrote to her longtime friend Margaret Bondfield.[2] Though 1949 was almost at an end, this trip to West Germany, which was the most significant thing Newman had done so far that year, boosted her both personally and professionally.

The time Newman and Miller had spent together in the months leading up to Newman's trip was devoid of the tension that had peppered so much of the past few years. She and Miller had rung in the New Year with friends. Earlier that year the pair treated themselves to their favorite pastimes, going to the theater and the movies. They enjoyed several plays, including *The Madwoman of Chaillot*, by French dramatist Jean Giraudoux, which concerned an eccentric woman living in Paris and struggling against the straitlaced authority figures in her life. They also sat rapt while watching *Mr. Roberts*, an adaptation of Thomas Heggen's 1946 novel about his experiences aboard the *USS Rotanin* and the *USS Virgo* in the South Pacific during World War II.[3]

Elisabeth, now twenty-six, was also making her way in the world. Having graduated from Vassar College, she had recently joined the International Labor Organization. Working in the former League of Nations Building, near the Lake of Geneva, Elisabeth was researching and doing editorial work, concentrating on women in the workplace, vocational training, and manpower. She was also becoming an accomplished economist. While working in Geneva in the later 1940s, she met Arthur David Kemp Owen. Born in 1904, David, as she called him, was nineteen years her senior. A graduate of Leeds University in England, Owen was a leading administrator and rising star in the newly established United Nations.

As Newman packed for her trip to Germany, she traced her finger along the white holly leaves and birds that decorated the red Christmas card from Miller. "Well, I hope it will not be too long before we will be together once again. It can't be too soon for me," Miller had written.[4] Newman put the card in her drawer, atop the recent Valentine's Day card showing a black kitten on the outside and a printed message on the inside that said, "A little note to YOU from me to tell you that I think we could make some PURR-FECT harmony!" Miller had added her own playful message: "What do *you* think? A little 'something' will follow."[5]

Now Newman stood in the midst of roofless apartment blocks and cratered streets and that Valentine's Day card was a world away, literally and figuratively. Here there were staircases that went nowhere; apartment buildings where rats were landlord and tenant; endless, snaking lines for bread, lines for fruit, lines for meat. Here a corner of a building remained. There a façade, with one intact window, underneath which a box of late-blooming roses flowered.[6] As she wrote to Rose Schneiderman, "It was a grim place for adults, let alone for children. No hope for improving their existence because Germany has no money. Nothing, nothing to look forward to, and yet they will welcome this rather than endure the life in the Russian zone!"[7] The construction crews faced a Sisyphean task.

Always a keen observer, Newman wrote draft after draft of what she saw, trying to make sense of the postwar landscape and America's place in it. She was working on a column for *Life and Labor* and finding it nearly impossible to adequately convey the degree of destruction and devastation she saw. She struggled to find the precise words to show the desperation carved into the faces of women who preferred living in rat-infested basements rather than the Soviet zone. "No one who has not seen it can even imagine," Newman wrote in a pre-Christmas column titled "It Hasn't All Been Easy" for the *Life and Labor* bulletin.[8]

Between visits to knitting factories and speaking with small groups of miners, Newman decided it was time to confront the horror of Nazi Germany's genocide-industrial complex. So late one December morning, she stood in the drizzle at the entrance to Dachau, located just eleven miles from Munich. It was the first of more than 4,400 concentration camps the Nazis established. The US military authority had returned the grounds to the Bavarian state just the year before. In silence she read the sign affixed to an iron gate noting that 240,000 men, women, and children were murdered there by the Germans. Seeing what she described as a place of "sadistic horror" left an indelible mark on her memory: "Here is the place where the blood hounds were kept—ready to pounce upon any one who attempted to escape. Here is the grave where the victims were buried en masse, here are trees—straight and sturdy, called the 'hanging trees,' from which countless human beings were hung. I am sick at heart. But I walk on."[9] She walked on to a building of gray brick and stone. Upon entering the large room, she learned that it was here where, before being gassed, victims were forced to undress for what they were told would be a shower. Upon leaving Dachau, Newman looked westward. The clouds had parted, she wrote, but her "heart ached and my mind was weary."[10]

In the article, Newman tiptoed up to, but did not delve into, what it meant as a Lithuanian Jew to stand in an extermination camp where her extended family was, quite possibly, murdered. She wrote with ease about how painful it was in a global sense, but, unlike the way she shared her personal experience and thoughts about what it was like to labor as a child in unsafe working conditions, she never once revealed what it meant to her personally.

After her visit, Newman returned to her hotel in Munich. As was her custom, she put pen to paper. Her account was widely read and discussed among her peers, many of whom reached out afterward to share their thoughts. Friends like Harry Wemple told her it wasn't until he read the piece, "which pictured those conditions with such stark clarity, that I fully sensed their enormity and their diabolical atrociousness."[11]

Shortly after Newman's visit, another colleague, Irvin R. Kuenzli, secretary-treasurer of the American Federation of Teachers, visited the camp. He snapped a series of Kodachrome pictures while walking along the train tracks that once had conducted so many lives to their deaths. Kuenzli wrote to Newman after the visit, a visit that, he said, shook him to his core. He also said he was deeply afraid that if the United States failed to reestablish labor unions, Nazism would reemerge: "I certainly agree that Nazism is not dead. The higher education is full of it. It was my feeling that the organized labor movement is the last resort in implementing school reform and that if school reform fails, World War III is almost a certainty."[12] Newman's article made such an impression among those who read it because, aside from reporting by journalists like Martha Gellhorn, the Holocaust in 1949 was not yet widely and openly discussed. Newman shared Kuenzli's concern. She too believed Germany would never be "free of the old ways and the old difficulties" without supporting unions.[13]

From Dachau, Newman traveled 140 miles to Nuremberg, where she and Southall spent an afternoon visiting a radio factory. Not one employee spoke of the war crimes trials that had been held just three years earlier. Instead, the conversation remained focused on labor relations: how to organize and form a union. It was as if a collective amnesia gripped the populace. In Berchtesgaden, where Hitler had a home in the German Alps, Southall convinced Newman to climb aboard a bus that would drive six thousand feet to the top. That and the fact that getting to the top meant riding in an elevator for the last four hundred feet almost deterred her, she wrote Miller: "Well, you know me, I did not want to go—was really scared—but would I miss it? No! So I went up and decided that the reason Hitler did not have any unemployment was because he had God knows, how many people building this damned thing!"[14] At the top they found three inches of snow.

After Berchtesgaden, Newman and Southall traveled directly to a shoe factory. They checked into the Graf Zeppelin Hotel that evening, rising early the next morning. Newman gamely sat for an interview with both the English and German press. She also squeezed in time for a reporter from the military newspaper *Stars and Stripes*. Newman took any opportunity to spread the word of their mission.

After three months abroad, Newman and Southall had accumulated more than enough material to prepare their "Report on Status of Women in Industry and Trade Unions in Germany" for the High Commissioner. It was an ungainly title for a simple message: It was imperative to consider the psychological effects of defeat and destruction as the United States helped reorient the German economy. Essentially the report advised that it was essential to bolster unions to act as a bulwark against any residual totalitarian tendencies that might lie just below the rubble of war-torn streets.[15]

Upon her return to the States, Newman was selected to sit on numerous international commissions, including the newly established United Nations Subcommittee on the Status of Women and the United Nations' International Labor Organizations. Both Miller and Schneiderman also served in the ILO; together they worked to change night-work laws around the world for women and children.

These appointments came on the heels of the dissolution of the WTUL. Back in April 1949, after thirty-one years as head of the WTUL and forty-five years in the labor movement, Schneiderman decided to step down. Upon Rose's retirement, Eleanor Roosevelt hosted a luncheon in her honor at a restaurant called Sherry's in New York City. During the small affair, to which only close associates and friends like Newman were invited, Schneiderman was presented with thirty-one American Beauty roses. Each bloom symbolized her more than three decades of service.[16] At sixty-seven, Schneiderman yearned to spend time pursuing her hobbies. One year after she retired, in June 1950, the WTUL held its last board meeting. A contemplative Newman remarked how the indefatigable women created allyships among and between classes, boosting the leadership roles of women. She also recognized that the nature of the labor fights was changing and that in time many other sectors would need organizing, from domestic and migrant workers to professors and government employees.

At the same time that Newman was navigating her new role as more of a labor organizer emeritus than direct activist, Miller was helping Elisabeth with wedding preparations. The occasion highlighted Newman's complicated position in their small family. Newman was not asked to be involved in the arrangements, and when Elisabeth and Owen married, only Miller's name would appear on the simply engraved wedding invitation despite Newman's close relationship with Elisabeth.[17] Owen became under-secretary-general for Economic Affairs and chairman of the Technical Assistance Board of the United Nations. The couple welcomed two sons in quick succession, Michael in 1952 and Hugh in 1954. Newman and Miller doted on the boys, Newman frequently babysitting them.

Michael Owen remembered that because his father worked for the United Nations, there "was a constant parade of people from all over the world who to me probably seemed a lot stranger and more foreign than PN [*sic*] and FM [*sic*] who were my affective grandmothers. That was not a source ever of tension with in the family," Michael said.[18]

While waiting for the tea kettle to whistle inside the cozy kitchen of the apartment she shared with Miller, Newman pulled an envelope from the pile and slit it open. It was from Miller, who was now vacationing, without her, in Canada, traveling from Lake Louise to Banff. Newman couldn't remember the last time she had taken a proper vacation. Then again, she never really relished traveling great distances for fun. As Newman's grandson Hugh Owen, said, "My grandmother Frieda was much more inclined to travel the world. Pauline was much more content to stay put."[19] Over the years this difference had become a source of friction between her and Miller, like a stone in a shoe. Newman also looked forward to some tranquility at their summer cottage in Coffeetown, Pennsylvania. Someday they would retire at the small house in Lehigh Valley, but for now they took great pleasure rambling about the property, hosting Sunday dinners, reading, and fishing. Having always maintained separate finances, they bought the house together. It was a leap of faith for the future. Later Michael Owen recalled spending endless summers there with Newman, whom he adored, describing her as one half of "this amazing odd couple."[20]

With Miller's absence, and with her grandchildren in Switzerland, Newman found ample time to write. In a September column for *The Forward* to commemorate Labor Day, titled "Labor's Unfinished Business," she spoke about the amount of progress that had been made along with expressing hope for a more united labor movement, equal pay for equal work, and more responsible positions for women: "Let Labor Day of 1952 be a day of decision—to organize, to educate, and to advance the position of women in our beloved country."[21] As she worked on this, she also worked to reach the public through frequent letters to the editor and carefully crafted opinion columns, all of them addressing the fact that although fifteen or sixteen states had equal pay for equal work laws on the statute books, "the enforcement of these laws, however, leaves much to be desired."[22]

Aside from the writing and speaking, Newman also continued overseeing renovations to their cottage. Just as with their weekend house in West Redding and their previous apartments, the responsibility of renovations and decorating largely fell to Newman. She re-tiled and weeded, even though Miller was the accomplished gardener.[23] She hired painters to stain the porch ceiling and an electrician to update the wiring. Unlike in the past, she found it increasingly difficult to conceal her frustration with Miller for leaving her with most of the work. She was feeling ever more cantankerous. She was also feeling lonely, although this time it wasn't the loneliness that comes from being physically separated from someone. It was the loneliness that comes from sensing a growing emotional gap.

Instead of dwelling on the separation, she unleashed her frustration on the Voice of America (VOA) radio service. Newman had written a piece, "Concerning American Working Women," which was about her personal experiences and observations in the movement over the past decades, a follow-up to the VOA's story about working women called "A Better Deal for the American Working Women."[24] The station, established in 1942 to fight Nazi propaganda, had changed tack. It now largely concentrated on spreading democratic ideals behind the Iron Curtain.

Newman praised the VOA for its timely coverage and for recognizing that wage-earning women deserved better, like universal national health insurance, which President Truman proposed, extending old-age insurance to farmworkers and domestic employees, as well as a minimum three-month paid maternity leave.[25] In brief, she and Miller wanted the United States to get in line with other countries. Indeed, Miller had testified in support of the 1945 universal health insurance bill, and she would continue to do so for the next five years.[26]

But Newman couldn't help herself. In her letter to the VOA, she enumerated several mistakes in the story. For example, the article said women workers didn't perform heavy labor. Instead, it said that female workers primarily worked only in schools, offices, and hospitals. "This picture of women's employment in the United States is, to put it mildly, fallacious," she pointed out. "Obviously whoever wrote the story did not know, or did not remember, the active existence of 'Rosie the Riveter' who was during the war years, and still is, the symbol of her sisters working at ship building, automobiles, airplanes, laundries and machine shops. I doubt whether anyone familiar with these industries would classify them as 'light'."[27]

It was classic Newman. She could be disdainful toward those who she didn't think were serious. If she felt someone interviewed her and had been remiss in doing their homework, she was impatient and gruff. "But she wasn't a snob," Elisabeth recalled.[28] "If something wasn't particularly to her liking, she'd go to whoever was in charge and confront them about what she thought wasn't right. That was Pauline. She wouldn't stand for anything that was the slightest bit wrong. She would speak her mind and was very clear on what she liked and didn't like," Michael Owen said.[29]

Although the radio program accurately portrayed how the Dreier sisters and Ava Belmont were strong allies of labor rights and suffrage, it neglected to mention that it was the legions of trade union women who stood on the front lines—the ones whose bodies were bruised in police beatings, the ones sent to jail, the ones stigmatized for raising their voices. Leaving them out of the story was not only unfair to those women; it also left the public with the false impression that it was solely women of wealth and influence who made social reform possible.

Lastly, Newman pointed out, the VOA story overlooked the role of the Women's Trade Union League, an organization that began with $104, speeches, and a literal soapbox:

> Today I can say without fear of contradiction that there is hardly a union with women members in the industrial centers of our land which does not—in part—owe its existence to the valiant efforts of the WTUL. This was more than "exercising persuasive pressure" upon the unions for greater recognition of women in the labor movement. *It actually organized them.*

It was August 1954 when Newman first suspected that Miller, her partner of more than three decades, had taken a male lover. Until then she had no inkling that something was amiss. She was unable to directly confront Miller, who was now in Stockholm. So she turned to Rose Schneiderman, her friend of forty-five years, for comfort. Schneiderman was of little help. Knowing that Newman was planning on moving permanently to Coffeetown, Pennsylvania, Schneiderman preferred to wax nostalgic. True, Newman and her "Paul dear" didn't see each other every day or every week, but the fact that "I could reach out to you by lifting the telephone receiver and talk to you at length was a great comfort to me. The worst thing about getting old is that we do not make new friends and we lose old friends by death. I am down to two, really dear and true friends that is you and Elisabeth."[30]

During that sweltering summer, Newman stayed holed up in Coffeetown as much as possible. Here she could distract herself with the fresh scent of lilacs and outings with friends. Hugh and Michael visited if they weren't in England during their father's home leave. "She [Pauline] was a great lady, as much my grandmother as my own flesh and blood," Hugh Owen said.[31] As always, she wrote frequent letters to Miller, who, at the request of President Dwight Eisenhower, was on a prolonged fact-finding tour to evaluate women's labor conditions in economically developing countries. For the next two years, Miller would travel by plane and boat through Burma, Ceylon, India, Indonesia, Japan, Pakistan, Philippines, and Thailand. This time Newman kept her letter light, deliberately peppering it with mundane anecdotes and advice. She cautioned Miller to "beware of bugs, and funny foods and be a good girl and don't go around alone in unknown places."[32] The letter closed on a poignant note. It was the longest period of time the two had spent apart since 1917, the year they met. Glancing out the window at the moon, Newman switched on the radio for a bit and wondered, again, how long "it will be before I will see you, and where and when I will meet you."[33]

Back in New York City, it was ninety degrees outside, and inside the stuffy apartment, the linens felt damp, the floorboards slick. Newman hoped to spend a few days in Coffeetown cooling off, but Hurricane Connie was about to slam into Pennsylvania.[34] After hitting North Carolina as a Category 2 hurricane, Connie churned up the Chesapeake Bay, hitting Pennsylvania between August 12 and 13. Authorities helped eight hundred Boy Scouts evacuate from a summer camp, and President Eisenhower canceled his flight from Gettysburg back to Washington, DC, being driven instead. The storm killed six people each in Pennsylvania and New Jersey, and fourteen in New York, where record rainfall flooded houses and subway lines.

If Connie was devastating, Diane was calamitous. Days later, this second hurricane hit as a Category 3, leaving death and destruction all around. Newman opened her lengthy letter to Miller with the stern request that she make time to read every word of it.[35] The first floor of their Coffeetown cottage was submerged. That's all Newman knew. She had planned to take the 10:55 a.m. train from Penn Station to see Miller, but the lingering rain and winds were still too powerful. There were no trains going to Pennsylvania. The storm had washed out all the roadbeds, and the Delaware River was forty feet above normal. She folded the letter and licked the envelope closed.

Around 4:00 p.m., Newman dialed her Coffeetown neighbors for the third time that day. No one answered. She puttered around the apartment, trying them on and off. She paced the room, telephone in hand. Finally she got through. They told her how bad the situation was. The town was under water, "bridges, homes, cattle all floating down the river!" The water was still rising and there wasn't much they could tell her about her house. When she could stand it no longer, she went to a bookstore and bought a thriller to read. Finally, sometime after 10:00 p.m., she fell into "a disturbed sleep."[36] Local newspapers like *The Morning Call* and the *Pittsburgh Post-Gazette* ran photo essays of what they described as "Lehigh Valley's worst flood."[37] The storm carved a swath of ruin in the Northeast. Connecticut was effectively split in two after bridges and communications were destroyed, and the storm caused the state's largest flood on record. The pummeling rains and winds damaged or destroyed 206 damns across New England and injured an estimated 7,000 people. In Pennsylvania, the storm was responsible for 101 deaths. The swollen Broadhead Creek flooded a summer camp, killing 37 people. It destroyed an estimated 150 bridges and roads. With an estimated $70 million in damage, the last time the state had experienced something of this magnitude was the 1889 Johnstown Flood.

Almost a week passed before Newman was able to make the trip to Coffeetown. She dropped her bags and took out her camera to document the damage. It was a lot to take in, and after tiring of snapping photos, she set to work on cleaning. She scraped mud from a tray Miller's grandfather had made and went down to an icy brook to scrub a green chair Elisabeth loved. It reminded her of going to the river in Kovno to do laundry with her mother and sisters. "Meanwhile, I wish you were here, tho what you could do, I know not except that when things are in such a state, company—is most desirable. No matter what the extent the damage we will have sustained, we are alive, and the house still stands," she wrote to Miller.[38]

Meanwhile, Miller was ten thousand miles away in Djakarta, recovering from an unspecified vitamin deficiency. Lying in bed, she read Newman's lengthy letter—page after page about the flood. She perked up when reading about her grandsons. Michael's first day of school was tearful. He had begged Elisabeth to stay with him. However, the next day David Owen took him to school and there was no difficulty about his staying. Newman wrote about going to the park and watching baby Hugh make mud pies in the sandbox like the older children. "What five months will do for a baby!" Newman said of the grandson Miller had yet to meet. Miller laughed at Newman's oh-so-serious report on which of the two boys was the better eater—Hugh loved seconds on soup; Michael quit after a few spoonfuls.[39]

Even though the long separation wore on the couple, neither could agree on a time or place to meet. Newman complained that the costly repairs awaiting them at Coffeetown took precedence over spending money on a vacation. She also said that if they did go on vacation, she preferred meeting someplace warm rather than Geneva in the cold weather. That didn't work for Miller. She told Newman she needed to stay in Geneva to write her report on her most recent fact-finding trip. Newman snapped back: "I fear that meeting you is out of the question."[40] But Miller persisted. She told Newman she was going to send her a check so that she could add it to her savings account. That way by next spring it would be enough for "you come to meet me in Italy or Spain."[41] They continued the negotiations, not reaching any satisfactory conclusion, and before long it was the holiday season.

Evergreen boughs and twinkling lights, colorful window dressings and ice skating on Wollman Rink; the festive facade of New York City in 1955 could not soften Newman's loneliness. After meeting her briefly, Miller was in Bangkok, only halfway through her ILO tour. Once again she was missing a family event—this time Elisabeth's thirty-third birthday. Newman, the inveterate organizer, was most definitely not a party planner. She wanted Michael and Hugh to know it was their mother's birthday, but she could hardly ask Elisabeth to arrange her own party. So she ordered a birthday cake and bought Elisabeth an elegant fountain pen and a few small things that would be from Michael and Hugh. It was the best she could do.[42]

After spending a short week together with Elisabeth and her grandsons, Newman attended a celebratory cocktail party hosted by Amalgamated Bank at the armory. Among the speakers were Eleanor Roosevelt and Governor Averell Harriman, who thanked her for helping elect him.[43] "Meanwhile, keep well, and 'whatever you do and wherever you are may you always see that guiding star.' I'll be with you wherever you may be. But would so much more love to have you here and—now. Lots of love to you," she wrote, making only passing mention that she now suffered from a vascular situation that made her dizzy when she stood.[44]

Newman kept her condition from her grandsons as well, instead delighting in preparing the living room of the apartment with a tall, tinsel-strung Christmas tree and shimmering ornaments. Michael and Hugh hung their stockings at the foot of their beds, chattering away about Santa Claus. After they were tucked in, Newman read them "The Night Before Christmas."[45] Newman marveled at the little boys. Michael, she decided, was a bit more reserved—like Miller and like Elisabeth. Hugh, on the other hand, was "the cheerful laughing playful cherub."

For all of 1956, Newman spent more time writing and telephoning Miller than seeing her in person. They were split between New York and Washington. It was a torment knowing that Miller was just cities away—she might as well have been across the ocean. Yet, Miller gave no indication that she wanted to slow down, let alone retire together in Coffeetown. "Paul Darling, I'd be very glad to quit if I had the wherewithal for living in retirement. It's the spur of necessity that drives me on now."[46] But as Newman knew, it wasn't the necessity of money; it was the necessity of purpose. And, truthfully, at sixty-six she felt the same way. Her knees might creak and her hair might be white, but she still felt the same drive.

13

"I Yield to No One"

Elisabeth and David Owen sat at the dinner table in their West Sixty-Seventh Street apartment facing a dejected Newman. Clearly, she didn't want to talk about it, but she knew she must. Later that night, she marked the evening with a single sentence in her daybook: "At E's talked with her and David re Frieda S Miller."[1] The crackling tension that underpinned the last few years had surfaced. It was 1958, and although Miller had physically returned from England to take a job in Washington, DC, mentally she seemed to remain abroad. Where the couple once exchanged views on everything from politics to books, a cold politeness now joined them whenever they were together at the dinner table.[2]

A misplaced—or perhaps subconsciously well-placed—letter confirmed Newman's suspicion that something was amiss. A few days before joining Elisabeth and David for dinner, she pulled open her drawer in the dresser that she and Miller shared. Nestled between her carefully folded clothes sat a letter addressed to Miller from "the man from Bombay."[3] As she read, she felt all the joy and happiness squeezed from her heart. Before she could catch her breath, she searched the rest of the dresser and found other letters—lots of them. Each one was addressed to "My own darling Frieda" and "My darling own Frieda." Each one expressing some variation of the theme "I love you and wish I was with you at coffeetown." Newman composed herself before writing a letter to Miller, saying, "It was not you; it could not be you whom he addressed as his wife; it just could not be true! Then the past rose before me—my God! Again? But why not tell me, why? And once again I felt the staggering blow and realized in agony that you have again decided to stab me in the back!"[4]

And just like that all the old wounds reopened. Newman reminded Miller that this was not her first affair. She reminded Miller that she had become more secretive in both cases. But the first time, Miller kept her affair secret until she became pregnant. It was only then that she asked Newman to stand by her side. "And so, despite my hurt and deep resentment against your cruel and uncalled for treatment—and perhaps against my better judgement, I decided to share your new life," Newman wrote. She did so even though she was forced to lie to friends about why they were going away and the circumstances. "But it was you and the one we both loved that mattered," she said referring to Elisabeth.[5]

More than a cry of despair, Newman's letter to Miller was a map of their life together. She reminded Miller of how she had helped her find employment (though she omitted how many times Miller, too, recommended her for various posts), how she had provided for Elisabeth's education since Miller wasn't earning enough at the time, how she had paid for Elisabeth's wedding (even though her name wasn't included on the invitation), how she was the one who had taken Elisabeth shopping for glasses and new dresses. She recalled how she was there for Hugh and Michael when Elisabeth learned her husband, David, died and she needed to fly to Europe. She was there when Elisabeth remarried Chester Burger, who owned a management consulting firm. Lest Miller think Newman was keeping score, she made it clear that helping raise and provide for Elisabeth gave her great happiness: "You know also that I did it because of my love for her. In that love I yield to no one—including yourself."[6]

Still, her greatest fear, the one she effectively kept tamped down for decades, was now a reality. The "breakup" was here. For decades Newman had ignored how Miller was also attracted to men. She ignored it until it broke up their relationship. Elisabeth never thought of her mother as bisexual, and both of Miller and Newman's grandsons described Newman as nonsexual. "She obviously loved Frieda very much and was very attached to her. Clearly, there had always been some underlying tension because of the fact that it wasn't a normal situation to bring up a girl who had a father, and there had always been this fear that Frieda would get into a relationship with another man and leave her out in the cold," Hugh Owen said.[7]

An exhausting sadness replaced Newman's initial rush of anger. She yearned for Miller to remember all the small things that made up their life—from the books they read, the music they loved, the walks they enjoyed, and all their conversations.[8] It was in that sadness that Newman let Miller know she intended to withdraw from Coffeetown. She had invested most of her life's savings into the property because she believed it was where they would retreat together when they retired. As bighearted and gruff and "give-them-hell" as ever, a large part of Newman's life centered on Miller. She closed the letter telling Miller that she harbored no hate or bitterness. Instead, she suffered the heartache that came from "something holy and noble gone wrong; of a sun gone under that will not rise again in the same way.'"[9] So unraveled the threads that had stitched their life together for forty-one years.

When Miller's answer arrived weeks later, it danced around the edges. "Human relationships are difficult and risky and that in them one has to take the bad with the good," Miller wrote.[10] Confused, Newman pressed Miller to tell her what had happened. Thus began the couple's epistolatory dissection of their decades-long relationship. Miller explained that their separation stemmed simply from a "divergence of interest." Miller enjoyed cruises; Newman did not. Newman enjoyed warmer climes; Miller did not. Newman conceded that point but also insisted those were surface differences. The two of them were bonded by Elisabeth, Michael, and Hugh, she pointed out. And they shared the same professional goals and their political views.[11] She tempered her attack on Miller, trying to remind her of the depth of their connection.

Even so, Newman laid the blame squarely at Miller's feet. After all, it was Miller, through her actions, who initiated the separation. It was Miller who never tried to find a job in New York where they lived. It was Miller who didn't appreciate that without a diploma it was not simple to find a full-time position in Washington, DC. In the end, it would have been kinder if Miller simply declared she was leaving Newman for "the man from Bombay."[12] Finally the two met face-to-face. They barely spoke, moving around each other like shadows: "Fried left on Sunday knowing that I was ill and in bed. She never called to find out how I am—it has come to that!"[13]

Her life in upheaval, Newman found solace in nature and in writing. But even the sunset seemed a metaphor for her life:

> Slowly, very slowly dark clouds are now replacing the blaze of colors and all the beauty and glory of the sun set must submit to the darkening of the night. Oh, how much more this beauty would mean if shared with one who at one time was there to do just that. Those days are gone. Never to return. Still the mind or memory clings to those days of deep friendship and understanding. To think of the present situation makes me sad and most unhappy. What an incredible end![14]

Yet, it wasn't the end. It was in some ways a beginning for this next phase of Newman's life. Newman, who disliked cruises, was now aboard the *Christof Colombo*, sailing along the Brazilian coast and writing to Miller. It had been a year since their relationship ruptured. Newman and Miller, both in their early seventies now, were estranged but not out of touch—hence the letter. Newman didn't love the cruise. In fact, she found a lot wrong with it, starting with the noise. She was forever looking for a quiet place, away from the "so-called music," and constant announcements over public speakers.[15] There was food aplenty for dinner but "nothing to write home about as to preparation and flavor." After breakfast she walked out on to the sun deck and people-watched: well-dressed women and tanned men in crisp suits, construction workers and shoe shiners, garment workers and common laborers. "All you have to do is look at their hands and at their tired faces and you know who they are and where they come from. Well, they are having a wonderful time. They have earned it," she said.[16]

At the end of the trip, Newman reunited with Elisabeth, David, Hugh, and Michael in Geneva. She was under no illusions about why she was there alone. She was still hurting; even if the pain had dulled, her disillusionment had not. As the extent of Miller's betrayal sank in, their letters became icy with anger. Where there was once "Much love" there was now "Sincerely." "Paul" was now "Pauline."[17] Sitting alone, Newman resolved to make the most of the present: "I have seen and felt the warmth of the sun, the blue of the sky and the fleecy clouds. I have seen the Mediterranean Sea, listened to the constant whisper of the waves. I am with the Owen family whom I love more than they will ever know."[18]

The pair also continued to sort their finances. Miller changed power of attorney from Newman to her son-in-law, Chester Burger. She recognized her financial indebtedness to Newman, who had generously contributed nine thousand dollars toward the purchase of the Coffeetown house as well as numerous repairs. Miller agreed to reimburse Newman, although she cautioned Newman that she would not be able to afford the full sum at that moment unless she mortgaged the house, which she did not want to do. She also told Newman that she was more than welcome to use the house whenever she wished until the money was repaid.[19] Newman raised a figurative eyebrow at this remark: "Perhaps I should have made this decision when, without consulting me, you announced to all our friends here and abroad that Coffeetown is the 'Miller House.' . . . I resented that act of yours and I still do," she wrote.[20] Nevertheless, perhaps it was a small sign that Miller was trying to thaw the ice that lay between them, a thaw that would take much more time to heal.

Newman threw herself single-mindedly into her work. It was that sense of renewed vigor that led her to become a delegate to the International Confederation of Free Trade Unions and a continued role with the United Nations Commission on the Status of Women. The work helped her put some distance between her and the places she and Miller once shared.

In a few more hours the silver-bodied airplane would make its final approach over Israel and touch down at Lod Airport (renamed Ben Gurion International Airport in 1973). Newman spent a restless night in her seat, and now as she looked out the oval window, she remembered a poem she wrote soon after President John F. Kennedy, sans overcoat despite the piercing cold, swore to uphold the Constitution and protect Americans from enemies foreign and domestic: "We can plunge into darkness beneath the sea; we master the wind, we count the stars, we fly into the sun, we can see for miles, soon we shall reach the moon; we have made the wind and the stars and water serve mankind. We have been able to do all this and more. And yet—mankind still seems to be unable to turn the 'swords into ploughshares so that there shall be war no more.'"[21]

In 1964, six years after reading the letter that shattered her life, Newman felt a renewed sense of purpose. Once it became clear to her that her relationship with Miller was over, she stepped up her work, relishing the role of labor organizer emeritus. She kept her office at the ILGWU, going there several times a week. She also accepted roles on advisory boards like the Labor Advisory Committee of the Women's Bureau. But this was her first visit to the young state of Israel. She was there on behalf of the ILGWU to gather information about the country's unions and health care system and to then present her findings to various social reform groups and Jewish groups when she returned to the States. She would also speak about her experience to the New York chapter of the Women's Division of Jewish Labor Organizations. In these later years, Newman engaged more directly with Jewish organizations, including the Jewish Federation. Though she wore her Jewish identity more easily in these later years, no longer trying as hard to cover her accent as she had back when she was speaking to socialites in the early days of the movement, she remained steadfastly secular.

Her itinerary also included visiting the Kupat Holim Central Hospital in Beersheba. The union hospital was the ILGWU's gift to Histadrut, the young country's labor union. The work interested her, and she filled notebooks with her thoughts about the country's potential, its chance to model union membership and affordable health care. She also relished the chance to play tourist, so once she finished her work in Israel, she left for Egypt, where she drove through the desert from Alexandria to Cairo. She walked around the port and bargained and browsed her way through various markets. She bought two blouses for Elisabeth, a sweater each for Michael and Hugh, and, despite everything that had happened in their relationship, she couldn't resist buying a small trinket for Miller.[22] Then it was onward to Greece. In the morning she stood on the same sun-warmed square where Socrates and Plato once held their dialogs. In the afternoon she stood atop the Acropolis à la Richard Halliburton. She capped off the day with an evening visit to the theater, where actors performed the dramas of Euripides and the comedies of Aristophanes: "In short, the places I read about I have been able to see with mine own eyes!"[23] Walking through the twisty streets, she was surprised to see how women across the Atlantic, from Syria to Jordan and from Greece to Yugoslavia, embraced the craze for miniskirts.

By the time Newman stepped aboard the plane that would take her home, she resolved to return to the region. Thus, she returned to Israel in 1967, four months after the Six Day War. After meeting with leaders from the country's insurance and medical services organization in Tel Aviv, she met with Arabic women in Jaffa. After that she traveled about seventy miles south to Beersheba, where she checked into the 120-room Beersheba Desert Inn, which, aside from offering swimming pools and horse, camel, and donkey rides, prided itself on being "the most modern and exotic hotel in Israel."[24] She arrived just in time for tea and a short rest before dinner. Casting an appraising eye about the lobby, she was impressed with the hotel's modern furnishings. "I wish I could say the same about the food which I think is awful! However, one can exist on tea and bread—for a time, anyway," she said.[25] She wasn't seeing the country entirely through rose colored glasses. Newman was well aware that the new country would need to contend with economic, political, and religious problems, yet she remained optimistic that "we who have been there are confident that these problems will be solved—it will have to be solved if Israel is to survive as a democratic nation."[26]

Before flying home Newman made one last stop. Standing before the Chagall-stained windows in the Hadassah Hospital and Medical Center, she watched the light dance across her hands. "I happened to be there when the rays of the setting sun illuminated those glorious colors—a beautiful sight to remember. From there I was driven to see the monument erected in memory of the six million Jews who were exterminated by Hitler and his henchmen—a most impressive monument," she wrote.[27]

Miller rhythmically chopped vegetables for soup as Newman sat at the table reading the newspaper with a magnifying glass, a basket of darned socks at her feet. There wasn't a lot of drama when she and Miller moved back in together in their West Sixty-Seventh Street apartment. The two had a very deep bond and were clearly emotionally inseparable from each other, Hugh Owen said. However, he added, "Frieda could also sometimes get a little impatient with Pauline, who was simpler. Usually Pauline had a kind of shrug it off mentality, but you could see sometimes the hurt by it if Frieda was a little unkind to her."[28] After swimming in angry estrangement for so many years, the couple fell into a familiar pattern—reading, writing, visiting with old friends. There was no passionate tear-filled reunion, no more mention about the man from Bombay. Instead they grew companionable—close, even—spending Sunday dinners with Elisabeth, David, Michael, Hugh, and friends. Miller was the chef; Newman was the dish washer.[29]

When Michael turned sixteen, he began to sense that something was wrong. He always appreciated how the two women "had this great ability to jibe each other to go back and forth," but as Miller's memory began to fade, "she became a bit more brittle personality." That give-and-take aspect of the two women's relationship became more argumentative. It was no longer amusing to watch them "go at each other . . . I think Pauline took it in stride. But something was changing," Michael said.[30] That something was the beginning of Miller's long downward spiral into poor health. After being admitted to the hospital for surgery, she suffered a stroke and never again came home. Newman, now eighty-two, had neither the space nor the money to care for Miller at home. After much discussion, she and Elisabeth decided it would be best to admit Miller to the Mary Manning Walsh Home and, when that was no longer feasible, to a nursing home on Long Island.

Newman couldn't believe her eyes when she walked into the room in the nursing home; there Miller sat, her hands and body strapped to a chair. The nurses had restrained her to stop her from wandering into other patients' rooms. Newman often stayed with Miller until well past 6:00 p.m. She would feed her and wipe her mouth. But mostly she talked to her, held her hand, and hoped that Miller did not understand what was happening. It twisted Newman's insides to see the fingers of this woman—a woman who loved poetry and music, walking and climbing, traveling and adventure—curl into themselves.[31] When she finally had to leave, the sight of tears leaking from Miller's eyes was too much to hold:

> For days and weeks I could not sleep—even a pill did not help much. I could not get rid of the vision—her sitting tied to a chair. The whole thing seemed so cruel! She who loved freedom of movement was forcibly prevented from moving at all. She who was company to all was no longer allowed to speak to anyone. All her activity cut off as by a sword, left to stare, just to stare and to wonder?[32]

Sometimes Newman sat quietly beside Miller. Sometimes she took pencils and a sketch pad from her bag and sketched her old, beloved companion as she looked out the window. As the pencil scratched across the white paper, stray thoughts and images, unbidden, popped into Newman's head. Sometimes it was her parents. Sometimes it was her sisters. Other times it was her grandsons building castles in the sand at the seashore, a field of wild gentian, Elisabeth as a toddler in West Redding. But mostly she thought about death: "My heart aches for her and for all of us."[33]

Frieda S. Miller died on July 23, 1972, and was cremated a day later in North Bergen, New Jersey. There would be no funeral, no grave, no stone, no place to lay a flower. "There is nothing left of you except your ashes. Only your spirit lives on and alive in my heart and mind and always will," a devasted Newman said.[34] The letters poured in—letters that spoke of the pioneering role the pair played, the life they shared, the daughter they raised. One letter read in part, "You know how tremendously I admire you and Frieda—and the women of your time—who went out and moved mountains—your accomplishments are for all times—and I wish some of our women libbers would do some homework and read history!"[35]

The *Washington Post* remarked that one of Miller's first jobs in 1924 as inspector for the Board of Sanitary Control was inspecting women's bathrooms: "It was nasty work but wonderful discipline."[36] A month later Newman was dealt another blow: Rose Schneiderman, her closest friend and confidante, died at age ninety.

On May 6, 1975, two years after Miller died, Newman joined Michael, Hugh, Elisabeth, and Elisabeth's second husband, Chester Burger, for Sunday dinner. After Burger gently teased Newman into talking about the old days, she agreed to talk about the seventy-fifth anniversary of the founding of the ILGWU. When everyone promised not to interrupt, she launched into a brief reminiscence about the early years, how the ILGWU got its charter in 1900, and the tragedy of the Triangle Shirtwaist Factory fire. "While we celebrate our 75th anniversary, it behooves all of us to remember those who fought and bled and died," Newman said, a trace of her Lithuanian accent showing through.[37]

A few months later, on July 2, almost two years to the day of Miller's death, Newman reflected on their life together: how they walked through the woods gathering "delicate little flowers" and how whenever Miller suffered from a migraine headache, she would ask Newman to play some music. And she reflected on Miller's death:

> For close to five years I watched you die. Part of me shared in your dying. I shall not ever forget the long and bitter years. Those were heartbreaking years—years that haunted me when you were still alive and haunt me still. I cannot forget the sadness and the pain in your eyes when I would leave you. You did not speak, but your eyes spoke. Why do you leave, why? You would just look at me, hold on to my hand, try to tell me something but by this time your speech was impaired and I could not understand what you were trying to say.

After Miller's death, Newman found solace in work and in her grandsons. It helped that as the boys grew, Newman became a valuable confidante for both of them, particularly for Hugh, who took long walks with his "Granny Pauline" to discuss religion and other weighty matters. "She was always concerned about me and very supportive. I could talk to her about all kinds of things. We had a lot of conversations about religion. I talked to her about her past, her childhood. We would take walks in the park before she got very old and frail," Hugh Owen reminisced.[38]

Newman remained active in the ILGWU, heading to the office several times a week. Shunning a large print edition of anything, she would read the newspaper with a magnifying glass. She wrote and she spoke to students. She opined on the Vietnam War and offered her—completely unsolicited—views about Watergate to President Gerald Ford. She corresponded with US secretary of state George Shultz about important events in American labor history. She also lamented that women still had not attained many top positions in the labor movement. "We still find that too few capable women have not reached the position they could so well fill sometimes," she said, adding that she didn't want to see women appointed to positions for the sake of their being women. Instead she maintained that there were numerous capable women who "should be utilized in the labor movement as well as in any other."[39]

Six years after Miller died, Newman slipped off a chair in her apartment. It was New Year's Eve, 1978. She didn't break any bones, and though she was shaken by the incident—realizing for the first time that she was growing frail—she insisted to Elisabeth that she could manage. But two weeks later things hadn't improved. In fact, they were getting worse. Her once robust body now looked thin in street clothes. If she wasn't using a cane, she held Elisabeth's elbow for balance.[40] Ever the organizer, Newman started putting her affairs in order. She told Elisabeth that she would do her best to sort through her possessions now, keeping some, disposing of others, "lessen the burden which will fall upon you—when the end comes. My hope is that I will not linger as long as Granny did, and that you and my doctor will do all that is possible to follow the instruction of the 'living will.'"[41] To that end she set money aside in a trust for Michael and Hugh and asked Elisabeth to donate her papers to the women's archives at Radcliffe. She also told Elisabeth to take Miller's sterling silver and whatever else she wanted from the armoire in the hall—a salad bowl, a glass platter, a clock radio, blankets, suitcases with some still containing Miller's clothes, shoes, letters, and snapshots.

Three years later, Elisabeth hired a home health care aide and insisted Newman move in with her; she refused to watch Newman deteriorate in a nursing home as her mother had done.[42] It was a generous gesture on Elisabeth's part. It also meant the atmosphere in the home she now shared with her second husband was "getting tense and angry."[43] Indeed, diary entries from this time show Newman's frustrations over not being able to care for herself, of being left alone, sometimes manifested in violent outbursts.[44] An entry in Elisabeth's diary read: "Pauline has been extremely bitter lately when we have gone out. She feels destitute, left with 'inferior' people . . . Perhaps the key factor is that, while she was independent on her own, she could move around and arrange to see people. Now she has lost control. That is what really makes her rage, quite literally."[45] Each month grew more difficult than the last. Most of her friends were dead; Clara Lemlich, the last of the original group, had died in 1982. With no appointments to keep, Newman swum between depression and anger. She no longer knew how to channel her feisty personality.

Newman died at age ninety-eight. On April 9, 1986, in New Jersey, she was cremated, as Miller had been. Throughout her life, the feminist icon wrote, lectured, and advised the next generation of women organizers:

> It might not be right to "hang on" to life when life becomes difficult. But the memory of walking through woods with your first friend looking for and finding the delicate and fragrant flowers or of a field of wild gentian, or the hilltop of daffodils at Coffeetown, or the unforgettable

sunsets reflected in the Hudson which I often marveled at its beauty—or watching the sunrise on a summers day; or remembering the voices of a Caruso, and other great artists of the 19th century, or with my mind's eye to once again watch Elisabeth playing "house" in West Redding, and later to watch her children Hugh and Michael building castles in the sand at the French riviera—all these memories pull you back from the inevitable end if only for a little longer—just to remember![46]

Epilogue

In 1965, Pauline Newman reflected on the decades she'd spent working to improve the lives of others, be it in making the air safer to breathe in a garment factory, securing higher wages for working men and women, or increasing access to health care for workers. She would go on to serve others for many more years, but as it became clearer to her that she had less time in front of her than she had behind her, she took time to acknowledge how privileged she had been to participate in bringing about societal changes.

Now, nearly four decades after her death in 1986, a new generation of labor activists have risen up. Together they are leading unionization efforts in all sectors of the economy, from manufacturing to distribution, from health care to education. In October 2023, United Auto Workers struck a tentative agreement with automakers. Hollywood writers won higher royalty payments, protections against artificial intelligence for scriptwriting, and mandatory staffing levels after striking for several months. About seventy-five thousand workers at Kaiser Permanente, one of the nation's largest health care consortiums, secured pay increases and higher staffing levels after a three-day-long strike. Although these are only a few examples, they occurred at a time when the public's approval of unions sits at the highest it's been in decades. According to a 2023 Gallup report, Americans' union-approval rating was at 67 percent, this after a low of 48 percent in 2009. At the time of this writing, women account for nearly 60 percent of newly organizing workers. As in Newman's day, they lead some of the largest labor movements in recent years: baristas at Starbucks and bakery workers, Etsy sellers who went on strike against transaction fee increases. More so, the gender gap in union representation has also narrowed. According to a 2021 Bureau of Labor Statistics report, about 10.6 percent of men are members of a union, compared to 9.9 percent of women. Once upon a time, Newman lamented the lack of women in leadership positions. Today women head unions, and the 2023 Nobel Prize in economics went to Claudia Goldin, a Bronx-born Jewish woman who helped deepen and advance our understanding of how gender differences play out in the labor market.

Throughout her illustrious career, Pauline Newman epitomized the indomitable spirit of women who dared to defy societal norms and reshape the landscape of social and political discourse. Her legacy serves as an enduring testament to the transformative power of individual action and a reminder that "there is a great deal to be done. It is going to take time and effort. It will require the same crusading spirit which spurred us on in days gone by. It is not going to be easy. But in the end we will get there."[1]

Notes

Chapter 1. The Land of Gold and Promise

1. Pauline Newman interview with Barbara Wertheimer, 1976, Manuscript Collection (hereafter, MC) 324, box 1, folder 6, Pauline Newman Papers (hereafter, PNP), Schlesinger Library, Radcliffe Institute, Harvard University, Cambridge, Massachusetts.

2. Newman interview with Wertheimer, 1976, PNP.

3. Newman interview with Wertheimer, 1976, PNP.

4. Newman interview with Wertheimer, 1976, PNP.

5. "History of Child Labor in the United States—part 2: The Reform Movement," January 2017, US Bureau of Labor Statistics, https://www.bls.gov/opub/mlr/2017/article/history-of-child-labor-in-the-united-states-part-2-the-reform-movement.htm, last accessed Oct. 11, 2023.

6. Letter to Michael and Hugh, 1965, MC 324, box 1, folder 3, PNP.

7. Newman interview with Wertheimer, 1976, PNP.

8. Letter to Michael and Hugh, 1965, PNP.

9. Letter to Michael and Hugh, 1965, PNP.

10. Letter to Michael and Hugh, 1965, PNP.

11. Pauline Newman interview for Thames Television, 1975, MC 324, box 1, folder 5, PNP.

12. Letter to Michael and Hugh, 1965, PNP.

13. Letter to Michael and Hugh, 1965, PNP.

14. Letter to Michael and Hugh, 1965, PNP.

15. Letter to Michael and Hugh, 1965, PNP.

16. Letter to Michael and Hugh, 1965, PNP.

17. Letter to Michael and Hugh, 1965, PNP.

18. Letter to Michael and Hugh, 1965, PNP.

19. Susan A. Glenn, *Daughters of the Shtetl: Life and Labor in the Immigrant Generation* (Ithaca, NY: Cornell University Press, 1990), 13.

20. Gus Tyler, *Look for the Union Label: A History of the International Ladies' Garment Workers' Union* (Armonk, NY: M.E. Sharpe, 1995), 9.

21. Glenn, *Daughters of the Shtetl*, 30–31.

22. "Russian Jewish Horrors: A Nine-Months' Record of Rape, Murder and Outrage," *New York Times*, Jan. 28, 1882.

23. Newman interview with Wertheimer, 1976, PNP.

24. Letter to Michael and Hugh, 1965, PNP.

25. Letter to Michael and Hugh, 1965, PNP.

26. Newman interview with Wertheimer, 1976, PNP.

27. Letter to Michael and Hugh, 1965, PNP.

28. Masha Greenbaum, *The Jews of Lithuania: A History of a Remarkable Community, 1316–1945* (Jerusalem: Gefen Books, 2018), 114–18.

29. Greenbaum, *Jews of Lithuania*, 114–18.

30. Greenbaum, *Jews of Lithuania*, 145–47.

31. Greenbaum, *Jews of Lithuania*, 187.

32. Greenbaum, *Jews of Lithuania*, 187.

33. Newman interview with Wertheimer, 1976, PNP.

34. Glenn, *Daughters of the Shtetl*, 42–43.

35. Glenn, *Daughters of the Shtetl*, 42–43.

Chapter 2. "Will It Ever Be Different?"

1. Pauline Newman interview with Barbara Wertheimer, 1976, MC 324, box 1, folder 6, Pauline Newman Papers (hereafter, PNP), Schlesinger Library, Radcliffe Institute, Harvard University, Cambridge, Massachusetts.

2. Letter to Michael and Hugh, 1965, MC 324, box 1, folder 3, PNP.

3. Newman interview with Wertheimer, 1976, PNP.

4. Newman interview with Wertheimer, 1976, PNP.

5. Letter to Michael and Hugh, 1965, PNP.

6. "Where 'Ah Goo' Is Heard in Tongues of Many Lands," *New York Times*, June 5, 1904, 26.

7. Susan A. Glenn, *Daughters of the Shtetl: Life and Labor in the Immigrant Generation* (Ithaca, NY: Cornell University Press, 1990), 62–63.

8. Glenn, *Daughters of the Shtetl*, 53.

9. Letter to Michael and Hugh, 1965, PNP.

10. Peter Stuyvesant, as quoted in Ira Wolfman, *Jewish New York: Notable Neighborhoods and Memorable Moments* (New York: Universe Publishing, 2003), 15.

11. Dutch East India Company to Peter Stuyvesant, as quoted in Wolfman, *Jewish New York*, 15.

12. Wolfman, *Jewish New York*, 2.

13. Sanford Sternlicht, *The Tenement Saga: The Lower East Side and Early Jewish American Writers* (Madison: University of Wisconsin Press, 2004), 8–9.

14. Newman interview with Wertheimer, 1976, PNP.

15. Laws of New York State, 1897, as quoted in Mable Hurd Willett, *The Employment of Women in the Clothing Trade*, Columbia University Studies in the Social Services (New York: AMS Press, 1968), 64. First published 1902.

16. Newman interview with Wertheimer, 1976, PNP.

17. Newman interview with Wertheimer, 1976, PNP.

18. Letter to Michael and Hugh, 1965, PNP.

19. Letter to Michael and Hugh, 1965, PNP.

20. Letter to Michael and Hugh, 1965, PNP.

21. Kim Kelly, *Fight Like Hell: The Untold History of American Labor* (New York: One Signal Publishers/Atria, 2022), 3.

22. Kelly, *Fight Like Hell.*

23. Carmen Nigero, "Beware of Zombies: The Grim Origins of Washington Square Park," *New York Public Library* (blog), March 10, 2011, https://www.nypl.org/blog/2011/03/10/grim-origins-washington-square-park.

24. Glenn, *Daughters of the Shtetl*, 53; Grace H. Dodge, ed., *Thoughts of Busy Girls: Written by a Group of Girls Who Have Little Time for Study and Yet Find Much Time for Thinking* (New York: Cassell, 1892), 74.

25. Letter to Michael and Hugh, 1965, PNP.

26. Charles Hirschman and Elizabeth Mogford, "Immigration and the American Industrial Revolution from 1880 to 1920," *Social Science Research*, 38, no. 4 (2009): 897–920. National Library of Medicine. https://www.ncbi.nlm.nih.gov/pmc/articles/PMC2760060/.

27. Glenn, *Daughters of the Shtetl*, 2.

28. Pauline Newman and Joan Morrison, "Working for the Triangle Shirtwaist Company," History Matters, http://historymatters.gmu.edu/d/178/.

29. Newman interview with Wertheimer, 1976, PNP.

30. Willett, *Employment of Women*, 37.

31. Letter to Michael and Hugh, 1965, PNP.

32. Glenn, *Daughters of the Shtetl*, 7, 92.

33. Newman interview with Wertheimer, 1976, PNP.

34. Newman interview with Wertheimer, 1976, PNP.

35. Report on Population, United States Census, 1890, part 2, as quoted in Willet, *Employment of Women*, 25.

36. Glenn, *Daughters of the Shtetl*, 80.

37. Newman interview with Wertheimer, 1976, PNP.

38. Letter to Michael and Hugh, 1965, PNP.

39. Letter to Michael and Hugh, 1965, PNP.

40. Letter to Michael and Hugh, 1965, PNP.

41. Letter to Michael and Hugh, 1965, PNP.

42. Albert Marrin, *Flesh and Blood So Cheap: The Triangle and Its Legacy* (New York: Alfred A. Knopf, 2011), 67–68.

43. J.A.H. Donhure to Pauline Newman, July 15, 1906, PNP, MC 324, box 9, folder 165.

44. Mary Van Kleeck, *Working Girls in Evening Schools: A Statistical Study*. (New York: Russell Sage Foundation, 1914), 11.

45. Van Kleeck, *Working Girls in Evening Schools*, 95.

46. Newman interview with Wertheimer, 1976, PNP.

47. Newman interview with Wertheimer, 1976, PNP.

48. Newman interview with Wertheimer, 1976, PNP.

49. Newman interview with Wertheimer, 1976, PNP.

50. Pauline Newman as quoted in Annelise Orleck, *Common Sense and a Little Fire: Women and Working-Class Politics in the United States, 1900–1965* (Chapel Hill: University of North Carolina Press, 1995), 40.

Chapter 3. East Side Joan of Arc

1. Letter to Michael and Hugh, 1965, MC 324, box 1, folder 3, Pauline Newman Papers (hereafter, PNP), Schlesinger Library, Radcliffe Institute, Harvard University, Cambridge, Massachusetts.

2. Letter to Michael and Hugh, 1965, MC 324, box 1, folder 3, PNP.

3. Annelise Orleck, *Common Sense and a Little Fire: Women and Working-Class Politics in the United States 1900–1965* (Chapel Hill: University of North Carolina Press, 1995), 35.

4. Pauline Newman interview with Barbara Wertheimer, 1976, PNP.

5. "Rent Day Is Like the Day of Judgement," *Jewish Daily Forward*, March 5, 1908.

6. "Women Resume Riots Against Kosher Meat Shops," *New York Times*, May 15, 1902.

7. Marjorie Ingall, "Lessons from the Kosher Meat Boycott," *Tablet Magazine*, May 6, 2019, https://www.tabletmag.com/sections/community/articles/lessons-from-the-kosher-meat-boycott (accessed March 2, 2023).

8. "Fierce Meat Riot on Lower East Side," *New York Times*, May 16, 1902, 1, 3.

9. "New Joan of Arc Leads Rent Strike," *New York Times*, Dec. 27, 1907, 4.

10. "To Starve Out Landlords: East Side Tenants Threatened to Inaugurate Rent Strike," *New York Times*, Dec. 26, 1907, 1.

11. "New Joan of Arc."

12. "New Joan of Arc."

13. "Rent Strike Spreads on the East Side," *New York Times*, Dec. 28, 1907, 2.

14. "Rent Strike Spreads on the East Side."

15. "Police Break Up Rent War Meetings," *New York Times*, Dec. 29, 1907, 14.

16. "Denouncing Police in Lower Rent War," *New York Times*, Dec. 30, 1907, 16.

17. Pauline Newman, as quoted in Ann Schofield, *To Do and To Be: Portraits of Four Women Activists, 1893–1986* (Boston: Northeastern University Press, 1997), 86.

18. "Denounce Police in Lower Rent War," *New York Times*, Dec. 30, 1907, 16.

19. Michael Owen interview with author, Feb. 13, 2023.

20. Abe Cahan, "What Sense Is There in These Rent Strikes," *Worker*, Apr. 17, 1904.

21. "Rent Strike Going," *New York Times*, 1907.

22. Jenna Weissman Joselit, "The Landlord as Czar; *Pre–World War I Tenant Activity*," in Ronald Lawson, *The Tenant Movement in New York City, 1904–1984*, pp. 39–50 (New Brunswick, NJ: Rutgers University Press 1986).

23. "Outcome of Rent Agitation: Charities and Commons," *New York Economic Journal*, Jan. 3, 1908, and Feb. 8, 1908.

24. "Outcome of Rent Agitation: Charities and Commons," Jan. 3, 1908.

25. Gerald Sorin, "Socialism in the United States," *The Shalvi/Hyman Encyclopedia of Jewish Women*, Jewish Women's Archive, last updated June 23, 2021, https://jwa.org/encyclopedia/article/socialism-in-united-states.

26. Letter to Michael and Hugh, 1965, PNP.

27. Orleck, *Common Sense*, 37.

28. Newman interview with Wertheimer, 1976, PNP.

29. Newman interview with Wertheimer, 1976, PNP.

30. Hugh Owen interview with author, Feb. 6, 2023.

31. "Mansfield to Act Ibsen's *Peer Gynt*; A Notable Event of the Theatrical Season," *New York Times*, Feb. 24, 1907, 2.

32. Newman interview with Wertheimer, 1976, PNP.

33. Newman interview with Wertheimer, 1976, PNP.

34. *The Forward*, https://www.nli.org.il/en/newspapers/frw? (accessed Nov. 8, 2023).

35. Pauline Newman as quoted in Orleck, *Common Sense*, 32.

36. Newman as quoted in Orleck, *Common Sense*, 32.

37. Philip S. Foner, *History of the Labor Movement in the United States, vol. 1: From Colonial Times to Founding of the American Federation of Labor* (New York: International Publishers, 1982), 500, 503.

38. Fannia M. Cohn, "History of the I.L.G.W.U.," unpublished, 1940, Kheel Center for Labor-Management Documentation and Archives, Martin P. Catherwood Library, Cornell University, 3.

39. Louis Levine, *The Women's Garment Workers* (New York: B. W. Heubsch, 1924).

40. Nancy Schrom Dye, *As Equals and as Sisters: Feminism, the Labor Movement, and the Women's Trade Union League of New York* (Columbia: University of Missouri Press, 1980), 13.

41. Cohn, "History of the I.L.G.W.U.," 38.

42. Cohn, "History of the I.L.G.W.U.," 38.

43. Mary E. Dreier, *Margaret Dreier Robins: Her Life, Letters, and Work* (New York: Island Cooperative Press, 1950), 21.

44. Kim Kelly, *Fight Like Hell: The Untold History of American Labor* (New York: One Signal Publishers/Atria, 2022), 6.

45. Reports of the Meetings Held for the Purpose of Organizing the Woman's Trade Union League in Boston, Nov. 14, 17, 19 in 1903, MC 324, box 4, folder 54, PNP.

46. Lillian Faderman, *To Believe in Women: What Lesbians Have Done for America—A History* (Boston: Houghton Mifflin, 1999), 106.

47. Dorothy Sue Cobble, *For the Many: American Feminists and the Global Fight for Democratic Equality* (Princeton, NJ: Princeton University Press, 2021), 16.

48. Cobble, *For the Many*, 15.

49. As quoted in Dye, *As Equals and as Sisters*, 35; "Paper Read before the Working Women's Society of New York," n.d. Schlesinger Library, Radcliffe Institute, Harvard University, Leonora O'Reilly Papers.

50. "Laborers Sip Tea in Fifth Avenue," *New York Times*, April 11, 1907, 8.

Chapter 4. Corsets and Cloak Makers

1. Nancy Schrom Dye, *As Equals and as Sisters: Feminism, the Labor Movement, and the Women's Trade Union League of New York* (Columbia: University of Missouri Press, 1980), 5, 90.

2. Philip S. Foner, *Women and the American Labor Movement: From Colonial Times to the Eve of World War One* (New York: Free Press, 1979), 497.

3. Kim Kelly, *Fight Like Hell: The Untold History of American Labor* (New York: One Signal Publishers/Atria, 2022), 12.

4. Gus Tyler, *Look for the Union Label: A History of the International Ladies' Garment Workers' Union* (Armonk, NY: M. E. Sharpe, 1995), 33.

5. M. Fannia Cohn, "History of the I.L.G.W.U.," unpublished, 1940, Kheel Center for Labor-Management Documentation and Archives, Martin P. Catherwood Library, Cornell University, 13.

6. "The New York Cloakmakers' Strike," *Journal of Political Economy* 19, no. 3 (March 1911), https://www.journals.uchicago.edu/doi/pdf/10.1086/251825 (accessed March 15, 2023).

7. Tyler, *Look for the Union Label*, 56.

8. Tyler, *Look for the Union Label*, 56.

9. Tyler, *Look for the Union Label*, 56.

10. *New York World*, Nov. 23, 1909, as quoted in Eric Foner and Steven H. Jaffe, "'I Am a Working Girl': Upheaval in the Garment Trades," in *Activist New York: A History of People, Protest, and Politics*, by Steven H. Jaffe (New York: NYU Press, 2018), https://muse.jhu.edu/pub/193/oa_monograph/chapter/3722808.

11. *New York World*, Nov. 23, 1909, as quoted in Foner and Jaffe.

12. Writings by Pauline Newman, including autobiographical notes, 1960–75, MC 324, box 4, folder 4, PNP.

13. Albert Marrin, *Flesh and Blood So Cheap: The Triangle Fire and Its Legacy* (New York: Alfred A. Knopf, 2011), 82.

14. Letter to Michael and Hugh, 1965, MC 324, box 1, folder 3, Pauline Newman Papers (hereafter, PNP), Schlesinger Library, Radcliffe Institute, Harvard University, Cambridge, Massachusetts.

15. "Waist Strike Is On," *New York Times*, Nov. 24, 1909.

16. Articles and notes, mostly by Pauline Newman re: PMN life, 83-M191, 83-M198, box 1, folder 1, PNP.

17. "New York Cloakmakers' Strike," *Journal of Political Economy*.

18. Steven Buechler, *Women's Movements in the United States: Woman Suffrage, Equal Rights, and Beyond* (New Brunswick, NJ: Rutgers University Press, 1990), 35.

19. Pauline Newman interview with Barbara Wertheimer, 1976, PNP.

20. Newman interview with Wertheimer, 1976, PNP.

21. Newman interview with Wertheimer, 1976, PNP.

22. Tyler, *Look for the Union Label*, 55.

23. "New York Cloakmakers' Strike," *Journal of Political Economy*, 160–61.

24. Susan A. Glenn, *Daughters of the Shtetl: Life and Labor in the Immigrant Generation* (Ithaca, NY: Cornell University Press, 1990), 54, 185.

25. Glenn, *Daughters of the Shtetl*, 55, 185.

26. "Shirtwaist Strike Peace Plan Fails," *New York Times*, Dec. 28, 1909, 5.

27. Cohn, "History of the I.L.G.W.U.," 16.

28. Newman interview with Wertheimer, 1976, PNP.

29. Pauline Newman as quoted in Nan Enstad, *Ladies of Labor, Girls of Adventure: Working Women, Popular Culture, and Labor Politics at the Turn of the Twentieth Century* (New York: Columbia University Press, 1999), 96.

30. Barbara Welter, "The Cult of True Womanhood: 1820–1860," *American Quarterly* 18, no. 2 (1966): 151–74.

31. Enstad, *Ladies of Labor*, 98.

32. Biographical: oral history interview for Thames Television, 1975, 1900–1980, MC 324, M-44, 5, box 1, PNP.

33. Newman interview with Wertheimer, 1976, PNP.

34. Sarah Comstock, "The Uprising of the Girls," *Collier's* 44 (Dec. 25, 1909): 14–16.

35. Joan Marie Johnson, *Funding Feminism: Monied Women, Philanthropy, and the Women's Movement, 1870–1967* (Chapel Hill: University of North Carolina Press, 2017), 43.

36. Johnson, *Funding Feminism*, 42.

37. "College Girls," *New York Times*, Dec. 19, 1909, 39.

38. Irving E. Doob, Letter to the Editor, *New York Times*, Jan. 23, 1910.

39. Untitled, *New York Call*, Dec. 16, 1909.

40. "Girl Strikers Tell Rich Their Woes," *New York Times*, Dec. 16, 1909, 3.

41. "Girl Strikers Tell Rich Their Woes," 3.

42. Johnson, *Funding Feminism*, 4.

43. Annelise Orleck, *Common Sense and a Little Fire: Women and Working-Class Politics in the United States 1900–1965* (Chapel Hill: University of North Carolina Press, 1995), 44.

44. Mary E. Dreier, *Margaret Dreier Robins: Her Life, Letters, and Work* (New York: Island Cooperative Press, 1950), 80.

45. Newman interview with Wertheimer, 1976, PNP.

46. Allan L. Benson, "Women in a Labor War," *Munsey's*, April 1910, 68–76.

47. Cohn, "History of the I.L.G.W.U.," 121, 227.

48. Pauline Newman as quoted in Enstad, *Ladies of Labor*, 95.

49. "Autos for Strikers in Shirtwaist War," *New York Times*, Dec. 21, 1909, 1.

50. Olmstead as quoted in Marrin, *Flesh and Blood*, 92.

51. Cohn, "History of the I.L.G.W.U.," 15.

52. "Autos for Strikers in Shirtwaist War," 1.

53. Newman interview with Wertheimer, 1976, PNP; Cohn, "History of the I.L.G.W.U.," 16.

54. From *Let's Sing!* (Educational Department, International Ladies' Garment Workers' Union, New York City), https://trianglefire.ilr.cornell.edu/primary/songsPlays/UprisingTwentyThousand.html.

55. Articles and notes, mostly by PMN re: PMN life, 83-M191, 83-M198, box 1, folder 1, PNP.

56. Cohn, "History of the I.L.G.W.U.," 16–17.

57. Newman interview with Wertheimer, 1976, PNP.

58. "Frankly Speaking," articles and notes, mostly by PMN re: PMN life, 83-M191, 83-M198, box 1, folder 1, PNP.

59. Writings by Pauline Newman, including autobiographical notes, MC 324, box 4, folder 3, PNP.

Chapter 5. The Union Label

1. "New Penn Station Is Opened; Train Serve Begins Sept. 8 in Largest Building in World Ever Built at One Time," *New York Times*, Aug. 29, 1910, 4.

2. Natalie Zarelli, "Early 1900s Women Had an Ingenious Method for Fending off Gropers," History.com, Nov. 1, 2017, https://www.history.com/news/how-women-defended-themselves-against-street-gropers-100-years-ago (last updated April 15, 2025).

3. Letter to Michael and Hugh, MC 324, box 1, folder 3, Pauline Newman Papers (hereafter, PNP), Schlesinger Library, Radcliffe Institute, Harvard University, Cambridge, Massachusetts.

4. Joan Morrison and Charlotte Fox Zabusky, *American Mosaic: The Immigrant Experience in the Words of Those Who Lived It* (Pittsburgh: University of Pittsburgh Press, 1980), 12.

5. "Switchmen in East Prepare for Strike," *New York Times*, Dec. 6, 1909, 1.

6. Dorothy Sue Cobble, Linda Gordon, and Astrid Henry, *Feminism Unfinished: A Short, Surprising History of American Women's Movements* (New York: Liveright, 2014), 10.

7. Letter to Michael and Hugh, PNP.

8. Nan Enstad, *Ladies of Labor, Girls of Adventure: Working Women, Popular Culture, and Labor Politics at the Turn of the Twentieth Century* (New York: Columbia University Press, 1999), 155.

9. Michael Owen interview with author, Feb. 13, 2023.

10. Hugh Owen interview with author, Feb. 6, 2023.

11. Letter to Michael and Hugh, PNP.

12. Letter to Michael and Hugh, PNP.

13. Joan Marie Johnson, *Funding Feminism: Monied Women, Philanthropy, and the Women's Movement, 1870–1967* (Chapel Hill: University of North Carolina Press, 2017), 100.

14. Untitled, *Union Labor Advocate*, Aug. 1907, 18.

15. Leonora O'Reilly as quoted in Johnson, *Funding Feminism*, 96.

16. Letter to Michael and Hugh, PNP.

17. Herve K. Fiske to Pauline Newman, n.d., MC 324, box 9, folder 165, PNP.

18. Morrison and Zabusky, *American Mosaic*, 12.

19. Letter to Michael and Hugh, PNP.

20. Letter to Michael and Hugh, PNP.

21. Letter to Michael and Hugh, PNP.

22. Letter to Michael and Hugh, PNP.

23. Letter to Michael and Hugh, PNP.

24. Letter to Michael and Hugh, PNP.

25. Pauline Newman as quoted in Enstad, *Ladies of Labor*, 105.

26. M. Fannia Cohn, "History of the I.L.G.W.U.," unpublished, 1940, Kheel Center for Labor-Management Documentation and Archives, Martin P. Catherwood Library, Cornell University.

27. Pauline Newman as quoted in Ann Schofield, *To Do and To Be: Portraits of Four Women Activists, 1893–1986* (Boston: Northeastern University Press, 1997), 92.

28. "Seamstress Rockefeller Will Sew a Union Label," *New York Times*, Jan. 9, 1959, 12.

29. Letter to Michael and Hugh, PNP.

30. Letter to Michael and Hugh, PNP.

31. Rheta Childe Dorr, *What Eight Million Women Want* (Boston: Small, Maynard, 1910), 28–29.

32. Lincoln Filene obituary, *New York Times*, Aug. 4, 1957.

33. Johnson, *Funding Feminism*, 82.

34. Grace H. Dodge, ed., *Thoughts of Busy Girls: Written by a Group of Girls Who Have Little Time for Study and Yet Find Much Time for Thinking* (New York: Cassell, 1892), 90–91.

35. "The NY Cloakmakers' Strike," *Political Economy*, 155.

36. Cohn, "History of the I.L.G.W.U.," 20.

37. Cohn, "History of the I.L.G.W.U.," 21.

38. "Right Wrong with Song," *New York Times*, Nov. 17, 1910.

39. Susan A. Glenn, *Daughters of the Shtetl: Life and Labor in the Immigrant Generation* (Ithaca, NY: Cornell University Press, 1990), 136, 205.

40. Pauline Newman, "Out of the Past—Into the Future," *Life and Labor*, June 1921.

41. Pauline Newman, "How About It Girls?" *Progressive Woman*, Convention Number, Progressive Woman Publishing Co., 7, MC box 10, folder 174, https://www.marxists.org/history/usa/pubs/socialist-woman/120500-progressivewoman-v5w60.pdf.

42. Pauline Newman to Rose Schneiderman, Aug. 9, 1911, MC 324 box 5, folder 77, PNP.

43. Glenn, *Daughters of the Shtetl*, 74, 191.

44. "The Cloakmakers' Strike," *Journal of Political Economy* 19, no. 3 (March 1911), https://www.journals.uchicago.edu/doi/pdf/10.1086/251825 (accessed March 15, 2023).

45. Cohn, "History of the I.L.G.W.U.," 23.

46. Pauline Newman to Rose Schneiderman, Oct. 19, 1910, PNP.

47. Percy Bysshe Shelly, "The Masque of Anarchy."

48. Annual Report, NWTUL executive board, 1937–1939; and letter to Michael and Hugh, PNP.

49. Rose Schneiderman to Pauline Newman, letters over the course of 1910, Rose Schneiderman Papers TAM 018, box 6, folder 1, Rose Schneiderman Papers (hereafter, RSP), Tamiment Library and Robert F. Wagner Labor Archive, Elmer Holmes Bobst Library, New York University.

50. Dorothy Sue Cobble, *Feminism Unfinished*, 13.

51. Rose Schneiderman Papers, April 1910, folder 1, box 5, RSP.

52. May 10, 1911, box 5, RSP, and box 6, folder 1.

53. Earl Mayo, "The Work That Kills," *The Outlook* 99 (1911): 205.

54. Pauline Newman interview with Barbara Wertheimer, 1976, MC 324, box 1, folder 6, PNP.

55. George Price, Diary, May 4, Kheel Center, Labor-Management Documentation & Archives, Cornell University.

56. George Price, Diary, May 4.

57. Pauline Newman, "Out of the Past—The Joint Board of Sanitary Control," MC 324, box 6, folder 109, PNP.

58. Morrison and Zabusky, *American Mosaic*, 13.

Chapter 6. The Triangle Fire

1. "Triangle Survivors Slid Down Cables," *New York Times*, Dec. 13, 1911, 20.

2. "Triangle Survivors Slid Down Cables," 20.

3. Frances Perkins as quoted in Albert Marrin, *Flesh and Blood So Cheap: The Triangle Fire and Its Legacy* (New York: Alfred A. Knopf, 2011), 3.

4. Dr. D. E. Keefe of St. Vincent's Hospital as quoted in Leon Stein, *The Triangle Fire: Centennial Edition* (Ithaca, NY: ILR Press, 1990), 16. (First published 1926.)

5. Mary E. Dreier, *Margaret Dreier Robins: Her Life, Letters, and Work* (New York: Island Cooperative Press, 1950), 77.

6. Stein, *Triangle Fire*, 73.

7. Pauline Newman interview with Barbara Wertheimer, 1976, MC 324, box 1, folder 6, Pauline Newman Papers (hereafter, PNP), Schlesinger Library, Radcliffe Institute, Harvard University, Cambridge, Massachusetts.

8. Anna Quindlen, "About New York: The Triangle Fire and a Lifetime of Union Service," *New York Times*, March 23, 1983, 31.

9. Manufacturers' Bulletin for Fire Protection Issued by the Joint Board of Sanitary Control (New York: The Board, 1915).

10. Letter to Michael and Hugh, MC 324, box 1, folder 6, PNP.

11. "Greed the Trouble, Clergymen Assert," *New York Times*, March 27, 1911, 5.

12. Manufacturers' Bulletin for Fire Protection.

13. Manufacturers' Bulletin for Fire Protection.

14. Manufacturers' Bulletin for Fire Protection.

15. Gus Tyler, *Look for the Union Label: A History of the International Ladies' Garment Workers' Union* (Armonk, NY: M. E. Sharpe, 1995), 86–87.

16. NOAA sunrise/sunset calculator, March 27, 1911, https://gml.noaa.gov/grad/solcalc/sunrise.html (accessed Feb. 25, 2023).

17. "Sad All-Day March to Morgue Gates," *New York Times*, March 27, 1911, 2.

18. Letter to Michael and Hugh, PNP.

19. Letter to Michael and Hugh, PNP.

20. "Greed the Trouble," *New York Times*, March 27, 1911, 5.

21. "Greed the Trouble," 5.

22. Rose Schneiderman Papers TAM 018, box 6, Tamiment Library/Robert F. Wagner Labor Archives, New York University.

23. Rose Schneiderman as quoted in Dreier, *Margaret Dreier Robins*, 77.

24. Tyler, *Look for the Union Label*, 91.

25. Susan A. Glenn, *Daughters of the Shtetl: Life and Labor in the Immigrant Generation* (Ithaca, NY: Cornell University Press, 1990), 122, 84.

26. Schneiderman as quoted in Annelise Orleck, *Common Sense and a Little Fire: Women and Working-Class Politics in the United States 1900–1965* (Chapel Hill: University of North Carolina Press, 1995), 66.

27. Schneiderman as quoted in Tyler, *Look for the Union Label*, 95.

28. Schneiderman as quoted in Tyler, *Look for the Union Label*, 95.

29. Schneiderman as quoted in Tyler, *Look for the Union Label*, 95.

30. Pauline Newman to Rose Schneiderman, May 17, 1911, MC 324, box 5, folder 77, PNP.

31. Newman to Schneiderman, May 17, 1911, PNP.

32. Newman to Schneiderman, May 17, 1911, PNP.

33. Newman to Schneiderman, May 17, 1911, PNP.

34. Newman interview with Wertheimer, 1976, PNP.

35. As quoted in Lillian Faderman, *To Believe in Women: What Lesbians Have Done for America—A History* (Boston: Houghton Mifflin, 1999), 111.

36. Lectures of Frances Perkins, Collection /3047, Sept. 30, 1964, Cornell University, Kheel Center for Labor-Management Documentation and Archives, Ithaca, NY.

37. Henry Moskowitz, "The Joint Board of Sanitary Control of the Cloak, Suit, and Skirt Industry," *Annals of American Academy of Political and Social Science* 44, Outlook for Industrial Peace (Nov. 1912): 39–58.

38. "Regrets Voting for Triangle Acquittal," *New York Times*, Dec. 29, 1911, 8.

39. "Girls Fought Vainly at Triangle Doors," *New York Times*, Dec. 12, 1911, 4.

40. "Regrets Voting," 8, 4; "Triangle Owners Acquitted by Jury," Dec. 28, 1911, http://www.law.umkc.edu/faculty/projects/ftrials/triangle/trianglenyt1228.html (accessed June 28, 2010).

41. "Regrets Voting," 8; "Triangle Owners Acquitted by Jury."

42. "Regrets Voting," 8.

43. Ernest Deutch to *New York Times*, Sept. 1, 1980, MC 324, box 9, folder 15, PNP.

Chapter 7. Hopscotching

1. M. Fannia Cohn, "History of the I.L.G.W.U.," unpublished, 1940, 28, Kheel Center for Labor-Management Documentation and Archives, Martin P. Catherwood Library, Cornell University.

2. Pauline Newman to Rose Schneiderman, July 14, 1911, MC 324, box 5, folder 77, Pauline Newman Papers (hereafter, PNP), Schlesinger Library, Radcliffe Institute, Harvard University, Cambridge, Massachusetts.

3. Annelise Orleck, *Common Sense and a Little Fire: Women and Working-Class Politics in the United States 1900–1965* (Chapel Hill: University of North Carolina Press, 1995), 69.

4. Pauline Newman to Rose Schneiderman, Nov. 12, 1911, TAM box 6, folder 2, Rose Schneiderman Papers (hereafter RSP), Tamiment Library/Robert F. Wagner Labor Archives, New York University.

5. Cohn, "History of the I.L.G.W.U.," 29–30.

6. As quoted in Lois Sharf, "The Great Uprising in Cleveland: When Sisterhood Failed," in *A Needle, a Bobbin, a Strike: Women Needleworkers in America*, ed. Joan M. Jensen and Sue Davidson (Philadelphia: Temple University Press, 1984).

7. Pauline Newman, "The Child Labor Law," June 13, 1911, *Progressive Woman*.

8. Pauline Newman to Rose Schneiderman, July 14, 1911, PNP.

9. Newman to Schneiderman, July 14, 1911, PNP.

10. Newman to Schneiderman, Oct. 29, 1911, PNP.
11. Newman to Schneiderman, Nov. 7, 1911, PNP.
12. Newman to Schneiderman, Nov. 7, 1911, PNP.
13. Newman to Schneiderman, Nov. 21, 1911, PNP.
14. Newman to Schneiderman, Nov. 21, 1911, PNP.
15. Newman to Schneiderman, Nov. 21, 1911, PNP.
16. Newman to Schneiderman, Nov. 21, 1911, PNP.
17. Julie Novkov, *Constituting Workers, Protecting Women: Gender, Law and Labor in the Progressive Era and New Deal Years* (Ann Arbor: University of Michigan Press, 2001), https://library.oapen.org/bitstream/handle/20.500.12657/64145/1/9780472904211.pdf (last accessed Oct. 25, 2023).
18. Lillian Faderman, *To Believe in Women: What Lesbians Have Done for America—A History* (Boston: Houghton Mifflin, 1999), 8.
19. Pauline Newman, "A Stove and I," MC 324, box 10, folder 176, PNP.
20. Pauline Newman, "The Workers of the World," *Progressive Woman* 5, no. 59 (April 1912: 7, MC 324, box 10, folder 174, PNP.
21. Newman, "Workers of the World."
22. Pauline Newman to Rose Schneiderman, Dec. 26, 1911, MC 324, box 5, folder 77, PNP.
23. Pauline Newman to Rose Schneiderman, Aug. 1912, folder 3, box 6, RSP.
24. Newman to Schneiderman, Aug. 1912, RSP.
25. Pauline Newman interview with Barbara Wertheimer, 1976, MC 324, box 1, folder 6, PNP.
26. A. B. Reeve, "The Death Roll of Industry," *Charities and the Commons* 17 (1907): 791.
27. Pauline Newman to Rose Schneiderman, Jan. 16, 1912, MC 324, box 5, folder 77, PNP.
28. Newman to Schneiderman, Jan. 16, 1912, PNP.
29. Newman to Schneiderman, March 26, 1912, PNP.
30. As quoted in Novkov, *Constituting Workers*, 165.
31. Pauline Newman, "Difficulties with Sister," *Labor Ages* 11, no. 4 (April 1912): 181, MC 324, box 10, folder 175, PNP.
32. Newman, "Workers of the World."
33. Pauline Newman, "How About It Girls?" *The Progressive Woman*, Convention Number, n.d., MC 324, box 10, folder 174, https://www.marxists.org/history/usa/pubs/socialist-woman/120500-progressivewoman-v5w60.pdf.

Chapter 8. "I Would Rather Be the Fighter"

1. Injunction 1912, MC 324, box 6, folder 95, Pauline Newman Papers (hereafter, PNP), Schlesinger Library, Radcliffe Institute, Harvard University, Cambridge, Massachusetts.

2. Pauline Newman to Rose Schneiderman, July 12, 1912, MC 324, box 5, folder 77, PNP.

3. M. Fannia Cohn, "History of the I.L.G.W.U.," unpublished, 1940, p. 36, Kheel Center for Labor-Management Documentation and Archives, Martin P. Catherwood Library, Cornell University.

4. Newman to Schneiderman, July 12, 1912, PNP.

5. Josephine Casey, "Letter from Prison," *Detroit Times*, May 4, 1912, https://www.marxists.org/subject/jewish/ilgwu-history/ilg-5.pdf (accessed Feb. 23, 2023).

6. Pauline Newman, "The Workers of the World," *The Progressive Woman* 5, no. 59 (April 1912): 7, MC 324, box 10, folder 174, PNP.

7. Newman to Schneiderman, July 11, 1912, PNP.

8. Pauline Newman, "From the Battle Front," MC 324, box 10, folder 174, PNP.

9. Cohn, "History of the I.L.G.W.U.," 36.

10. Ellen Munroe, "On 'Woman's Weakness,'" *Boston Bee*, reprinted in *Voice of Industry*, March 13, 1945, https://www.industrialrevolution.org/women-weakness (last accessed Nov. 27, 2023).

11. Munroe, "On 'Woman's Weakness.'"

12. Brian Donovan, "Respectability on Trial: Sex Crimes in New York City, 1900–1918," *New York History* 99, nos. 3/4 (2018): 478–81.

13. Newman as quoted in Nancy Schrom Dye, *As Equals and as Sisters: Feminism, the Labor Movement, and the Women's Trade Union League of New York* (Columbia: University of Missouri Press, 1980).

14. Pauline Newman as quoted in Ann Schofield, *To Do and To Be: Portraits of Four Women Activists, 1893–1986* (Boston: Northeastern University Press, 1997), 90.

15. Dreier as quoted in Joan Marie Johnson, *Funding Feminism: Monied Women, Philanthropy, and the Women's Movement, 1870–1967* (Chapel Hill: University of North Carolina Press, 2017), 98.

16. Pauline Newman, "An Inspector's Point of View," *The Message* 4, no. 4 (Feb. 1917): 46 (published by ILGWU).

17. Newman, "Inspector's Point of View."

18. "Roosevelt Talks to Wrapper Strikers on Visits to Halls," *ILGWU News History*, Fiftieth Anniversary Convention Issue, Jan. 22, 1913, https://www.marxists.org/subject/jewish/ilgwu-history/ilg-5.pdf (last accessed March 3, 2023).

19. Cohn, "History of the I.L.G.W.U.," 45.

20. Cohn, "History of the I.L.G.W.U.," 49.

21. Alice Kessler-Harris, *Out to Work: A History of Wage Earning Women in the U.S.* (New York: Oxford University Press, 1982).

22. Manufacturers' Bulletin for Fire Protection Issued by the Joint Board of Sanitary Control (New York: The Board, 1915), 3, Kheel Center.

23. Manufacturers' Bulletin for Fire Protection, 7.

24. Mary Van Kleeck, *Working Girls in Evening Schools: A Statistical Study* (New York: Russell Sage Foundation, 1914), 91.

25. "The Message," MC 324, box 10, general, 1910–1964, PNP.

26. Paul Buhle and Jennifer Buhle, *The Concise History of Woman Suffrage: Selections from History of Woman Suffrage, by Elizabeth Cady Stanton, Susan B. Anthony, Matilda Joslyn Gage, and the National American Woman Suffrage Association* (Champaign: University of Illinois Press, 2005).

27. Pauline Newman, "Insuring Motherhood," *American Hebrew and Jewish Messenger*, Sept. 15, 1916, 590, MC 324, box 10, folder 175, PNP.

28. Newman, "Insuring Motherhood."

29. Newman, "Insuring Motherhood."

30. Pauline Newman, "Mid-Atlantic Interstate Conference of WTUL," Dec. 1 to 3, 1916, MC 324, box 4, folder 57, PNP.

31. Newman, "Mid-Atlantic Interstate Conference of WTUL."

Chapter 9. Finding Frieda

1. Frieda S. Miller to Pauline Newman, Sept. 11, 1918, MC 324, box 6, folder 87, Pauline Newman Papers (hereafter, PNP), Schlesinger Library, Radcliffe Institute, Harvard University, Cambridge, Massachusetts.

2. Miller to Newman, Sept. 11, 1918, PNP.

3. Lillian Faderman, *To Believe in Women: What Lesbians Have Done for America—A History* (Boston: Houghton Mifflin, 1999), 7.

4. Sophonisba P. Breckinridge to the Editor, *University of Chicago Magazine*, Nov. 1938, MC 324, A-37, box 1, folder 4, Frieda Segelke Miller Papers (hereafter, FMP), Schlesinger Library, Radcliffe Institute, Harvard University, Cambridge, Massachusetts.

5. General correspondence, 1913–1965, MC 324, box 6, folder 87, PNP.

6. Elisabeth Burger Miller interview with Jodie Rodberg, 2003, MC 868, box 1, folder 5, Elisabeth Burger Miller Papers (hereafter, EBP), Schlesinger Library, Radcliffe Institute, Harvard University, Cambridge, Massachusetts.

7. Elisabeth Burger Miller interview with Eva Mosely, MC 868, box 1, folder 4, EBP.

8. "The American Expeditionary Forces," Stars and Stripes Collection, Library of Congress, https://www.loc.gov/collections/stars-and-stripes/articles-and-essays/a-world-at-war/american-expeditionary-forces/ (accessed Oct. 19, 2023).

9. John F. Hart as quoted in Philip S. Foner, *History of the Labor Movement in the United States*, vol. 7: *Labor and World War I, 1914–1916* (New York: International Publishers, 1987), 3.

10. Pauline Newman interview with Barbara Wertheimer, 1976, MC 324, box 1, folder 6, PNP.

11. Dorothy Sue Cobble, *For the Many: American Feminists and the Global Fight for Democratic Equality* (Princeton, NJ: Princeton University Press, 2021), 41–42.

12. Foner, *History of the Labor Movement*, 7:40.

13. Hart quoted in Foner, *History of the Labor Movement*, 7:197.

14. Hart quoted in Foner, *History of the Labor Movement*, 7:198.

15. Foner, *History of the Labor Movement*, 7:199.

16. Foner, *History of the Labor Movement*, 7:199; Samuel Gompers, "Don't Sacrifice Womanhood, *American Federationist* (Aug. 1917): 747–49.

17. Foner, *History of the Labor Movement*, 7:200; Samuel Gompers, "There Is No Shortage of Labor," *American Federationist* 24 (Oct. 1917): 22–25.

18. Pauline Newman, "An Old Problem—To Be Faced Anew," MC 324, box 10, folder 176, PNP.

19. Sarah Cory Rippey to Pauline Newman, Dec. 10, 1919, MC 324, box 6, folder 87, PNP.

20. Pauline Newman, "Lest We Forget," 1918, MC 324, box 10, folder 175, PNP.

21. Rose Schneiderman to Pauline Newman, Aug. 11, 1917, MC 324, box 5, folder 78, PNP.

22. Grace H. Dodge, ed., *Thoughts of Busy Girls: Written by a Group of Girls Who Have Little Time for Study and Yet Find Much Time for Thinking* (New York: Cassell, 1892), 16.

23. Dodge, *Thoughts of Busy Girls*, 22–23.

24. Newman interview with Wertheimer, 1976, PNP.

25. Rose Schneiderman to Pauline Newman, Nov. 2, 1918, MC 324, box 5, folder 77, PNP.

26. Faderman, *To Believe in Women*, 109.

27. Faderman, *To Believe in Women*, 110–11.

28. "Evelyn Nesbitt in Film: "Redemption" Somewhat Resembles Actress's Life Story," *New York Times*, May 22, 1917.

29. Newman interview with Wertheimer, 1976, PNP.

30. Lindsey Clark, "How the 1918 Flu and COVID-19 Pandemics Transformed Women's Lives," March 2, 2021, American Society for Microbiology, https://asm.org/Articles/2021/March/How-the-Spanish-Flu-and-COVID-19-Pandemics-Transfo (accessed Dec. 18, 2022).

31. "Tahiti Builds Pyres of Influenza," *New York Times*, Dec. 25, 1918; "Care for Jewish Orphans," *New York Times*, Nov. 30, 1918, 8.

32. Rose Schneiderman to Pauline Newman, Oct. 16, 1918, MC 324, box 5, folder 78, PNP.

33. Newman interview with Wertheimer, 1976, PNP.

34. Newman interview with Wertheimer, 1976, PNP.

35. Leonora O'Reilly to Pauline Newman, Nov. 14, 1918, MC 324, box 5, folder 78, PNP.

36. O'Reilly to Newman, Nov. 9, 1918, PNP.

37. O'Reilly to Newman, Nov. 9, 1918, PNP.

38. Writings by Pauline Newman, including autobiographical notes, 1960–75, MC 324, box 5, folder 4, PNP.

39. Newman as quoted in Ann Schofield, *To Do and to Be: Portraits of Four Women Activists, 1893–1986* (Boston: Northeastern University Press, 1997), 93.

40. Pauline Newman, "To the men and women of the 13th" a.d., MC 324, box 10, folder 176, PNP.

41. Pauline Newman, Oct. 11, 1912, "The Workers of the World," *The Progressive Woman* 5, no. 59 (April 1912): 7.

42. Newman interview with Wertheimer, 1976, PNP.

43. Pauline Newman, "Organized Labor Battles Hotel and Restaurant Employers," professional letters/speeches, MC 324, box 8, folder 129, PNP.

44. Pauline Newman to Rose Schneiderman, and Rose Schneiderman to Pauline Newman, Nov. 20, 1919, both in MC 324, box 5, folder 78, PNP.

45. Frieda Segelke Miller telegram to Pauline Newman, Dec. 25, 1919, MC 324, box 2, folder 35, PNP.

Chapter 10. Working Mothers

1. Undated love letter to Frieda Miller from Charles Kutz, Elisabeth Burger Papers (hereafter, EBP), MC 868, box 27, folder 6, Schlesinger Library, Radcliffe Institute, Harvard University, Cambridge, Massachusetts.

2. Ada Broughton to Pauline Newman, June 8, 1923, MC 324, box 10, folder 166, Pauline Newman Papers (hereafter, PNP), Schlesinger Library, Radcliffe Institute, Harvard University, Cambridge, Massachusetts.

3. Mary Bondfield to Pauline Newman, Jan. 9, 1923, MC 324, box 8, folder 142, PNP.

4. Bondfield to Newman, Jan. 9, 1923, PNP.

5. "Birth," MC 868, box 1, folder 7, EBP.

6. "Birth," EBP.

7. "Adoption," MC 868 box 1, folder 2, EBP.

8. Elisabeth Burger Miller interview with Josie Rodberg, 2003, MC 868, box 1, folder 5, EBP.

9. Frieda Miller, notes on caring for baby, MC 868, box 27, folder 12, EBP.

10. Pauline Newman interview with Barbara Wertheimer, 1976, MC 324, box 1, folder 6, PNP.

11. Pauline Newman, "The Voice of Labor at the National Health Conference," speeches and statements, MC 324, box 10, folder 182, PNP.

12. Newman, "Voice of Labor," PNP.

13. Pauline Newman, "A Dream Realized," p. 6, MC 324, box 10, folder 174, PNP.

14. Matthew Lavine, "The Early Clinical X-Ray in the United States: Patient Experiences and Public Perceptions," *Journal of the History of Medicine and*

Allied Sciences 67, no. 4 (2012): 587–625, doi: 10.1093/jhmas/jrr047. Epub 2011 Sep 6. PMID: 21896562.

15. Lavine, "Early Clinical X-Ray."

16. As quoted in Gus Tyler, *Look for the Union Label: A History of the International Ladies' Garment Workers' Union* (Armonk, NY: M. E. Sharpe, 1995), 131.

17. Tyler, *Look for the Union Label*, 131–32.

18. Lillian Faderman, *To Believe in Women: What Lesbians Have Done for America—A History* (Boston: Houghton Mifflin, 1999), 111.

19. "Eva Le Galliene, A Wistful Peter Pan," *New York Times*, Nov. 27, 1928, 27.

20. Frieda Segelke Miller Papers (hereafter, FMP), Frieda Miller to Pauline Newman, n.d., 83-m191. 83-m198, box 1, folder 8, Schlesinger Library, Radcliffe Institute, Harvard University, Cambridge, Massachusetts.

21. Burger Miller interview with Rodberg, 2003, EBP.

22. Michael Owen interview with author, Feb. 13, 2023.

23. Michael Owen interview with author, Feb. 13, 2023.

24. Michael Owen interview with author, Feb. 13, 2023.

25. Michael Owen interview with author, Feb. 13, 2023.

26. Faderman, *To Believe*, 4.

27. Pauline Newman letter to David Leab, editor of *Labor History*, Oct. 27, 1976, pn papers addenda, MC 324, folder 2, box 1, PNP.

28. Original language of Equal Rights Amendment as quoted from https://www.alicepaul.org/equal-rights-amendment-2/ (last accessed May 6, 2025).

29. Dorothy Sue Cobble, Linda Gordon, and Astrid Henry, *Feminism Unfinished: A Short, Surprising History of American Women's Movements* (New York: Liveright, 2014), 11–12.

30. Cobble et al., *Feminism Unfinished*, 12–13.

31. The Progressive opposition to the ERA was vastly different from the reasons the conservative movement, under Phyllis Schlafly, opposed it starting in the 1970s. The conservative lawyer argued the ERA would rip the social fabric of the United States asunder. Ratification of the ERA would lead to gender-neutral bathrooms, same-sex marriage, and women in combat. When Schlafly's campaign proved successful, Republicans, which had been first party to endorse the amendment back in 1940, denounced it.

32. Newman as quoted in Ann Schofield, *To Do and To Be: Portraits of Four Women Activists, 1893–1986* (Boston: Northeastern University Press, 1997), 65.

33. Pauline Newman, "Difficulties with Sister," *Labor Ages* 11, no. 4 (April 1912): 1819, MC 324, box 10, folder 175, PNP.

34. Burger Miller interview with Rodberg, 2003, EBP.

35. Kate M. to Pauline Newman, March 1928, MC 324, box 10, folder 166, PNP.

36. Burger Miller interview with Rodberg, 2003, EBP.

37. Burger Miller interview with Rodberg, 2003, EBP.

38. Burger Miller interview with Rodberg, 2003, EBP.

39. Pauline Newman to Frieda S. Miller, Aug. 23, 1972, A-37, box 1, folder 8, FMP.

40. Newman to Miller, Aug. 23, 1972, FMP.

41. Newman to Miller, Aug. 23, 1972, FMP.

42. Newman to Miller, Aug. 23, 1972, FMP.

43. Newman to Miller, Aug. 23, 1972, FMP.

44. Jacob Panken to Pauline Newman, Oct. 31, 1929, MC 324, box 10, folder 166, PNP; "Socialists Name Woman to Sheriff," *New York Times*, July 12, 1929, 16.

45. Michael Owen interview with author, Feb. 13, 2013.

46. Solomon Lowenstein to Pauline Newman, Nov. 6, 1929, MC 324, box 10, folder 166, PNP.

47. Pauline Newman speech on minimum wage, MC 324, box 8, folder 130, PNP.

48. Pauline Newman, letter to the editor, *New York Times*, March 15, 1933, MC 324, box 9, folder 153, PNP.

49. Sophonisba P. Breckinridge letter to the editor, *University of Chicago Magazine*, Nov. 1938, AC-37, box 1, folder 4, FMP.

50. Frieda S. Miller to Pauline Newman, Dec. 14, 1935, AC-37, box 1, folder 1, FMP.

51. "Yule Party Given by Mrs. Roosevelt," *New York Times*, Dec. 22, 1934, 3.

Chapter 11. Eight Days in the White House

1. "15 Trades Union Girls Thrilled by Life as White House Guests," *New York Times*, May 5, 1936, 25.

2. Pauline Newman interview with Barbara Wertheimer, 1976, MC 324, box 1, folder 6, Pauline Newman Papers (hereafter, PNP), Schlesinger Library, Radcliffe Institute, Harvard University, Cambridge, Massachusetts.

3. ILGWU Collection, *Justice*, Sept. 1, 1934, "Seven Days That Shook the World," Microfilm vols. 15–19, 1933–1937, Kheel Center for Labor-Management Documentation and Archives, Martin P. Catherwood Library, Cornell University.

4. Dorothy Sue Cobble, Linda Gordon, and Astrid Henry, *Feminism Unfinished: A Short, Surprising History of American Women's Movements* (New York: Liveright, 2014), 16.

5. Kirsten Downey, *The Woman Behind the New Deal: The Life and Legacy of Frances Perkins—Social Security, Unemployment Insurance, and the Minimum Wage* (New York: First Anchor Books Edition, 2009), 157.

6. Dorothy Sue Cobble, *For the Many: American Feminists and the Global Fight for Democratic Equality* (Princeton, NJ: Princeton University Press, 2021).

7. Eleanor Roosevelt, "My Day, May 5, 1936," Columbian College of Arts and Sciences, George Washington University, *The Eleanor Roosevelt Papers Digital Edition* (2017), Eleanor Roosevelt Papers Project.

8. "Attacks Women's Party," *New York Times*, April 21, 1936, 9.

9. "15 Trades Union Girls Thrilled," 25.

10. "15 Trades Union Girls Thrilled," 25.

11. Pauline Newman, *Life and Labor*, 1936, "PMN's corner" post-election notes, MC 324, box 6, folder 90, Articles and speeches by PN 1923, PNP.

12. Landon R. Y. Storrs, *The Second Red Scare and the Unmaking of the New Deal Left* (Princeton, NJ: Princeton University Press, 2013), 124.

13. Pauline Newman, Poem, MC 324 21v-39, folder 37, poetry by and for PN, n.d., PNP.

14. Mary Dreier to Pauline Newman, MC 324, box 5, folder 85, PNP.

15. Newman to Dreier, PNP, unpublished, n.d.

16. Downey, *Woman Behind the New Deal*, 218.

17. "Attacks Women's Party," 9; "Minimum Pay Law Asked for Women," *New York Times*, April 1, 1935, 13.

18. Pauline Newman, "First Minimum Wage Law Goes into Effect," *American Labor World* (Nov. 1933): 17.

19. "Attacks Women's Party," 9.

20. "Attacks Women's Party," 9.

21. Pauline Newman to E. Worth Higgins, July 28, 1938, MC 324, box 6, folder 103, PNP.

22. Pauline Newman, "Labor's Contribution to the Field of Industrial Dentistry," typed notes for speech, Oct. 27, 1931.

23. Pauline Newman to Eleanor Roosevelt, May 27, 1936, MC 324, box 5, folder 86, PNP.

24. Freida Miller to Pauline Newman, undated postcard, MC 324, box 26, folder 4, PNP.

25. Frieda Miller to Pauline Newman, Feb. 10, 1950, MC 324, box 8, folder 119, PNP.

26. Pauline Newman to Frieda Miller, June 1, 1936, Frieda S. Miller Papers (hereafter, FMP), 1909–1973, A-37, folder 8.

27. Elisabeth Miller Burger interview with "Jodie R," 2003, Elisabeth Burger Papers (hereafter, EBP), MC 868, box 1, folder 5.

28. Newman to Miller, June 1, 1936, FMP.

29. "80 Sign to Oppose Rights Amendment," *New York Times*, Aug. 19, 1943.

30. Cobble et al., *Feminism Unfinished*, 42.

31. Rossiter Johnson, "A Bold Guess What Equal Rights," *New York Times*, Oct. 28, 1923, 65.

32. Newman to Miller, June 1, 1936, FMP.

33. Elisabeth Miller Burger interview with "JR," 2003, MC 868, box 1, folder 5, EBP.

34. Sen. W. Borah to Pauline Newman, Feb. 9, 1938, MC 324, box 9, folder 164, PNP.

35. Pauline Newman, "Equal Rights' Amendment," *American Federationist*, Aug. 1938, 815–17.

36. Dorothy Straus to Pauline Newman, Dec. 12, 1938, MC 324, box 8, folder 136, PNP.

37. NYWTUL statements, 1934, MC 324, box 4, folder 68, PNP; *American Federationist* 45, no. 8 (Aug. 1938), MC 324, box 6, folder 90, PNP.

38. Cobble, *For the Many*, 173.

39. Cobble, *For the Many*, 173.

40. Mary Dreier to Pauline Newman, 1934–1939, MC 324, box 5, folder 85 and MC 324, box 5, folder 78, PNP.

41. Rose Schneiderman to Cordell Hull, Dec. 9, 1938, MC 324, box 5, folder 79, PNP.

42. Elisabeth C. to Pauline Newman, April 15, 1938, MC 324, box 5, folder 81, PNP.

43. Cobble, *For the Many*, 180.

44. National WTUL executive board, 1937–1939, MC 324, box 3, folder 60, PNP.

45. Elisabeth Miller Burger interview with Eva M., MC 868, box 1, folder 4, EBP.

46. Michael Owen interview with author, Feb. 13, 2023.

47. Michael Owen interview with author, Feb. 13, 2023.

48. Pauline Newman to Frieda S. Miller, March 15, 1941, MC 324, box 3, folder 49, PNP.

49. Pauline Newman to Frieda S. Miller, March 17, 1941, PNP.

50. Pauline Newman to Frieda S. Miller, March 18, 1941, PNP.

51. Rose Schneiderman to Franklin Delano Roosevelt, Dec. 10, 1941, MC 324, box 5, folder 1, PNP.

52. "Women and Post–WWII Wages," Nov. 1, 2003, National Bureau of Economic Research, https://www.nber.org/digest/nov02/women-and-post-wwii-wages (last accessed May 8, 2025).

53. Pauline Newman to Mary Dreier, May 26, 1941, MC 324, box 5, folder 85, PNP.

54. Newman to Dreier, May 26, 1941, PNP.

55. Pauline Newman radio interview, Aug. 24, 1943, MC 324, box 10, folder 183, PNP.

56. Cobble, *For the Many*, 240.

57. Pauline Newman to Elisabeth Burger, 1943, 1969, Additional papers of Pauline Newman, 1926–1982, 83-M191, 83-M198, 4, box 1, PNP.

58. Pauline Newman to Frieda S. Miller, Dec. 30, 1943, MC 868, box 26, folder 4, PNP.

59. Newman to Miller, Dec. 30, 1943, PNP.

60. Newman to Miller, Dec. 30, 1943, PNP.

61. Newman to Miller, Dec. 30, 1943, PNP.

62. Pauline Newman to Frieda S. Miller, Aug. 30, 1943, A-37, box 1, folder 8, FMP.

63. Pauline Newman to Frieda S. Miller, March 3, 1943, FMP.

Chapter 12. Miles of Ruins

1. Report with Sara Southall, "Recommendations excerpted from the Report on Status of Women in Industry and Trade unions in Germany submitted to the high commissioner," MC 324, box 8, folder 126, Pauline Newman Papers (hereafter, PNP), Schlesinger Library, Radcliffe Institute, Harvard University, Cambridge, Massachusetts.

2. As quoted in Dorothy Sue Cobble, *For the Many: American Feminists and the Global Fight for Democratic Equality* (Princeton, NJ: Princeton University Press, 2021), 291.

3. Diaries, 1949, Feb. 21, 1949, and Feb. 22, 1949, MC 324, M-44, 8v., box 1, PNP.

4. Pauline Newman to Frieda S. Miller, "greeting cards," A-37, box 1, folder 11, Frieda S. Miller Papers (hereafter, FMP), Schlesinger Library, Radcliffe Institute, Harvard University, Cambridge, Massachusetts.

5. Frieda Miller to Pauline Newman, greeting card, 1949, MC 324, box 3, folder 48, PNP.

6. "Germany," MC 324, box 8, folder 126, PNP.

7. Pauline Newman to Rose Schneiderman, Frankfurt, Sept. 11, 1949, MC 324, 8v, 1949, PNP.

8. Articles and notes, mostly by Pauline Newman re: PMN life, Dec. 1949, no. 107 Newman, 83-M191, 83-M198, box 1, folder 1, PNP.

9. Pauline Newman to *New York Times*, Sept. 17, 1958, MC 324, box 9, folder 153, PNP.

10. Newman to *New York Times*, Sept. 17, 1958, PNP.

11. Harry D. Wemple to Pauline Newman, Dec. 20, 1949, MC 324, box 8, folder 126, PNP.

12. "Germany," PNP.

13. Frieda S. Miller to Pauline Newman, Sept. 26, 1949, MC 868, box 26, folder 6, PNP.

14. Pauline Newman to Frieda S. Miller, Aug. 20, 1949, MC 868, box 26, folder 6, PNP.

15. Report with Sara Southall, "Recommendations," PNP.

16. Eleanor Roosevelt to Pauline Newman, May 10, 1949, MC 324, 8v, 1949, PNP.

17. Michael Owen reflections, Sept. 7, 1992, MC 868, box 26, folder 1, Elisabeth Miller Burger Papers (hereafter, EBP), Schlesinger Library, Radcliffe Institute, Harvard University, Cambridge, Massachusetts.

18. Michael Owen reflections, Sept. 7, 1992, EBP.

19. Hugh Owen interview with author, Feb. 6, 2023.

20. Michael Owen reflections, Sept. 7, 1992, EBP.

21. Pauline Newman, "Labor's Unfinished Business," *Live and Labor*, Dec. 1949, no. 107, 83-M191, 83-M198, box 1, folder 3, PNP.

22. Pauline Newman to *New York Times*, Aug. 10, 1951, MC 324, box 9, folder 153, PNP.

23. Hugh Owen interview with author, Feb. 6, 2023.

24. Pauline Newman, "Concerning American Working Women," MC 324 box 6, folder 90, Publicity: articles and speeches by Pauline Newman, 1923, n.d., PNP.

25. Dorothy Sue Cobble, Linda Gordon, and Astrid Henry, *Feminism Unfinished: A Short, Surprising History of American Women's Movements* (New York: Liveright, 2014), 32–33.

26. Cobble et al., *Feminism Unfinished*, 32–33.

27. Pauline Newman, MC 324 box 6, folder 90, Publicity: articles and speeches by Pauline Newman, 1923, n.d., PNP.

28. Elisabeth Miller Burger to Jodie Roden, 2003, MC 868, box 1, folder 5, EBP.

29. Michael Owen interview with author, Feb. 13, 2023.

30. Rose Schneiderman to Pauline Newman, Aug. 11, 1954, 83-M191, 83-M198, box 1, folder 3, PNP.

31. Hugh Owen interview with author, Feb. 6, 2023.

32. Pauline Newman to Frieda S. Miller, July 20, 1955, AS-37, box, 1, folder 8, FMP.

33. Newman to Miller, July 22, 1955, FMP.

34. Newman to Miller, Aug. 1, 1955, FMP.

35. Newman to Miller, Aug. 19, 1955, FSM MC 811, box 1, folder 1, PNP.

36. Newman to Miller, Aug. 19, 1955, PNP.

37. "Complete Picture Coverage of Valley's Worst Flood," *The Morning Call*, Aug. 20, 1955.

38. Newman to Miller, Aug. 19, 1955, PNP.

39. Newman to Miller, Aug. 19, 1955, PNP.

40. Newman to Miller, Aug. 19, 1955, PNP.

41. Miller to Newman, Oct. 11, 1955, MC 811, box 3, folder 41, PNP.

42. Newman to Miller, Dec. 10, 1955, FMP.

43. Newman to Miller, Dec. 10, 1955, FMP.

44. Newman to Miller, Dec. 10, 1955, FMP.

45. Pauline Newman to Frieda S. Miller, Jan. 4, 1956, MC 811, box 1, folder 1, PNP.

46. Miller to Newman, as quoted in Annelise Orleck, *Common Sense and a Little Fire: Women and Working-Class Politics in the United States 1900–1965* (Chapel Hill: University of North Carolina Press, 1995), 281.

Chapter 13. "I Yield to No One"

1. Pauline Newman daybook, April 27, 1958, 83-M191, box 1, folder 4, Pauline Newman Papers (hereafter, PNP), Schlesinger Library, Radcliffe Institute, Harvard University, Cambridge, Massachusetts.
2. Pauline Newman to Frieda S. Miller, July 1958, MC 868, box 26, folder 6, Elisabeth Burger Papers (hereafter, EBP), Schlesinger Library, Radcliffe Institute, Harvard University, Cambridge, Massachusetts.
3. Newman to Miller, July 1958, EBP.
4. Newman to Miller, July 1958, EBP.
5. Newman to Miller, July 1958, EBP.
6. Newman to Miller, July 1958, EBP.
7. Hugh Owen interview with author, Feb. 6, 2023.
8. Newman to Miller, July 1958, EBP.
9. Newman to Miller, July 1958, EBP.
10. Elisabeth Burger, MC 868, box 26, folder 6, EBP.
11. Newman to Miller, July 1958, EBP.
12. Newman to Miller, July 1958, EBP.
13. Pauline Newman Daybook, Oct. 11, 1958, MC 324, box 3, folder 4, PNP.
14. Writings by PN, including autobiographical notes, 1960–75, MC 324, box 1, folder 4, PNP.
15. Pauline Newman to Frieda S. Miller, June 5, 1959, MC 811, box 1, folder 2, PNP.
16. Newman to Miller, June 5, 1959, PNP.
17. Newman to Miller, June 5, 1959, PNP.
18. Newman to Miller, June 5, 1959, PNP.
19. Frieda S. Miller to Pauline Newman, June 1, 1959, MC 868, box 26, folder 6, EBP.
20. Miller to Newman, June 1, 1959, EBP.
21. Pauline Newman, Feb. 18, 1961, writings by PN, including autobiographical notes, 1960–7, MC 324, box 1, folder 4, PNP.
22. England, Scotland, Greece and Israel, 1967, MC 324, 21v-39, box 2, folder 36, PNP.
23. England, Scotland, Greece and Israel, 1967, PNP.
24. Beersheba Desert Inn Vintage postcard, 1967, author's own collection.
25. England, Scotland, Greece and Israel, 1967, PNP.
26. England, Scotland, Greece and Israel, 1967, PNP.
27. England, Scotland, Greece and Israel, 1967, PNP.
28. Hugh Owen interview with author, Feb. 6, 2023
29. Michael Owen interview with author, Feb. 13, 2023.
30. Michael Owen interview with author, Feb. 13, 2023.
31. Pauline Newman to Elisabeth Miller Burger, July 15, 1969, 83-M191, 83-M198, box 1, folder 4, PNP.
32. Newman to Miller Burger, July 15, 1969, PNP.

33. Pauline Newman daybook, Dec. 5, 1970, 83-M191, box 1, folder 4, PNP.

34. Pauline Newman daybook, July 2, 1975, MC 868, box 1, folder 11, EBP.

35. Re: Death of FSM, 1973, MC 324, box 3, folder 50, PNP.

36. Frieda Miller obituary, *Washington Post*, July 24, 1973.

37. Pauline Newman taped dinner conversation, May 6, 1975, courtesy Michael Owen.

38. Hugh Owen interview with author, Feb. 6, 2023.

39. Letter to Hugh and Michael, MC 324, box 1, folder 3, PNP.

40. Elisabeth Burger diary entry, Jan. 17, 1979, MC 868, box 2, folder 2, EBP.

41. Elisabeth Burger diary entry, Nov. 27, 1973, MC 868, box 31, folder 11, EBP.

42. Michael Owen, interview with author, Feb. 13, 2023.

43. Elisabeth Burger diary entries, Jan. 1, 1979–April 21, 1981, MC 868, box 1, folder 11, EBP.

44. Elisabeth Burger diary entries, Jan. 17, 1979–April 21, 1981, MC 868, box 1, folder 11, EBP.

45. Elisabeth Burger diary, Jan. 1, 1985–March 14, 1987, MC 868, box 2, folder 3, EBP.

46. Writings by PN, including autobiographical notes, 1960–75, MC 324, box 1, folder 4, PNP.

Epilogue

1. Pauline Newman, draft of address "It Has Not All Been Easy," MC 324, box 10, folder 182, speeches/states 1914, 1918, n.d., Pauline Newman Papers, Schlesinger Library, Radcliffe Institute, Harvard University, Cambridge, Massachusetts.

Selected Bibliography

Archival Sources

Columbian College of Arts and Sciences, George Washington University:

The Eleanor Roosevelt Papers Digital Edition (2017), Eleanor Roosevelt Papers Project

Kheel Center for Labor-Management Documentation and Archives, Martin P. Catherwood Library, Cornell University, Ithaca, New York:

International Ladies' Garment Workers' Union Collection
Lectures of Frances Perkins, Collection / 3047.
Pauline Newman Collection

Schlesinger Library, Radcliffe Institute, Harvard University, Cambridge, Massachusetts:

Elisabeth Burger Papers, 1980–2013 (inclusive), 1940–2000 (bulk)
Frieda S. Miller Papers, 1909–1973. A-37
Pauline Newman Papers, 1900–1980. MC 324; M-44
Leonora O'Reilly Papers, 1861–1928. A-39
Papers of the Women's Trade Union League and Its Principal Leaders. Microfilm

Tamiment Library and Robert F. Wagner Labor Archive, Elmer Holmes Bobst Library, New York University:

Rose Schneiderman Papers

Books and Articles

Albert, Marta. "Not Quite 'A Quiet Revolution': Jewish Women Reformers in Buffalo, New York, 1890–1914." *Shofar* 9, no. 4 (1991): 62–77. Special Issue: Eastern European Jewish Women Immigrants: To America and to Pre-State Israel.

Benson, Allan L. "Women in a Labor War." *Munsey's*, April 1910, 68–76.

Buechler, Steven. *Women's Movements in the United States: Woman Suffrage, Equal Rights, and Beyond*. New Brunswick, NJ: Rutgers University Press, 1990.

Buhle, Paul, and Jennifer Buhle. *The Concise History of Woman Suffrage: Selections from History of Woman Suffrage, by Elizabeth Cady Stanton, Susan B. Anthony, Matilda Joslyn Gage, and the National American Woman Suffrage Association*. Champaign: University of Illinois Press, 2005.

Clark, Lindsey. "How the 1918 Flu and COVID-19 Pandemics Transformed Women's Lives," March 2, 2021, American Society for Microbiology. https://asm.org/Articles/2021/March/How-the-Spanish-Flu-and-COVID-19-Pandemics-Transfo (accessed Dec. 18, 2022).

"The Cloakmakers' Strike." *Journal of Political Economy* 19, no. 3 (1911), https://www.journals.uchicago.edu/doi/pdf/10.1086/251825.

Cobble, Dorothy Sue. *For the Many: American Feminists and the Global Fight for Democratic Equality*. Princeton, NJ: Princeton University Press, 2021.

Cobble, Dorothy Sue, Linda Gordon, and Astrid Henry. *Feminism Unfinished: A Short, Surprising History of American Women's Movements*. New York: Liveright, 2014.

Cohn, M. Fannia. "History of the I.L.G.W.U." Unpublished, 1940. Kheel Center for Labor-Management Documentation and Archives, Martin P. Catherwood Library, Cornell University.

Comstock, Sarah. "The Uprising of the Girls." *Collier's* 44 (Dec. 25, 1909): 14–16.

"Conditions in the Cloak, Suit and Skirt Trades in New York." *Monthly Labor Review* 23, no. 1 (July 1926).

Dodge, Grace H., ed. *Thoughts of Busy Girls: Written by a Group of Girls Who Have Little Time for Study and Yet Find Much Time for Thinking*. New York: Cassell, 1892.

Donovan, Brian. "Respectability on Trial: Sex Crimes in New York City, 1900–1918." *New York History* 99, nos. 3/4 (2018): 478–81.

Dorr, Rheta Childe. *What Eight Million Women Want*. Boston: Small, Maynard, 1910.

Downey, Kirsten. *The Woman Behind the New Deal: The Life and Legacy of Frances Perkins—Social Security, Unemployment Insurance, and the Minimum Wage*. New York: First Anchor Books Edition, 2009.

Dreier, Mary E. *Margaret Dreier Robins: Her Life, Letters, and Work*. New York: Island Cooperative Press, 1950.

Dye, Nancy Schrom. *As Equals and as Sisters: Feminism, the Labor Movement, and the Women's Trade Union League of New York*. Columbia: University of Missouri Press, 1980.

Enstad, Nan. *Ladies of Labor, Girls of Adventure: Working Women, Popular Culture, and Labor Politics at the Turn of the Twentieth Century*. New York: Columbia University Press, 1999.

Faderman, Lillian. *To Believe in Women: What Lesbians Have Done for America—A History*. Boston: Houghton Mifflin, 1999.

Foner, Eric, and Steven H. Jaffe. "'I Am a Working Girl': Upheaval in the Garment Trades." In *Activist New York: A History of People, Protest, and Politics,* by Steven H. Jaffe. New York: NYU Press, 2018.

Foner, Philip S. *History of the Labor Movement in the United States.* Vol. 7: *Labor and World War I, 1914–1916.* New York: International Publishers, 1987.

Foner, Philip S. *Women and the American Labor Movement: From Colonial Times to the Eve of World War One.* New York: Free Press, 1979.

Glenn, Susan A. *Daughters of the Shtetl: Life and Labor in the Immigrant Generation.* Ithaca, NY: Cornell University Press, 1990.

Gompers, Samuel. "Don't Sacrifice Womanhood." *American Federationist* (Aug. 1917): 747–49.

Gompers, Samuel. "There Is No Shortage of Labor." *American Federationist* 24 (Oct. 1917): 22–25.

Greenbaum, Masha. *The Jews of Lithuania: A History of a Remarkable Community 1316–1945.* Jerusalem: Gefen Books, 2018.

Hirschman, Charles, and Elizabeth Mogford. "Immigration and the American Industrial Revolution from 1880 to 1920." *Social Science Research,* 38, no. 4 (2009): 897–920.

ILGWU, *Justice.* 1 September 1934. "Seven Days That Shook the World." Microfilm Vols. 1519, 19331937, United Archives, Kheel Center, Cornell University, Ithaca, New York.

ILGWU News History. *Fiftieth Anniversary Convention Issue,* "Roosevelt Talks to Wrapper Strikers on Visits to Halls," 1.

Johnson, Joan Marie. *Funding Feminism: Monied Women, Philanthropy, and the Women's Movement, 1870–1967.* Chapel Hill: University of North Carolina Press, 2017.

Joselit, Jenna Weissman. "The Landlord as Czar; *Pre–World War I Tenant Activity.*" In Ronald Lawson, *The Tenant Movement in New York City, 1904–1984.* New Brunswick, NJ: Rutgers University Press 1986.

Kelly, Kim. *Fight Like Hell: The Untold History of American Labor.* New York: One Signal Publishers/Atria, 2022.

Kessler-Harris, Alice. *Out to Work: A History of Wage Earning Women in the U.S.* New York: Oxford University Press, 1982.

Lavine, Matthew. "The Early Clinical X-Ray in the United States: Patient Experiences and Public Perceptions." *Journal of the History of Medicine and Allied Sciences* 67, no. 4 (2012): 587–625.

Lawson, Ronald. *The Tenant Movement in New York City, 1904–1984.* New Brunswick, NJ: Rutgers University Press, 1986.

Lemlich, Clara. "The Inside of a Shirtwaist Factory." *Good Housekeeping* 64 (March 1912): 367. https://digital.library.cornell.edu/catalog/hearth6417403_1340_004 [https://perma.cc/R9EH-T5JV].

Levine, Louis. *The Women's Garment Workers.* New York: B. W. Heubsch, 1924.

London, Jack. "The Scab." *The Atlantic.* January 1904. https://www.theatlantic.com/magazine/archive/1904/01/the-scab/306194/.

Manufacturers' Bulletin for Fire Protection Issued by the Joint Board of Sanitary Control. New York: The Board, 1915. Kheel Center.

Marrin, Albert. *Flesh and Blood So Cheap: The Triangle Fire and Its Legacy*. New York: Alfred A. Knopf, 2011.

Morrison, Joan, and Charlotte Fox Zabusky. *American Mosaic: The Immigrant Experience in the Words of Those Who Lived It*. Pittsburgh: University of Pittsburgh Press, 1980.

Moskowitz, Henry. "The Joint Board of Sanitary Control of the Cloak, Suit, and Skirt Industry." *Annals of American Academy of Political and Social Science* 44, Outlook for Industrial Peace (Nov. 1912): 39–58.

Newman, Pauline. "The Child Labor Law." *Progressive Woman*. June 13, 1911.

Newman, Pauline. "Difficulties with Sister." *Labor Ages* 11, no. 4 (April 1912): 181.

Newman, Pauline. "Equal Rights' Amendment." *American Federationist*, Aug. 1938, 815–17.

Newman, Pauline. "First Minimum Wage Law Goes into Effect." *American Labor World* (Nov. 1933): 17.

Newman, Pauline. "How About It Girls?" *The Progressive Woman*, Convention Number, n.d., Progressive Woman Publishing Co., 7, https://www.marxists.org/history/usa/pubs/socialist-woman/120500-progressivewoman-v5w60.pdf.

Newman, Pauline. "An Inspector's Point of View." *The Message* 4, no. 4 (Feb. 1917): 4 (published by ILGWU).

Newman, Pauline. "Insuring Motherhood." *American Hebrew and Jewish Messenger*, Sept. 15, 1916, 590.

Newman, Pauline. "Labor's Constitution to the Field of Industrial Dentistry." Typed notes for speech, Oct. 27, 1931.

Newman, Pauline. "The Workers of the World," *The Progressive Woman* 5, no. 59 (April 1912): 7.

Newman, Pauline, and Joan Morrison. "Working for the Triangle Shirtwaist Company." History Matters, http://historymatters.gmu.edu/d/178/.

Nigero, Carmen. "Beware of Zombies: The Grim Origins of Washington Square Park." *New York Public Library* (blog). March 10, 2011.

Novkov, Julie. *Constituting Workers: Protecting Women: Gender, Law and Labor in the Progressive Era and New Deal Years*. Ann Arbor: University of Michigan Press, 2001.

Orleck, Annelise. *Common Sense and a Little Fire: Women and Working-Class Politics in the United States 1900–1965*. Chapel Hill: University of North Carolina Press, 1995.

Perkins, Frances. "The Committee of Safety." *Bulletin of the Joint Board. Manufacturers' Bulletin for Fire Protection*. Issued by the Joint Board of Sanitary Control, March 1915, Kheel Center.

Reeve, A. B. "The Death Roll of Industry," *Charities and the Commons 17* (1907): 791.

Report of the Joint Relief Committee, Ladies' Waist and Dressmakers' Union No. 25 on the Triangle Fire Disaster, Jan. 15, 1913. New York.

Report of the Ladies' Waist and Dressmakers' Union Loc. 25 to the Convention of the International Ladies' Garment Workers' Union, 1916.

Schofield, Ann. *To Do and To Be: Portraits of Four Women Activists, 1893–1986*. Boston: Northeastern University Press, 1997.

Sharf, Lois. "The Great Uprising in Cleveland: When Sisterhood Failed." In *A Needle, a Bobbin, a Strike: Women Needleworkers in America*, ed. Joan M. Jensen and Sue Davidson. Philadelphia: Temple University Press, 1984.

Stein, Leon. *The Triangle Fire: Centennial Edition*. Ithaca, NY: ILR Press 1990. First published 1926.

Sternlicht, Sanford. *The Tenement Saga: The Lower East Side and Early Jewish American Writers*. Madison: University of Wisconsin Press, 2004.

Storrs, Landon R. Y. *The Second Red Scare and the Unmaking of the New Deal Left*. Princeton, NJ: Princeton University Press, 2013.

Tyler, Gus. *Look for the Union Label: A History of the International Ladies' Garment Workers' Union*. Armonk, NY: M. E. Sharpe, 1995.

Van Kleeck, Mary. *Working Girls in Evening Schools: A Statistical Study*. New York: Russell Sage Foundation, 1914.

Welter, Barbara. "The Cult of True Womanhood: 1820–1860." *American Quarterly* 18, no. 2 (1966): 151–74.

Willett, Mable Hurd. *The Employment of Women in the Clothing Trade*. Columbia University Studies in the Social Services. New York: AMS Press, 1968. First published 1902.

Wolfman, Ira. *Jewish New York: Notable Neighborhoods and Memorable Moments*. New York: Universe Publishing, 2003.

Zarelli, Natalie. "Early 1900s Women Had an Ingenious Method for Fending off Gropers." History.com. Nov. 1, 2017. Last updated April 15, 2025. https://www.history.com/news/how-women-defended-themselves-against-street-gropers-100-years-ago.

Index

CATHRYN J. PRINCE is an adjunct professor of journalism at Fordham University. Her books include *Queen of the Mountaineers: The Trailblazing Life of Fanny Bullock Workman* and *American Daredevil: The Extraordinary Life of Richard Halliburton, the World's First Celebrity Travel Writer.*

The University of Illinois Press
is a founding member of the
Association of University Presses.

Composed in 10.5/13 Mercury G1
with display
by Kirsten Dennison
at the University of Illinois Press
Manufactured by Sheridan Books, Inc.

University of Illinois Press
1325 South Oak Street
Champaign, IL 61820-6903
www.press.uillinois.edu